Conor Mc Guckin and Lucie Corcoran (Eds.)

Cyberbullying: Where Are We Now? A Cross-National Understanding

This book is a reprint of the Special Issue that appeared in the online, open access journal, *Societies* (ISSN 2075-4698) from 2014–2015, available at:

http://www.mdpi.com/journal/societies/special_issues/cyberbulling

Guest Editors
Conor Mc Guckin
School of Education, Trinity College Dublin
Ireland

Lucie Corcoran
School of Education, Trinity College Dublin
Ireland

Editorial Office
MDPI AG
St. Alban-Anlage 66
Basel, Switzerland

Publisher
Shu-Kun Lin

Assistant Editor
Hui Liu

1. Edition 2017

MDPI • Basel • Beijing • Wuhan • Barcelona • Belgrade

ISBN 978-3-03842-310-2 (Hbk)
ISBN 978-3-03842-311-9 (electronic)

Table of Contents

List of Contributors

Ikuko Aoyama Office for the Promotion of Global Education Programs, Shizuoka University, Shizuoka Prefecture 432-8561, Japan.

Meghan Benson Planned Parenthood of Wisconsin, Madison, WI 53713, USA.

Lucie Corcoran School of Arts, Dublin Business School, Dublin 2, Ireland.

Francine Dehue Faculty of Psychology and Educational Sciences, Open University The Netherlands, Valkenburgerweg 177, PO Box 2960, 6419 AT Heerlen, The Netherlands.

Thuy Dinh Centre for Social and Educational Research, Dublin Institute of Technology, Grangegorman, Dublin 7, Ireland.

Lesley-Anne Ey School of Education, University of South Australia, St Bernard's Road, Magill SA 5072, Australia.

Linda Goossens Faculty of Psychology and Educational Sciences, Open University The Netherlands, Valkenburgerweg 177, PO Box 2960, 6419 AT Heerlen, The Netherlands.

Conor Mc Guckin School of Education, Trinity College Dublin, Dublin 2, Ireland.

Niels C. L. Jacobs Faculty of Psychology and Educational Sciences, Open University The Netherlands, Valkenburgerweg 177, PO Box 2960, 6419 AT Heerlen, The Netherlands.

Marianne Junger Industrial Engineering and Business Information Systems, University of Twente, P. O. Box 217, 7500-AE Enschede, The Netherland.

Shanmukh V. Kamble Department of Psychology, Karnatak University, Karnataka State 580 003, India.

Rajitha Kota Department of Pediatrics, University of Wisconsin-Madison, Madison, WI 53792, USA.

Lilian Lechner Faculty of Psychology and Educational Sciences, Open University The Netherlands, Valkenburgerweg 177, PO Box 2960, 6419 AT Heerlen, The Netherlands.

Li Lei Department of Psychology, Renmin University of China, Beijing 100872, China.

Zheng Li Department of Psychology, Renmin University of China, Beijing 100872, China.

Katja Machmutow Department of Psychology, University of Zurich, Binzmühlestrasse 14, CH-8050 Zürich, Switzerland.

Ersilia Menesini Department of Educational Sciences and Psychology, University of Florence, Via di S. Salvi, 12, Complesso di S. Salvi, Padiglione 26, 50135 Firenze, Italy.

Megan A. Moreno Center for Child Health, Behavior and Development, Seattle Children's Research Institute, Seattle, WA 98121, USA; Division of Adolescent Medicine, University of Washington, Seattle, WA 98121, USA.

Matt R. Nobles Department of Criminal Justice & Criminology, Sam Houston State University, Huntsville, TX 77341, USA.

Annalaura Nocentini Department of Educational Sciences and Psychology, University of Florence, Via di S. Salvi, 12, Complesso di S. Salvi, Padiglione 26, 50135 Firenze, Italy.

Brian O'Neill Centre for Social and Educational Research, Dublin Institute of Technology, Grangegorman, Dublin 7, Ireland.

Benedetta Emanuela Palladino Department of Educational Sciences and Psychology, University of Florence, Via di S. Salvi, 12, Complesso di S. Salvi, Padiglione 26, 50135 Firenze, Italy.

Sonja Perren Department of Empirical Educational Research, University of Konstanz/Thurgau University of Teacher Education, Bärenstrasse 38, CH-8280 Kreuzlingen, Switzerland.

Garry Prentice School of Arts, Dublin Business School, Dublin 2, Ireland.

Ryan Randa Department of Criminal Justice & Criminology, Sam Houston State University, Huntsville, TX 77341, USA.

Bradford W. Reyns Department of Criminal Justice, Weber State University, Ogden, UT 84408, USA.

Shari Schoohs Department of Pediatrics, University of Wisconsin-Madison, Madison, WI 53792, USA.

Chang Shu Department of Psychology, Renmin University of China, Beijing 100872, China.

Ruthaychonee Sittichai Faculty of Humanities and Social Sciences, Prince of Songkla University, Muang, Pattani 94000, Thailand.

Shruti Soudi Department of Psychology, Karnatak University, Karnataka State 580 003, India.

Barbara Spears School of Education, University of South Australia, St Bernard's Road, Magill SA 5072, Australia.

Ariane Stauber Department of Psychology, Swiss Distance University, Überlandstrasse 12, CH-3900 Brig, Switzerland.

Fabio Sticca Department of Empirical Educational Research, University of Konstanz/Thurgau University of Teacher Education, Bärenstrasse 38, CH-8280 Kreuzlingen, Switzerland.

Carmel Taddeo School of Education, University of South Australia, St Bernard's Road, Magill SA 5072, Australia.

Trijntje Völlink Faculty of Psychology and Educational Sciences, Open University The Netherlands, Valkenburgerweg 177, PO Box 2960, 6419 AT Heerlen, The Netherlands.

Sebastian Wachs Department of Educational Studies, University of Bremen, Bibliothekstr. 1-3, 28359 Bremen, Germany.

Michelle F. Wright Faculty of Social Studies, Masaryk University, Brno 60200, Czech Republic.

About the Guest Editors

Conor Mc Guckin is an Assistant Professor based in the School of Education at Trinity College, Dublin. His research interests are in the areas of bully/victim problems among children and adults, psychology applied to educational policy and processes, and the need for a fully inclusive education environment for all children and young people (e.g., special educational needs, disability). Conor has a long track record of involvement in, and management of, collaborative research projects. Conor gained his Ph.D. in Psychology for his research exploring bully/victim problems among Northern Ireland's school pupils. This thesis explored the prevalence of bully/victim problems from a multiple indicator approach, explored differential psychometric measurement issues, and the association between involvement in bully/victim problems and various individual difference variables.

Lucie Corcoran is a psychology lecturer and researcher based in the School of Education at Trinity College, Dublin. Lucie's research has largely focused on school bullying and cyber aggression since the emergence of cyberbullying research globally. This research has explored various aspects of bullying and aggression including definitional considerations, prevalence assessment, and exploration of psychological correlates such as personality, self-concept, empathy, psychological health, and coping styles/strategies. The purpose of such research is to contribute to current knowledge and inform best practice at the national- and international-level.

Preface to "Cyberbullying: Where Are We Now? A Cross-National Understanding"

The current publication provides a state-of-the-art review of key concerns in cyberbullying research; focusing on fundamental issues such as the conceptualisation of cyberbullying (or cyber aggression), cyberbullying as experienced by different age groups, correlates of cyberbullying involvement, cross-national research, and coping with cyberbullying.

To begin, Corcoran, Mc Guckin and Prentice examine the definition of cyberbullying and its conceptualisation as a 'cyber version' of school/traditional bullying. Corcoran and colleagues argue that in light of a number of factors — such as recent Irish data, the unique nature of cyberspace, and the restrictive characteristics of school bullying — consideration should be given to cyber aggression as a more appropriate concept for examination. Taking a similar focus, Randa, Nobles, and Reyns examine the relationship between cyberbullying and traditional bullying amongst adolescents. Specifically, Randa et al. seek to advance the understanding of whether cyberbullying is an extension of school bullying, or a distinct, stand-alone phenomenon. Highlighting the complexity of the relationship between the forms of aggression, this paper indicates an overlap between the phenomena, as well as indicating a uniqueness of the cyberbullying phenomenon.

Focusing on a somewhat under-researched aspect of cyberbullying, Ey, Taddeo and Spears explore the phenomenon at primary school level. The authors report the findings of a systematic literature review which focused on studies published from 2009–2014 with the purpose of examining cyberbullying amongst children aged 5–12 years of age. This paper has important implications for future research with this age group, including aspects of the phenomenon, and appropriate methodologies. Also examining an age-group which has been infrequently researched with regard to cyberbullying, Kota, Schoohs, Benson and Moreno provide a paper which discusses this issue from a college-age perspective. Qualitative data allowed the authors to gain insights into perceptions of cyberbullying on college campuses. This research sheds light on definitional issues discussed in other papers within this Special Issue; highlighting a lack of consensus on a cyberbullying definition and the relationship between traditional bullying and cyberbullying. Furthermore, the paper examines the potentially different presentation/manifestation and impact of cyberbullying among a college sample as opposed to an adolescent sample.

A number of papers in the current Issue provide a cross-national perspective on cyberbullying. For instance, Wachs, Junger and Sittichai explore the relationship between involvement in traditional bullying, cyberbullying, or both in relation to risky activities both online and offline, amongst German, Dutch, and Thai adolescents. Wachs and colleagues provide important insights regarding the relationships between risk and bullying involvement, whilst also indicating implications for teaching life skills to adolescents as opposed to exclusively focusing on reducing risks. Wright, Aoyama, Kamble, Li, Soudi, Lei and Shu investigated differences in cyber aggression involvement across China, India, and Japan whilst also examining the role of peer attachment. This paper provides insight on the nature of attachment as it relates to cyber aggression and also highlights the paucity of cyber aggression research in India. O'Neill and Dinh report on cyberbullying across seven European nations; suggesting that cyberbullying may begin to overtake traditional bullying in terms of prevalence. The data reviewed suggests that online bullying has increased and O'Neill and Dinh examine the factors which allow cyberbullying to become more prevalent.

Three of the papers in this Special Issue also focus on the coping aspect of cyberbullying. Jacobs, Goossens, Dehue, Völlink and Lechner contribute a better understanding of how cybervictims in the Netherlands experience/perceive cyberbullying, and feel motivated to cope in specific ways. Focus groups revealed that traditional bullying may be considered to be worse than cyberbullying. With regard to coping, Jacobs and colleagues found that victims tended to react to victimization with non-help-seeking. The methodology used in this study is proposed to be an approach which may allow for further insight than self-report data collection. Jacobs, Völlink, Dehue and Lechner discuss the development of a measure of coping with cyberbullying. In this endeavour, the authors sought to overcome the short-comings of other efforts to measure this construct. From their work, a Cyberbullying Coping Questionnaire was developed which showed good internal consistency, acceptable test-retest reliability, and good discriminant validity. The measure assesses various strategies: cognitive; behavioral; approach; and avoidance. Finally, Sticca et al. also report on efforts to develop a valid and reliable measure of coping in response to cyberbullying; the Coping with Cyberbullying Questionnaire. The paper details the five-stage process of its development. Longitudinal research in Switzerland along with data collection in Italy and Ireland contributed to the questionnaire version outlined in the current paper. Sticca et al. highlight the importance of such methodological advances to support intervention and prevention efforts.

This Special Issue allows readers to better understand key issues in the field of cyberbullying: including the difficulty of reaching a consensus on the conceptualisation of cyberbullying and the urgent need to reach an agreement regarding the phenomenon of cyberbullying; the need to continue to develop methods of research (accessing student voice via qualitative studies and progressing the development of robust quantitative measures); the importance of cross-cultural and global research in the context of increasing and rapid access to mobile technologies; and the need to provide better understandings of coping strategies in response to cyberbullying as some are helpful, others unhelpful and even potentially harmful.

Conor Mc Guckin and Lucie Corcoran
Guest Editors

Cyberbullying or Cyber Aggression?: A Review of Existing Definitions of Cyber-Based Peer-to-Peer Aggression

Lucie Corcoran, Conor Mc Guckin and Garry Prentice

Abstract: Due to the ongoing debate regarding the definitions and measurement of cyberbullying, the present article critically appraises the existing literature and offers direction regarding the question of how best to conceptualise peer-to-peer abuse in a cyber context. Variations across definitions are problematic as it has been argued that inconsistencies with regard to definitions result in researchers examining different phenomena, whilst the absence of an agreed conceptualisation of the behaviour(s) involved hinders the development of reliable and valid measures. Existing definitions of cyberbullying often incorporate the criteria of traditional bullying such as intent to harm, repetition, and imbalance of power. However, due to the unique nature of cyber-based communication, it can be difficult to identify such criteria in relation to cyber-based abuse. Thus, for these reasons cyberbullying may not be the most appropriate term. Rather than attempting to "shoe-horn" this abusive behaviour into the preconceived conceptual framework that provides an understanding of traditional bullying, it is timely to take an alternative approach. We argue that it is now time to turn our attention to the broader issue of cyber aggression, rather than persist with the narrow focus that is cyberbullying.

Reprinted from *Societies*. Cite as: Corcoran, L.; Guckin, C.M.; Prentice, G. Cyberbullying or Cyber Aggression?: A Review of Existing Definitions of Cyber-Based Peer-to-Peer Aggression. *Societies* **2015**, *5*, 245–255.

1. Introduction

This paper asserts a position to progress the conceptualisation and definition of cyber-based aggressive behaviours, generally classed under the term cyberbullying. A review of definitional approaches to both traditional bullying and cyberbullying is provided so as to highlight the similarities but, also, crucially, the differences between the "real world" and cyber settings. In this way, it becomes evident that the traditional bullying definitional criteria do not provide an easy match to the cyber context. In addition, different theoretical perspectives on the conceptualisation of cyberbullying further emphasise the need to consider different perspectives on cyber-based aggression [1]. Whilst it is acknowledged that important contributions have been made to progressing the definition of cyberbullying [2], recent findings [3] have highlighted the need to adopt a different approach. Ultimately, we will present a synopsis of the problematic nature of the label "cyberbullying" and current definitions, and we will present a way forward for the research community. In order to gain insight regarding the rationale for cyberbullying definitions, it is important to first review the defining components of traditional bullying.

2. Defining Bullying for a "Real World" Setting

Presently there is an ongoing debate regarding the existence of cyberbullying, the extent of the problem, and the threat that cyber-based abuse carries (see Olweus and Smith for a scholarly engagement [4,5]). Central to this debate is how we delineate the behaviours and actions that are commonly labelled as "cyberbullying"; that is, how we identify the parameters of the phenomenon, what we recognise as the inclusion and exclusion criteria as part of the definitional stance, and importantly, how we conclude that cyberbullying is in fact the correct term for the behaviour that we are exploring.

Within the realm of "traditional bullying" research, sometimes referred to as face-to-face (f2f) bullying [6], there is wide consensus regarding the defining criteria, namely (a) intent to cause harm [7,8], (b) repetition of the behaviour over time [7,9,10], and (c) an imbalance of power between the victim(s) and bully(ies) [7,8,10]. However, with the emergence of cyberbullying, the central question for researchers and practitioners relates to the extent to which the same criteria could be "plugged into" a definition of cyberbullying.

Definitions of traditional bullying have reflected the static nature of the "real world" setting, which is characterised by boundaries of time and geography (e.g., school, home). However, abuse of peers is no longer confined to the school setting, nor is it restricted to the typical daily routines of human interaction; characteristics that bind instances of traditional bullying. Indeed, the capacity to use electronic devices and media to attack someone in almost any location, and at any time, is a distinctive feature of cyber-based abuse [11]. Moreover, there is the potential for abusive or humiliating content to be disseminated to an audience of unknown size and location [12]. This allows for the notion of "repetition" in operational definitions to take a different form in the cyber world, as abusive behaviour need not be repeated on the part of the aggressor [13] in order for the target to experience repeated victimization, as the bystanders take a central role in cyber-based abuse through their viewing, "sharing", and "liking" of humiliating content, such as comments (e.g., tweets, texts), pictures, and videos. Moreover, the element of "power", another central aspect of operational definitions of traditional bullying, is somewhat more difficult to determine in a cyber context. For example, power could be characterised by the ability to remain anonymous in cyberspace, or the ability to capitalise on superior technological skills [13]. It could also be characterised by the immediacy of the dissemination and the capacity to humiliate on a grand scale [14]. Moreover, the

2

challenges faced by researchers do not end here—the very nature of cyberspace as an evolving entity presents a formidable challenge.

3. Defining Cyberbullying in an Ever Changing Cyber Environment

The term "cyberbullying" was initially a convenient label for abusive behaviour perpetrated through the use of mobile telephones and computers with Internet access. However, in less than ten years, and in homage to Moore's Law [15], the exponential development of the consumer technology market has witnessed the migration from immobile desktop computers with slow, dial-up Internet connections, to tablets and pocket size Smartphones, which allow for recording and publishing of material online in mere seconds. Thus, unlike their Cro Magnon ancestors who " . . . may have had to settle for daubing unflattering pictures of their peers on cave walls . . . " [16] (p. 679), the tools of modernity enable the children and adolescents of today to paint unflattering pictures in a more remote, covert, and insidious manner.

Thus, attempting to operationally define cyberbullying in a world which is in constant flux, could be likened to asking time to stand still. The evolving features of the available technology only intensify the unique nature of the communication. Indeed, whilst we debate and dialogue about the defining characteristics of cyberbullying, we must remain cognisant that by the time we reach some form of consensus, children and adolescents will, in all likelihood, be using technology and social communication tools that do not yet exist. What we as researchers and practitioners refer to as bully/victim problems must be understood in the context of this post-modern world. Perhaps the most important question that requires attention is: how do we operationalise and define these behaviours and intentions for the children of the 21st Century?

4. Practical Implications of Cyberbullying Definitions

This issue becomes particularly important at a practical level. The importance is evident in relation to the application of knowledge to prevention and intervention efforts (e.g., CyberTraining: http://www.cybertraining-project.org; CyberTraining-4-Parents: http://cybertraining4parents.org). Past research has provided a wealth of evidence that there is an overlap between traditional bullying and cyberbullying (e.g., Olweus, 2012 [4]), and therefore the literature pertaining to traditional bullying intervention and prevention efforts can inform our efforts to counter cyberbullying. Therefore, it would be important to establish whether the same degree of overlap remains if the focus were to shift to cyber aggression more broadly rather than cyberbullying specifically. In other words, if the characteristics of cyber-based aggression are in fact different to those of traditional bullying, can we still make clear links between the two forms of aggression when designing prevention and intervention initiatives for cyberspace? Overall, a better approach to defining and measuring cyber-based aggressive behaviour would support better intervention and prevention efforts intended to reduce the incidence of such harmful behaviours. Evidence informed interventions and preventative mechanisms cannot have a secure and robust evidence base if there is uncertainty regarding the operational definition of the key terminology for research purposes (see Menesini and colleagues [2] for an overview of work by the COST [European Cooperation in Science and Technology] IS0801 network: https://sites.google.com/site/costis0801).

The impact of cyber-based abuse can be best understood in terms of "coping"—whether at the systemic, familial, or personal level [17]. That is, coping can be viewed on distinct levels, including policy implementation (e.g., corporate social responsibility activities of organizations involved in hardware/software components of the industry) and legislation, and by extension quasi-legislative instruments such as the EU Convention on the Rights of the Child. At a national level, responses and policies become important vessels for disseminating guidance and support for the population (see O'Moore *et al.* [18] for overview of the work by the COST (European Cooperation in Science and Technology) IS0801 network: https://sites.google.com/site/costis0801). For instance, the Irish Department of Education and Skills [19] have updated their Anti-Bullying Procedures for Primary and Post-Primary Schools, and it would be hoped that this iterative development reflects the work regarding definitions of the aforementioned groups. It is important that both the conceptualisation and operationalisation of cyberbullying by researchers and practitioners is appropriate as we develop our understanding of the ways in which individuals cope effectively (see Mc Guckin and colleagues [20] for an overview of the literature pertaining to coping as part of the work by the COST [European Cooperation in Science and Technology] IS0801 network). Despite the limitations and challenges to impose traditional bullying criteria in a cyber setting, efforts to define cyberbullying to date have largely centred on this approach.

Finally, the way in which we label and define problematic cyber-based behaviour has real implications for protecting mental health. Due to the fact that there is potential for wide public access to online content, a single cyberbullying incident could have a serious and lasting harmful effect on the victimised person. Therefore, refining the definition and conceptualisation of cyber-based aggression could have serious implications for protecting mental health, as no longer would a young person have to endure multiple episodes of victimization before the behaviour could be recognised as cyberbullying. By removing the component of repetition from the conceptualisation of cyber aggression, we would be recognising the potential for one single act to cause psychological harm to a targeted person.

5. How We Have Defined Cyberbullying Thus Far?

Offering one of the earliest definitions, Belsey [21] defined cyberbullying as " ... the use of information and communication technologies to support deliberate, repeated, and hostile behaviour by an individual or group, that is intended to harm others". Applying the existing criteria regarding traditional bullying, and alluding to the potential power imbalance, Smith and colleagues [22] later defined cyberbullying as an " ... aggressive intentional act carried out by a group or individual, using electronic forms of contact, repeatedly and over time against a victim who cannot easily defend him or herself" (p. 376). Perhaps the most comprehensive and useful early definition was offered by Tokunaga [23], who built upon existing definitions to define cyberbullying as " ... any behavior performed through electronic or digital media by individuals or groups that repeatedly communicates hostile or aggressive messages intended to inflict harm or discomfort on others" (p. 278). However, considering the unique aspects of cyberspace, one must question how appropriate the label of cyberbullying and, by extension, existing definitions, really are.

Langos [14] argued that the core elements of traditional bullying (*i.e.*, repetition, power imbalance, intention, and aggression) also underpin cyberbullying, but insisted that we must distinguish between direct (private communications such as a text message) and indirect (communication in a public domain, such as a social networking site) forms of cyberbullying. Langos [14] argued that the repetitious nature of the behaviour is more evident in direct cyberbullying where repeated actions on the part of the cyberbully are necessary to characterise repetition. It was suggested that repeated actions on the part of the cyberbully may also indirectly expose the criterion of intent to cause harm. As the intent may be more difficult to identify in cases of indirect cyberbullying, Langos [14] recommended that intentionality is determined based upon how a reasonable person would assess the aggressor's conduct. However, taking an alternative perspective by focusing on cyber aggression in a broader sense, Grigg [1] has made an important contribution to the debate.

6. An Alternative Approach—What about Cyber Aggression?

Grigg [1] took a rather different approach, arguing that the term cyberbullying raises a number of difficulties. With respect to the element of power, Grigg [1] argued there is little evidence to suggest that cyberbullies have superior technological skills, and additionally indicates that there is a lack of clarity regarding whether responsibility lies with the cyberbully or the bystanders when repetition takes the form of repeated views of humiliating content. Considering the broad range of negative acts that can occur in cyberspace, Grigg [1] defined "cyber aggression" as " ... intentional harm delivered by the use of electronic means to a person or a group of people irrespective of their age, who perceive(s) such acts as offensive, derogatory, harmful, or unwanted" (p. 152). This argument, that there is a need to look at aggression more broadly, is one that has received little consideration since its publication, but must be given regard in light of the difficulties in achieving a satisfactory cyberbullying definition.

Pyżalski [24] proposes a typology of electronic aggression based on the identity of the targeted individual(s), arguing that the framing of cyberbullying within the school bullying conceptualisation involves the assumption that all aggressive behaviours occur within the peer group. Therefore, Pyżalski's typology [24] includes both peer-directed cyber aggression and electronic aggression targeting celebrities, groups, vulnerable individuals, school staff, and random victims. In a large scale study of Polish adolescents, Pyżalski [24] measured electronic aggression (characterised by intention as a traditional bullying criterion), and cyberbullying (also including the characteristics of repetition and power imbalance). In this way, similar to Grigg's approach, an important distinction was made between the traditional bullying criteria and cyber aggression more broadly. However, an important voice which also deserves attention, is that of our research population—children and adolescents. Pyżalski's typology [24] of electronic aggression was in fact based on qualitative interviews with teachers and students. This leads us to a vital consideration—if we create a cyberbullying concept which does not fit with the youth perspective, then what use is it?

7. How to Approach This Issue—Bottom-Up or Top-Down?

If the academic literature asserts that the negative experiences of children in cyberspace can be conceptualised as cyberbullying with agreed definitional parameters, the question arises, does this hold true for what children and young people think? In essence, are we applying a top-down approach to the area whereby experts deliver the terminology and definition as dogma without any reflection upon the voice of children, or their ability to co-construct meaning with researchers [25]? As we know from the literature regarding traditional bullying, when asked and involved in research which takes a bottom-up approach, children and young people may report a different perspective [26]. Menesini [27] provides an overview of recent research which has consulted student voice in an attempt to counter the "top-down" approach to definitions and labelling, and reports that the criteria for traditional bullying are also relevant for cyberbullying. Further, Menesini [27] states that whilst the additional aspects of publicity and anonymity can be useful in relation to identifying the severity of the cyber-based abuse, the relationship between the aggressor and victim, as well as the response from the victim, these aspects are not necessary for recognising behaviour as cyberbullying.

8. Involving Student Voice

An important contribution in this area was that by Menesini and colleagues as part of an international collaborative initiative (the COST [European Cooperation in Science and Technology] IS0801 network). In order to consider and advance the definition of cyberbullying, Menesini and colleagues [2] collected qualitative data from young people via focus groups across Italy, Spain, Germany, Sweden, and Estonia, as well as quantitative research via a questionnaire with the same countries and France in addition. Acknowledging the debate as to whether the criteria for defining traditional bullying are relevant for cyberbullying, the research group also sought to ascertain if the cyber-specific components of publicity and anonymity were key criteria. The focus groups revealed that intent, effect on the victim (as part of a power imbalance), and repetition (can indicate the intent and severity of the victimization) were all recognised as criteria for defining cyberbullying. Questionnaire results revealed that the power imbalance (in the form of consequences for the victim and inability to defend themselves) and intent were perceived as key criteria, whilst repetition was not regarded as a key characteristic.

Based on the overall analysis, Menesini and colleagues [2] drew conclusions regarding the appropriate defining components. One of the focus groups revealed that intentionality was less important for defining cyberbullying than the effect on the victim, as unintentionally harmful acts can have a detrimental effect on the victim. Therefore, Menesini and colleagues [2] concluded that intent should be considered a criterion for cyberbullying, although it remains unclear whether the perpetrator or victim perspective is more important. With respect to power imbalance, Menesini and colleagues [2] concluded that although it is difficult to define precisely how someone is less powerful in cyberspace compared with another person, the power imbalance can take different forms and makes the victim feel less powerful and causes difficulty in relation to defending him/herself. Power imbalance was considered by the research team to be a more important criterion than intentionality. Although repetition did not emerge as a key criterion from the questionnaire results, and despite their acknowledgement of the complex nature of repetition in a cyber context, Menesini and colleagues [2] suggest that it is a relevant criterion for defining cyberbullying as it distinguishes a joke from cyberbullying and it also highlights the distinction between cyberbullying and cyber aggression (as cyber aggression does not require repetition). Additionally, anonymity and publicity were considered to be significant factors but not defining characteristics of cyberbullying. Overall Menesini and colleagues [2] argued for the inclusion of intentionality and power imbalance to be included as key defining criteria of cyberbullying, whilst repetition received a lower level of agreement as a key criterion. The important research conducted by Menesini and colleagues [2] does much to progress the development of an agreed-upon definition of cyberbullying. However, it also highlights the complex nature of defining cyberbullying and reveals differing perspectives—even among students.

In addition, Vandebosch and Van Cleemput [28] collected data from 53 focus groups involving students aged from 10 to 18 years, with results supportive of the traditional bullying frame. Consistent with traditional bullying definitional criteria, "true" cyberbullying was found to be characterised by intention to cause hurt and perception of the behaviour as hurtful (by the victim), repetition of negative offline or online behaviours, and a power imbalance (based on "real-life" factors such as physical strength and/or on ICT-related criteria such as anonymity). With respect to repetition, just one online negative act in combination with traditional bullying was considered to constitute cyberbullying. Still, in light of the varying responses found by Menesini and colleagues [2] and also considering the challenges of traditional bullying criteria already outlined in this paper, is it in fact time for a fresh approach?

9. Time for a Fresh Approach—Evidence from Irish Research

Corcoran and Mc Guckin [3] provide evidence that the ways in which we label and measure cyber-based abuse can lead to marked differences in the reporting of victimization and perpetration of such behaviours. Using a survey approach, based on that designed by Swiss researchers [29], Corcoran and Mc Guckin [3] measured involvement in cyber aggression and cyberbullying among a sample of 2474 Irish second-level students aged between 12 and 19 years. Cyber aggression was measured using two nine-item scales (victimization and perpetration). With respect to cyber aggression, no definition was offered, but respondents were asked about the frequency of their experiences of specific aggressive behaviours in a cyber setting during the previous three months. By contrast, involvement in cyberbullying was measured by providing respondents with a definition of cyberbullying before presenting one item pertaining to perpetration of cyberbullying and one item pertaining to victimization by cyberbullying. Although both approaches were measuring the concept recognised in the academic literature as cyberbullying, the scale approach did not include a definition involving the traditional bullying criteria. Results revealed that, with a frequency of about once a month or more often, about once a week, or (almost) daily, 10.83% of respondents (n = 267) reported involvement as a victim of cyber aggression and 5.15% (n = 126) reported perpetration of cyber aggression. By contrast, just 2.24% of respondents (n = 55) indicated victimization by cyberbullying and 1.12% (n = 24) reported perpetration of cyberbullying. This provides some support for Olweus' assertion that cyberbullying is a low prevalence phenomenon [4]. As Tokunaga [23] suggests, and repeatedly emphasised by Mc Guckin [17] regarding traditional bullying, the inconsistencies across the various operational definitions (e.g., time reference periods for events to have happened) have resulted in researchers exploring different phenomena whilst using the same label (*i.e.*, cyberbullying). Furthermore, where one researcher might insist on repetition for an experience to be considered cyberbullying, another will accept just one incident as cyberbullying. Findings by Corcoran and Mc Guckin [3] constitute an important signpost for researchers—highlighting the need to look at definitional and conceptual issues with "fresh eyes" and to be open to the possibility of an alternative approach. In other words, it is time to reframe the problem, rather than persisting with trying to "fit a round peg in a square hole".

10. Why We Need to Reframe the Issue of Cyber-Based Abuse

In sum, a number of factors lead to the conclusion that the term cyber aggression may be a more appropriate term and concept than cyberbullying. First, cyberbullying implies a behaviour that is the cyber-based equivalent of traditional bullying, which in turn entails specific criteria (*i.e.*, repetition, power imbalance, and intent to cause harm). However, the contextual features of cyberspace mean that such criteria are not easily applied. Secondly, despite research exploring young people's perceptions of cyberbullying [2,28,30], there has been some difficulty in reaching a clear consensus regarding the defining aspects of cyberbullying. Thirdly, bullying is a form of social aggression [31] and thus cyberbullying would exclude incidents in which the aggressor(s) and victim(s) are strangers (e.g., happy slapping which would include acts such as using a camera phone to film a physical assault on a victim for the purpose of sharing it), which has implications in that education intended to prevent and counter cyberbullying would have a rather narrow scope. Surely it is more important to address all forms of aggression. Fourth, the findings of Corcoran and Mc Guckin [3] highlight the incompatibility between the academic understanding of cyberbullying and the student perception. Although this may highlight a need to educate students on the meaning of cyberbullying, perhaps the term cyber aggression would better serve our objectives. Indeed, the scale approach to assessing peer abuse in cyberspace revealed the incidence of behaviours which researchers and practitioners wish to better understand. Perhaps the term cyberbullying is in fact redundant and confusing. Fifth, the term cyberbullying may also carry a stigma which could account for the low incidence rate found by Corcoran and Mc Guckin [3]. This would further highlight the need for an alternative approach, and so a new focus on peer-directed cyber aggression is suggested.

11. Conclusion: A New Way Forward

Whilst Menesini [27] poses the question "How and to what extent might cyberbullying be underestimated if we neglect its specificity?" (p. 544), the present article poses the question, to what extent might we be underestimating the incidence and effects of cyber-based peer-to-peer abuse by constraining its conceptualisation and operationalisation with inappropriate criteria and labels? Perhaps the definition of aggression [32] which states that aggression is " … any behavior intended to harm another person that the target person wants to avoid" (p. 222) could be adapted for the purposes of cyber aggression. Therefore, also considering Langos' suggestion regarding appraisal of intent [14] and Pyżalski's inclusion of intent (but not repetition or power imbalance) when measuring electronic aggression [24], the following definition is proposed—"Cyber aggression refers to any behaviour enacted through the use of information and communication technologies that is intended to harm another person(s) that the target person(s) wants to avoid. Intent to cause harm should be judged on the basis of how a reasonable person would assess intent." In this way, the shackles of the traditional bullying framework can be removed, allowing a different path forward. Combined with Pyżalski's approach of examining the identity of the targeted individual(s) [24], it is possible to distinguish between peer-directed cyber aggression and other-directed cyber aggression. There is already acknowledgement that cyber aggression is a behaviour which can be identified as, for example, online harassment or Internet harassment [2], and Grigg [1] has hinted at the " … vagueness, restrictiveness and ambiguity … " (p. 152) of the term cyberbullying and suggested that perhaps the focus needs to shift towards this broader approach—a suggestion worth considering as research, practice, and prevention work matures.

Author Contributions: Lucie Corcoran was the primary author of this paper and was responsible for the write up and revisions to the manuscript. Conor Mc Guckin was involved in the planning of the paper and also contributed feedback, and editing throughout the writing process. Garry Prentice contributed feedback and editing throughout the writing process.

Conflicts of Interest: The authors declare no conflict of interest.

References

1. Grigg, D.W. Cyber-Aggression: Definition and Concept of Cyberbullying. *Aust. J. Guid. Counsell.* **2010**, *20*, 143–156.
2. Menesini, E.; Nocentini, A.; Palladino, B.E.; Scheithauer, H.; Schultze-Krumbholz, A.; Frisén, A.; Berne, S.; Luik, P.; Naruskov, K.; Ortega, R.; *et al.* Definitions of cyberbullying. In *Cyberbullying through the New Media: Findings from An International Network*; Smith, P.K., Steffgen, G., Eds.; Psychology Press: Oxfordshire, UK, 2013; pp. 23–36.
3. Corcoran, L.; Mc Guckin, C. The incidence of bullying and aggression in Irish post-primary schools: An investigation of school and cyber settings. In Proceedings of Annual Conference of the Educational Studies Association of Ireland, Sheraton Hotel, Athlone, Ireland, 10–12 April 2014.
4. Olweus, D. Cyberbullying: An overrated phenomenon? *Eur. J. Dev. Psychol.* **2012**, *9*, 520–538.
5. Smith, P.K. Cyberbullying: Challenges and opportunities for a research program—A response to Olweus (2012). *Eur. J. Dev. Psychol.* **2012**, *9*, 553–558.

6. Mc Guckin, C.; Cummins, P.K.; Lewis, C.A. f2f and cyberbullying among children in Northern Ireland: Data from the Kids Life and Times Surveys. *Psychol. Soc. Educ.* **2010**, *2*, 83–96.
7. Whitney, I.; Smith, P.K. A survey of the nature and extent of bullying in junior/middle and secondary schools. *Educ. Res.* **1993**, *35*, 3–25.
8. Campbell, M.A. Cyber Bullying: An Old Problem in a New Guise? *Aust. J. Guid. Counsell.* **2005**, *15*, 68–76.
9. Olweus, D. *Bullying At School: What We Know and What We Can Do*; Blackwell: Oxford, UK, 1993.
10. Farrington, D.P. Understanding and preventing bullying. *Crim. Justice* **1993**, *17*, 381–458.
11. O'Moore, M.; Minton, S.J. Cyber-bullying: The Irish experience. In *Handbook of Aggressive Behaviour Research*; Tawse, S., Quin, C., Eds.; Nova Science Publishers, Inc.: New York, NY, USA, 2009; pp. 269–292.
12. Kowalski, R.M.; Limber, S.P.; Agatston, P.W. *Cyber Bullying: Bullying in the Digital Age*; Blackwell: Malden, MA, USA, 2008.
13. Vandebosch, H.; Van Cleemput, K. Cyberbullying among youngsters: Profiles of bullies and victims. *New Media Soc.* **2009**, *11*, 1349–1371.
14. Langos, C. Cyberbullying: The challenge to define. *Cyberpsychol. Behav. Soc. Netw.* **2012**, *15*, 285–289.
15. Moore, G.E. Cramming more components onto integrated circuits. *Electronics* **1965**, *38*, 114–117.
16. Drogin, E.Y.; Young, K. Forensic Mental Health Aspects of Adolescent Cyber Bullying: A Jurisprudent Science Perspective. *J. Psychiatr. Law* **2008**, *36*, 679–690.
17. Mc Guckin, C. School bullying amongst school pupils in Northern Ireland: How many are involved, what are the health effects, and what are the issues for school management? In *Bullying in Irish Education*; O'Moore, A.M., Stevens, P., Eds.; Cork University Press: Cork, Ireland, 2013; pp. 46–64.
18. O'Moore, M.; Cross, D.; Valimaki, M.; Almeida, A.; Berne, S.; Kurki, M.; Olenik-Shemesh, D.; Heiman, T.; Deboutte, G.; Fandrem, H.; *et al.* Guidelines to prevent cyber-bullying: A cross-national review. In *Cyberbullying through the New Media: Findings from An International Network*; Smith, P.K., Steffgen, G., Eds.; Psychology Press: Oxfordshire, UK, 2013; pp. 136–161.
19. Anti-Bullying Procedures for Primary and Post-Primary Schools. Available online: http://www.education.ie/en/Publications/Policy-Reports/Anti-Bullying-Procedures-for-Primary-and-Post-Primary-Schools.pdf (accessed on 10 September 2014).
20. Mc Guckin, C.; Perren, S.; Corcoran, L.; Cowie, H.; Dehue, F.; Ševčíková, A.; Tsatsou, P.; Völlink, T. Coping with cyberbullying: How can we prevent cyberbullying and how victims can cope with it. In *Cyberbullying through the New Media: Findings from An International Network*; Smith, P.K., Steffgen, G., Eds.; Psychology Press: Oxfordshire, UK, 2013; pp. 120–135.
21. Belsey, B. Cyberbullying.ca. Available online: http://www.cyberbullying.ca (accessed on 10 September 2014).

22. Smith, P.K.; Mahdavi, J.; Carvalho, M.; Fisher, S.; Russell, S.; Tippett, N. Cyberbullying: Its nature and impact in secondary school pupils. *J. Child Psychol. Psychiatr.* **2008**, *49*, 376–385.

23. Tokunaga, R.S. Following you home from school: A critical review and synthesis of research on cyberbullying victimization. *Comput. Hum. Behav.* **2010**, *26*, 277–287.

24. Pyżalski, J. From cyberbullying to electronic aggression: Typology of the phenomenon. *Emot. Behav. Diffic.* **2012**, *17*, 305–317.

25. Carr-Fanning, K.; Mc Guckin, C.; Shevlin, M. Using student voice to escape the spider's web: A methodological approach to de-victimizing students with ADHD. *Trinity Educ. Papers* **2013**, *2*, 85–111.

26. Guerin, S.; Hennessy, E. Pupils' definitions of bullying. *Eur. J. Dev. Psychol.* **2002**, *17*, 249–261.

27. Menesini, E. Cyberbullying: The right value of the phenomenon. Comments on the paper "Cyberbullying: An overrated phenomenon?". *Eur. J. Dev. Psychol.* **2012**, *9*, 544–552.

28. Vandebosch, H.; Van Cleemput, K. Defining cyberbullying: A qualitative research into the perceptions of youngsters. *CyberPsycho. Behav.* **2008**, *11*, 499–503.

29. Sticca, F.; Ruggieri, S.; Alsaker, F.; Perren, S. Longitudinal risk factors for cyberbullying in adolescence. *J. Community Appl. Soc. Psychol.* **2013**, *23*, 52–67.

30. Nocentini, A.; Calmaestra, J.; Schultze-Krumbholz, A.; Scheithauer, H.; Ortega, R.; Menesini, E. Cyberbullying: Labels, Behaviours and Definition in Three European Countries. *Aust. J. Guid. Counsell.* **2010**, *20*, 129–142.

31. Björkqvist, K.; Ekman, K.; Lagerspetz, K. Bullies and victims: Their ego picture, ideal ego picture and normative ego picture. *Scand. J. Psychol.* **1982**, *23*, 307–313.

32. DeLamater, J.D.; Myers, D.J. *Social Psychology*; Wadsworth: Belmont, CA, USA, 2011.

Is Cyberbullying a Stand Alone Construct? Using Quantitative Analysis to Evaluate a 21st Century Social Question

Ryan Randa, Matt R. Nobles and Bradford W. Reyns

Abstract: Using a subsample of the 2009 National Crime Victimization Survey, School Crime Supplement (NCVS-SCS), the present study explores the nature of the relationship between cyberbullying and traditional bullying victimization among students aged 12–18. One question of particular interest in the recent cyberbullying literature regards the classification of cyberbullying relative to traditional school yard bullying. As is the case in the cyber victimization literature in general, the question has become whether cyberbullying is an extension of traditional bullying or whether it is a unique independent phenomenon. Using the available data we attempt to address this question by exploring cyberbullying victimization as a standalone construct. Results of exploratory factor analyses suggest that cyberbullying victimization is both interlaced with traditional bullying modalities, and experienced as a unique phenomenon. Our results contribute a 21st century texture and dimension to the traditional construct.

Reprinted from *Societies*. Cite as: Randa, R.; Nobles, M.R.; Reyns, B.W. Is Cyberbullying a Stand Alone Construct? Using Quantitative Analysis to Evaluate a 21st Century Social Question. *Societies* **2015**, *5*, 171–186.

1. Introduction

In America, a large majority of teens have their own cell phone, and almost two thirds of school age children (age 12–17) go online daily [1,2]. Social media and social networking online have emerged as a cultural reality over the past 25 years. By September 14, 2012 Facebook reportedly reached 1 billion registered users worldwide. Online experiences have become progressively integrated into all aspects of life, so much so that for today's tech savvy youth, an online presence is an expected part of their social life. The reality of their modern social experience is that being social means being online and mobile. As such, the separation of social contexts—online *versus* offline—may be an old way of thinking.

The social processes that are augmented, replaced, or otherwise affected by pervasive forms of personal technology are myriad. Individuals across continents can work together seamlessly in real time. Friends can stay in contact via their mobile web apps, and countless other innovations have made life better with the use of technology. While the benefits of these new ways of forming and maintaining social connections may seem countless, these developments also create divergent, and new negative social experiences. Of particular concern to contemporary youth is cyberbullying victimization—a subject that continues to garner interest in both academia and general public forums. To the casual observer, cyberbullying continues to be highlighted in the news media as a new and growing threat to youth in America. For example, as of 25 November 2014 the New York Times has published over 190 articles related to cyberbullying since 2003, 22 of which were printed since 2013. This attention may come in spite of research suggesting trends in cyber bulling victimization appear stable [3].

More empirical work on cyberbullying victimization continues to emerge that in many respects confirms the media message that cyberbullying victimization is serious, and has significant negative effects for victims. For example, cyberbullying victimization has been linked to a number of negative consequences including decreased academic performance, diminished perceptions of safety, depression, anxiety, reduced self-esteem, self-harm, emotional distress, and suicidal ideation among others [4–14]. Recent work has also explored the link between online victimization and "real world" behavioral consequences [15,16]. The present study explores the relationship between traditional bullying victimization and cyberbullying victimization with the intent to better understand how these forms of bullying relate to one another among a large national level sample of American youth. Over time, one of the questions that has emerged from the empirical cyberbullying literature has been—is cyberbullying an extension of traditional bullying victimization? As we see it, the question is—is cyberbullying victimization nested within the broader context of traditional bullying victimization, or is cyberbullying an isolated free standing construct?

2. Literature Review

2.1. Traditional Bullying

Research on bullying began appearing in the social science literature base with regularity in the latter part of the 1970s. Most of this work was European, (particularly Scandinavian) and since that time the base of knowledge on this topic has become increasingly mainstream and global [17–22]. While the majority of students do not experience bullying (e.g., [16]) research suggests that males are significantly more involved as both bullies and victims [18,22,23]. Students who are new to high school (incoming freshmen) experience more bullying victimization [23]. Unnever and Cornell [24] find bullying victimization was reported more frequently by girls and students in the lower grades. Bullying victimization has been linked to forms of aggressive behavior such as frequent fighting, fighting-related injury and weapon carrying for both boys and girls [18,25].

Longstanding definitions of the phenomenon generally refer to three major components of behavior which have been codified as distinguishing bullying from other forms of conflict among youth: (1) the intent to harm; (2) repeated behavior; and (3) and an imbalance of power [26]. Additionally bullying has been identified as repeated acts of physical or verbal aggression with intent to humiliate the victim [21]. Over time, specific attention has been paid to the *classification* of bullying through establishing more nuanced typologies; direct overt bullying (including verbal and physical) and indirect (social and relational which can include social exclusion) [27–30]. Others have classified bullying typologies as physical, verbal, and relational [31]. While these typologies are inclusive, encompassing a wide range of bullying forms and tactics, what remains to be seen is just how "typical" manifestations of *cyberbullying* will, or will not, fit within them. Are they more appropriately conceptualized within verbal bullying due to the distal nature of interactions, alongside verbal and physical bullying as a core typology due to conceptual or operational overlap with both forms, or separately from traditional bullying altogether?

2.2. Cyberbullying

In contrast to the traditional bullying literature, which has evolved over time to include well-accepted definitions, refined measures, and empirical examination across diverse populations, the cyberbullying research base is still comparatively young. Research into the extent and nature of cyberbullying began in earnest less than 10 years ago, but in that time tremendous progress has been made in understanding its prevalence, victims, perpetrators, and consequences. Yet, important questions remain surrounding this relatively new form of victimization. As is the case with other related forms of cybercrime victimization, such as cyberstalking or online harassment, it is not clear whether cyberbullying is a unique behavior, separate and distinct from its physical counterpart or simply an extension of traditional bullying carried out in cyberspace [32].

Most definitions of cyberbullying implicitly suggest that cyberbullying is essentially "bullying in cyberspace." For example, von Marées and Petermann [33], (p. 468) define cyberbullying as " ... bullying via the use of the internet, mobile phone, or a combination of both ... " Similarly, Patchin and Hinduja [10], (p. 152) explain that cyberbullying is "willful and repeated harm inflicted through the medium of electronic text." A more detailed definition provided by Smith *et al.* [34], (p. 367) describes cyberbullying as "An aggressive, intentional act carried out by a group or individual, using electronic forms of contact, repeatedly and over time against a victim who cannot easily defend him or herself." The common thread underlying each of these definitions is intentional harm experienced by victims through an electronic medium. The operational definition of cyberbullying for the current study

15

reflects this focus on the consequences experienced by the victim, and the commission of the cyberbullying act through electronic means.

Opportunities for cyberbullying victimization have grown with the expansion and integration of technology in society. Indeed, convenient communication tools such as emails, instant messages, and text messages delivered by phones, tablets, laptops, and even videogame devices have made these opportunities nearly ubiquitous. It is important to point out, however, that estimates of the extent of cyberbullying differ depending on cyberbullying definitions, measurement choices, and populations being studied by researchers. With this caveat in mind, estimates of the prevalence of cyberbullying are widely varied, and occasionally provide an inconsistent portrayal of the nature and scope of victimization. For example, in 2006 Li [35] reported that about 25% of students in a Canadian sample of adolescents had experienced cyberbullying, whereas a 2010 work by Mishna and colleagues [36] reported that half of their sample of Canadian middle and high schools students had been victims of cyberbullying. Examining a global convenience sample of adolescent Internet users in 2008, Hinduja and Patchin [37] reported cyberbullying victimization estimates of 32% for boys and 36% for girls (though they also noted no statistically significant difference between boys and girls as either victim or offender, p. 142). These three studies are fairly representative of the vast body of work that has estimated the prevalence of cyberbullying victimization, in addition to illustrating the point that these estimates are wide-ranging [34,38–40].

In addition to being prevalent, cyberbullying is also harmful. While cyberbullying experiences will be unique with distinct effects, an increasing number of studies suggest that experiencing cyberbullying can be very emotionally damaging to victims. Victims can experience a host of negative consequences ranging from self-harm to avoiding school to depression [6,13,16]. For example, Hinduja and Patchin [41] have suggested that cyberbullying victimization can lead to offline behavioral problems such as delinquency. Kowalski and colleagues [42] concluded that those who experience cyberbullying victimization often themselves become cyberbullies and vice versa.

As the previous discussion illustrates, much is known about the nature of cyberbullying. This knowledge base continues to grow as global research emerges addressing the extent to which victims of traditional bullying who are targets of threats, rumors, insults, exclusion, exploitation, and physical assault are also targeted online by their bullies in the form of cyberbullying [4,9,43]. Common cyberbullying behaviors include these same traditional behaviors, such as receiving threats and insults carried out through various online communications such as online gaming forums, text messages, social networks, emails, and other websites. Cyberbullies may also exclude victims from online activities, such as multiplayer videogame channels. If bullies are expanding their domain to into these online realms, it suggests that cyberbullying may be an extension of the traditional behaviors that victims are enduring at school. If, however, cyberbullying victims tend to only experience these online harms then cyberbullying may indeed be a distinct form of victimization [44,45].

While some contextualized research supports the assertion that there is overlap between bullying victimization and cyberbullying victimization [38,46] scholars have not fully investigated which bullying and cyberbullying victimization experiences overlap. The current study focuses on comparing and contrasting several potential indicators of conceptual and measurement overlap in a large, nationally representative sample of victims. Addressing this issue is important for the ongoing study of both bullying and cyberbullying in America. Any conceptual and measurement similarities and differences have the potential to inform future research, inductive theory development, and policy related youth victimization.

3. Data and Methods

Data for the present study originated from the 2009 National Crime Victimization Survey—School Crime Supplement (NCVS-SCS). The School Crime Supplement of the NCVS is considered an "occasional" supplement, but it has been collected with regularity since 1995 (every 2 years beginning 2003). This supplement collects interview data from NCVS household members age 12–18 who had attended a qualifying school in the past six months (typically between January and June), and asks them to reference the current school year. The 2009 SCS sample nets nearly 4000 cases in a national level multi-stage cluster sample. Within this sample 1232 students reported experiencing some form of traditional bullying victimization, and 269 reported a least one cyberbullying victimization experience.

The analyses included three stages, with each stage designed to allow differences between traditional bullying and cyberbullying to emerge. In the first stage we present simple cross tabulations of traditional bullying victimization and cyberbullying victimization to illustrate the degree of overlap that exists between them. We attempt to provide evidence which would facilitate either a "grand" bullying variable in the future—or on the other hand—support including cyberbullying as an additional measure in future bullying research. In the second stage of analysis we further assess the constructs of traditional bullying *vs.* cyberbullying using a technique similar to alpha modeling to assess the relative stability of these phenomena both independently and collectively. Given the prevalence of overlap between victimization types, the common theme of bullying victimization, and the research questions at hand, we proceed by generating a single reliability score to illustrate congruity in bullying victimization types. Finally, we explore similarities and differences in the constructs through exploratory factor analysis techniques, which articulate the unique characteristics of cyberbullying victimization. Conducting an exploratory factor analysis allows us to further

17

investigate the relationship between traditional and cyberbullying victimization responses, specifically assessing cross-item associations that exist in the data. Across these techniques we adjust for the dichotomous nature of our victimization indicators by using a tetrachoric correlation matrix. Most readers are familiar with the typical Pearson correlation matrix and the corresponding coefficients presented (r). However, when exploring entirely discrete data the most suitable process differs from the traditional method.

The principal question addressed in this study hinges on how bullying, both traditional and cyber forms, are conceptualized and measured in quantitative research. More specifically, how do they fit together for quantitative analysis? To that end, we use a number of advanced, and in some cases non-traditional analytical techniques, to explore a unified bullying construct.

Bullying Variables

The 2009 NCVS-SCS included 13 different items that address bullying in general. Seven of these are suited to address the more traditional concepts of schoolyard bullying. The remaining six items have been tailored to address technology-driven bullying victimization experiences. Each of these items are dichotomous in nature, students reporting yes or no answers. The individual items were introduced to the respondent through the following statement: "Now I have some questions about what students do that could occur anywhere and that make you feel bad or are hurtful to you. You may include events you told me about already. During this school year, has another student...." Traditional *Bullying* is addressed through SCS items including: " ... has another student ... " (1) "Made fun of you, called you names, or insulted you?"; (2) "Spread rumors about you?"; (3) "Threatened you with harm?"; (4) "Pushed you, shoved you, tripped you, or spit on you?"; (5) "Tried to make you do things you did not want to do, for example, give them money or other things?"; (6) "Excluded you from activities on purpose?"; and (7) "Destroyed your property on purpose?" Collectively, any positive response to any of these categories results in a score of *Bullying* $\alpha = 0.75$, suggesting a certain degree of success in the measurement of traditional bullying.

The cyberbullying items included in the survey were: (1) "Posted hurtful information about you on the Internet, for example, on a social networking site like MySpace or Facebook?"; (2) "Threatened or insulted you through email?"; (3) "Threatened or insulted you through instant messaging?"; (4) "Threatened or insulted you through text messaging?" (5) "Threatened or insulted you through online gaming, for example, while playing a game, through Second Life, or through XBOX [Live]?"; and (6) "Purposefully excluded you from an online community, for example, a buddy list or friends list?" These six items when combined would result in a *Cyberbullying* score of α = 0.63. [1]

Interestingly, the school crime supplement has evolved over time and added questions related to cyberbullying as they emerge in social sphere. The online social world changes very quickly and seemingly overnight the online social experience can evolve. The 2009 iteration adds questions related to victimization on specific online communities that cater to youths playing online video games. Cyberbullying item 5 addresses these online communities and provides us an opportunity to capture and include possible trends in victimization occurring on the leading edges of American youths social experiences.

4. Results

Our primary question addressed the classification of cyberbullying in relation to traditional bullying victimization. Specifically, does cyberbullying victimization typify an "extension" of school yard bullying, or does it manifest as a separate and distinct construct? In general, our results provided mixed support for either position.

4.1. Bivariate Associations

Table 1 presents a two-way table relating the prevalence of traditional bullying victimization to cyberbullying victimization. First, it should be noted that 29% of the sample reported some form of bullying victimization within the past school year. In Table 1, we present the distribution of cases, percentages (by row, column, and total N), and ultimately the bivariate correlation between cyberbullying victimization and traditional bullying victimization (rho = 0.67; $p < 0.000$). A large majority (83.27%) of cyberbullying victims report also experiencing traditional bullying victimization. And another 18.18% of traditional bullying victims report experiencing cyberbullying, supporting the intuitive position that traditional bullying and cyberbullying are indeed related. Importantly, we find that cyberbullying victimization is experienced outside of traditional bullying victimization. In this sample, 16.73% of those students reporting cyberbullying victimization report no traditional bullying victimization experiences. These results suggest that to some degree cyberbullying victimization is not an entirely collateral experience and is experienced by some as a separate form of victimization. There may be key features of the offenders, the victims, or the situations themselves that are accountable for the discrepancy in modalities. That being said, the majority of cyberbullying victimization is experienced by those already exposed to traditional school yard bullying.

---

[1] Original responses were coded categorically where respondent options included "never", "once or twice this school year", "once or twice a month", "once or twice a week", and "almost every day".

Table 1. Two-way presentation of Bullying and Cyberbullying Victimization.

			Bullying				
			No		Yes		Total
Cyberbullying	No	3087 ** 98.56%	* 75.38%	1008 ** 81.82%	* 24.62%	4095 93.8%	
	Yes	45 ** 1.44%	* 16.73%	224 ** 18.18%	* 83.27%	269 6.2%	
	Total	3132		1232		4364	

Pearson χ^2	438.157	$p < 0.000$
Tetrachoric rho	0.674	$p < 0.000$

Note: * Row Percent; ** Column Percent.

Table 2 elaborates on the basic association between bullying and cyberbullying victimization presented in Table 1 by further unpacking the individual cyberbullying elements relative to the victims' broad scale victimization experiences. This table (Table 2) presents the number of individuals reporting each of the specific forms of cyberbullying victimization as well as a proportion of the number of line item victims that also reported traditional bullying victimization. Of the six different cyberbullying victimization line items, five items display a substantial proportion of their victims also experiencing traditional forms of bullying. Among the cyberbullying items, the lowest proportion reporting traditional bullying experiences is the item Cyber 5, which refers to victimization through online gaming outlets such as XBOX Live (0.69). Based on these results, and the need for clarity regarding the position of cyberbullying in the broader scheme of victimization, we further explore evidence that would illustrate the clearest picture in conceptual overlap and/or differentiation. Stage two of the analysis therefore explores deeper connections between individual elements of bullying victimization.

Table 2. Comparison of Victims of Cyberbullying (Only) to Victims of Both Forms of Bullying.

Variable		Traditional Bullying (NO)		Traditional Bullying (YES)		Total	Proportion Overlapping
		n	% of Sample	n	% of Sample		
Cyber 1	(Facebook)	13	0.4%	78	6%	91	0.857
Cyber 2	(Email)	9	0.3%	49	4%	58	0.845
Cyber 3	(IM)	6	0.2%	73	6%	79	0.924
Cyber 4	(Texts)	15	0.5%	119	10%	134	0.888
Cyber 5	(Games)	10	0.3%	22	2%	32	0.688
Cyber 6	(Forums)	2	0.1%	35	3%	37	0.946

4.2. Item Reliability Analysis

Alpha reliability coefficients (Cronbach's alpha) are regularly used to demonstrate internal consistency, or the strength of a collection of variables to represent a construct [46]. This consistency or strength is then conveyed through a score between 0 and 1 that represents the inter-item correlation. More generally speaking, the higher this score, the more we assume the items to be congruent in capturing the same broad construct. As noted earlier, using entirely discrete data can be problematic. However, the Kuder-Richardson method compensates for, or accommodates binary data. Thus results displayed here in Table 3 can be interpreted as they would in a traditional alpha reliability analysis, yet the figures are derived from an alternative formula. As noted above there are several items available in the NCVS-SCS that address issues of bullying victimization as well as items that address cyberbullying victimization. As a part of the exploratory process we evaluate the alpha scores associated with the two possible conceptual classifications: (1) cyberbullying as a standalone construct; and (2) cyberbullying as a nested component of a more inclusive general bullying phenomenon. The results of this modeling process are presented in Table 3.

Table 3. Combined Bullying Victimization Kuder-Richardson Reliability Modeling ($N = 4346$).

Item	Brief Description	Item Difficulty	Item-Rest Correlation	Item Variance
Traditional 1	(Making Fun)	0.1871	0.5493	0.1521
Traditional 2	(Spreading Rumors)	0.1661	0.5741	0.1385
Traditional 3	(Threatening)	0.0575	0.4669	0.0542
Traditional 4	(Pushing, Shoving)	0.0916	0.5143	0.0832
Traditional 5	(Coercion)	0.0359	0.3856	0.0346
Traditional 6	(Exclusion)	0.0458	0.4557	0.0437
Traditional 7	(Destroying Property)	0.0324	0.4013	0.0314
Cyber 1	(Facebook)	0.0209	0.3125	0.0205
Cyber 2	(Email)	0.0133	0.2913	0.0132
Cyber 3	(IM)	0.0182	0.3803	0.0178
Cyber 4	(Texts)	0.0308	0.3976	0.0299
Cyber 5	(Games)	0.0071	0.0998	0.0071
Cyber 6	(Forums)	0.0083	0.2641	0.0082
Test		0.550	0.3918	
K-R Coef.				0.7628

First, we address the combined traditional and cyberbullying measures in one cumulative bullying construct, for which the Kuder-Richardson coefficient is 0.76. Second, we assess the constructs independently. The coefficient for the traditional bullying items alone is 0.75, and finally, the "alpha" score for the collection of cyberbullying items alone is 0.63. [2] Each of these scores individually suggests that the internal consistency of the measured concept is fair to acceptable. The comparatively lower alpha score for the cyberbullying measures alone does not necessarily mean it is a poorer construct; fewer items and fewer cases available for that portion of the analysis make a lower score somewhat justifiable. In sum, there are two key results to note from the examination of item reliability. First, both the traditional bullying items and the cyberbullying items create relatively stable and consistent independent constructs. And second, the inclusion of cyberbullying elements into a cumulative "grand" bullying measure does not markedly increase the stability of the traditional bullying scale.

4.3. Principal Components Analysis (PCA)

Classification of cyberbullying can also be addressed through further exploratory analysis. This process allows us, in essence, to process a number of individual items in such a way that their natural correlational patterns will produce variable clustering (or loadings). While there are a number of potential factor analytic solutions, the simplest and most direct for our purpose is a variation on the principal components method. Specifically, the nature of the research question suggests the possibility of correlated factors, supporting oblique (promax) rotations that naturally accommodate correlation of the factors rather than the alternative orthogonal (varimax) rotations. Table 4 presents a principal components analysis, derived from the tetrachoric correlation matrix, and the factor from a promax rotated solution when limiting to two factors. The two loaded components closely align with traditional bullying victimization and cyberbullying victimization constructs. Interestingly, initial extractions of bullying elements (Table 4) produce three components with Eigenvalues over 1.0. Entering all 13 items in a principal components analysis, we find that the elements of traditional bullying cluster on one factor and elements of cyberbullying victimization will cluster on another when constrained; when unconstrained, however, more interesting results emerge. Unlike simple evaluation of item reliability using alpha scores, principal components analysis yields a variety and depth of useful, textured results. Traditional bullying literature suggests that there are a number of identified modes of bullying victimization, yet the seven items representing traditional bullying victimization did not initially break out by verbal,

---

[2] The removal of one cyberbullying variable addressing victimization through online gaming mediums improves the Cronbach's alpha score of the cyberbullying composite, suggesting a possible sub group or sub form related specifically to online gaming.

22

physical, and relational forms, they remained clustered while cyber elements loaded separately on another factor.

Table 4. Exploratory PCA, Promax Rotated Solution, Two Factors (tetrachoric matrix).

Variable	Component 1	Component 2	Unexplained
Traditional 1	0.445		0.204
Traditional 2	0.285		0.228
Traditional 3	0.404		0.311
Traditional 4	0.414		0.259
Traditional 5	0.356		0.390
Traditional 6	0.368		0.311
Traditional 7	0.341		0.359
Cyber 1		0.389	0.353
Cyber 2		0.478	0.221
Cyber 3		0.483	0.114
Cyber 4		0.374	0.282
Cyber 5			0.736
Cyber 6		0.385	0.311

In the interest of better understanding a data driven classification scheme, Table 5 represents a variation in the classification scheme that parses cyberbullying elements into two sub-groups. The larger of the two groups features Cyber elements 1–4 which address email, instant messaging, text messaging and internet postings, where Cyber element 5 ("Has another student: threatened or insulted you through online gaming?") and Cyber element 6 ("Has another student purposefully excluded you from an online community?") appear to diverge from the remainder of the cyberbullying elements in constituting the third factor. The relative strength of the online gaming element in the third factor may be important in understanding and developing the most appropriate means for classification of these types of victimization.

The final exploratory factor analysis provides similar results, but expands the number of allowable components to five. This expansion presented in Table 6 facilitates further discriminatory analysis on which elements of bullying and cyberbullying will cluster differently than expected, if allowed. The resulting component formations are a departure from the findings from the previous rotations in Tables 4 and 5, and generally represent a "spectrum" of victimization experiences, some of which involve clustered behaviors and some of which integrate aspects of both traditional and cyberbullying. Traditional bullying elements break out into a mix of relational and physical typologies seen in component 2. Component 5 is dominated by the measure of traditional bullying associated with "making you do something you don't want to" which we have previously labeled as 'coercion'.

Bullying in the form of purposeful exclusion takes form in component 3, consisting of a traditional bullying item regarding exclusion from activities (Traditional 6 "Exclusion") in combination with a cyberbullying item focusing on exclusion from online communities (Cyber 6). Component 1 consists of cyber items pertaining to email, text, instant message and internet postings. Lastly, consistent with the results in Table 4, component 4 stands alone with the single item referencing online gaming.

Table 5. Promax Rotated Principal Components (Comp.) Extraction of Bullying Items (Three Factors).

	Comp. 1	Comp. 2	Comp. 3	Unexplained
Traditional 1	0.444			0.198
Traditional 2	0.281			0.179
Traditional 3	0.399			0.264
Traditional 4	0.415			0.251
Traditional 5	0.378			0.377
Traditional 6	0.369			0.299
Traditional 7	0.345			0.296
Cyber 1		0.470		0.245
Cyber 2		0.461		0.219
Cyber 3		0.469		0.113
Cyber 4		0.443		0.202
Cyber 5			0.821	0.094
Cyber 6		0.309	0.292	0.278

Table 6. Promax Rotated Principal Components Extraction of Bullying Items (Five Factors).

	Comp. 1	Comp. 2	Comp. 3	Comp. 4	Comp. 5	Unexplained
Traditional 1		0.296				0.190
Traditional 2			0.229			0.170
Traditional 3		0.368				0.250
Traditional 4		0.646				0.137
Traditional 5					0.900	0.051
Traditional 6			0.758			0.090
Traditional 7		0.558				0.222
Cyber 1	0.474					0.244
Cyber 2	0.543					0.098
Cyber 3	0.463					0.107
Cyber 4	0.450					0.183
Cyber 5				0.850		0.088
Cyber 6			0.327			0.148
* Proportion	0.30	0.20	0.12	0.11	0.09	

* Proportion of variance accounted for by component.

5. Discussion and Conclusion

The overarching purpose of this study was to evaluate competing conceptual and measurement approaches to the operationalization and classification of cyberbullying victimization. More simply, the goal of this work was to examine whether cyberbullying victimization was truly a unique phenomenon when exploring a large data set. Each of the preceding analyses has contributed insight to a data driven, framework aided, classification process whereby we attempt to find the best fit for cyberbullying victimization relative to the broader bullying victimization scheme. Results show that in this sample traditional bullying and cyberbullying victimization experiences are generally associated (rho = 0.67) and there is a great deal of overlap in the experience of both traditional and cyber victimization. However, the empirical data supports operationalization and measurement of cyberbullying victimization as a distinct outcome. The exploration of these constructs allows us to go beyond simple bivariate associations to contrast dimensional stability when operationalizing in several different ways. We found early evidence that a "grand" bullying variable is viable, but not necessarily more stable than traditional bullying alone. We also find that cyberbullying elements can arguably stand alone as a separate but related construct. Yet, critical to this is the exposure to victimization via online gaming communities.

Exploratory factor analysis produced a more detailed specification of bullying which delineates traditional bullying elements including physical, verbal, and exclusion bullying, but importantly adds dimension to cyberbullying in the context of a grand bullying victimization scheme where online gaming stands out from other mediums such as email, text, instant message and online postings. In particular, this collection of findings has great potential to create future avenues of research in the cyber-social realm of youths. While cyberbullying victimization has the potential to fall within the traditional rubric of relational bullying dimensions as the wording of these items addresses 'threat and insults', and those items (traditional or cyber) addressing exclusion load together (purposeful exclusion), we have exposed an area where there is much to learn: online gaming communities. Today's youth experience their social lives in such a way that online gaming environments may share distinct similarities with the traditional playground. So powerful are these dimensional differences that in all of our presented exploratory models, victimization in gaming environments commanded its own recognition. While other included mediums for experiencing victimization such as text or instant message could be considered facilitators of traditional relational bullying, online gaming may be a separate form of social world which traditional forms of bullying take place within. Thus, while in answering the question we set out to, we can suggest that with the exception of the online gaming environment, "cyberbullying" is a means to experience relational bullying. Yet, we cannot exclude the gaming environment as it is a part of the ever

25

changing cyber social reality. As such, the online gaming world needs exploration to establish whether it should be considered a tool for delivery or a nested cyber social world in which traditional forms of victimization take place. The real value of this exploration may be in the admission that classifying the victimization experience is conceivably unrelated to what we understand about perpetration. The victimization experience may be more a reflection of the tools available within one's social circles. If traditional and cyber bullying are expressions of power within the confines of a social circle rather than a physical space, the dimensions of victimization are likely to reflect the contextualized means of the group. Perhaps the isolation of the recognition of the online gaming group within the data is a reflection of a uniquely clustered social structure among American youth. It may be that while many youth play video games as a part of their social experience, some small number of them live their entire social life within this arena. Further research is required in the area of bullying modality in concordance to group social settings.

Several ancillary findings also arise here, some of which may be instrumental in discussions about policy as well as theory. For example, while bullying and cyberbullying outcomes may be considered independent but related constructs, among these respondents experiencing cyberbullying without traditional bulling is uncommon. Among cyberbullying victims, only 16.73% reported not experiencing traditional bullying, and only 1% of all respondents reported experiencing cyberbullying without having experiencing any form of traditional bullying victimization. Conversely, and perhaps equally important, we find that a large majority (83%) of cyberbullying victims report experiencing both cyber and traditional bulling victimization. Furthermore, nearly 1 in 5 victims of traditional bullying is also being victimized 'online'. These findings are strongly suggestive that a comprehensive and integrated approach to prevention is appropriate. Further, the apparent predominance of overlap between the two forms inspires numerous questions about the etiology of offending. For example, do bullies specialize in one form over another, perhaps as a function of rational choice considerations about skill, expertise, or detectability? As the multi-disciplinary study of bullying and cyberbullying moves forward, there will undoubtedly be opportunities to apply traditional criminological theories to better understand these complicated dynamics.

As with any exploratory research, several limitations of the present study must be noted. First, a common feature of virtually all empirical analysis of cyberbullying to date is that datasets that include measures of cyberbullying are still relatively limited. Even when a nationally representative sample from the NCVS is used, as in this study, the relatively broad spectrum of victimization experiences and relatively few cyberbullying cases available presents challenges for analysis. Although it might be insightful to work with particular subsets of cases in order to identify relationships between specific risk factors and victimization sequelae (e.g., gendered or race-based cyberbullying), these relationships are difficult to explore with the available secondary data. Second, the results presented here cannot address a fundamental issue with time ordering. Thus, while some of the findings suggest that the majority of victims of bullying also experience cyberbullying, without a more extensive understanding of ordering, we cannot conclude that cyberbullying victimization is a logical extension of the school yard experience. Third, the data here are a secondary and many readers familiar with the bullying literature will note deviations from the contemporary structuring of questions and examination of victim-offender overlap. As these elements are not a part of the survey's design, we sacrifice specificity for a large sample of students from across the United States. Finally, a common feature of bullying definitions is the power imbalance between bully and victim which cannot be addressed here. The result of this may be that we have cast a wider net which would include fighting among peers.

Similar to other emerging areas of literature, most notably the stalking/cyberstalking nexus, criminologists will soon be forced to confront nuanced conceptual and measurement problems when determining how to appropriately classify and accurately capture these experiences. Relatively little work to date has been published related to the similarities and differences in bullying and cyberbullying victimization in the United States, despite the growing volume of work globally. Our results suggest that bullying victimization can be experienced with conceptual distinction and empirical overlap among American youth, but replication with richer and larger data is a logical next step. Moreover, future researchers will need to ask why bullying victimization clusters along dimensions as they do here. As the field builds evidence-based consensus on these issues, the next generation of researchers will be in position to move forward with theoretical as well as policy-oriented work.

Author Contributions: R. Randa and M. R. Nobles conceived of the modeling process. R. Randa completed the modeling and constructed the tables, wrote the methods, results, and drafted the discussion and conclusion sections. B. W. Reyns wrote the introduction and literature review and aided in the construction of the remainder of the paper, as well as the revisions. M. R. Nobles aided in the completion of the manuscript and the interpretation of the findings.

Conflicts of Interest: The authors declare no conflict of interest.

References

1. Lenhart, A.; Ling, R.; Campbell, S.; Purcell, K. *Teens and Mobile Phones*; Pew Research Center: Washington, DC, USA, 2010. Available online: http://www.pewinternet.org/files/old-media//Files/Reports/2010/PIP-Teens-and-Mobile-2010-with-topline.pdf (accessed on 29 August 2014).

2.   Lenhart, A.; Purcell, K.; Smith, A.; Zickuhr, K. *Social Media & Mobile Internet Use Among Teens and Young Adults*; Pew Research Center: Washington, DC, USA, 2010. Available online: http://www.pewinternet.org/files/oldmedia//Files/Reports/2010/PIP_Social_Media_and_Young_Adults_Report_Final_with_toplines.pdf (accessed on 29 August 2014).

3.   Beran, T.; Li, Q. The relationship between cyberbullying and school bullying. *J. Stud. Wellbeing* **2007**, *1*, 15–33.

4.   Olweus, D. Cyberbullying: An overrated phenomenon? *Eur. J. Dev. Psych.* **2012**, *9*, 520–538.

5.   Esbensen, F.A.; Carson, D.C. Consequences of being bullied results from a longitudinal assessment of bullying victimization in a multisite sample of American students. *Youth Soc.* **2009**, *41*, 209–233.

6.   Hay, C.; Meldrum, R. Bullying victimization and adolescent self-harm: Testing hypotheses from general strain theory. *J. Youth Adolesc.* **2010**, *39*, 446–459.

7.   Hinduja, S.; Patchin, J.W. Bullying, cyberbullying and suicide. *Arch. Suicide Res.* **2010**, *14*, 206–221.

8.   Houbre, B.; Tarquinio, C.; Thuillier, I.; Hergott, E. Bullying among students and its consequences on health. *Eur. J. Psychol. Educ.* **2006**, *21*, 183–208.

9.   Juvonen, J.; Gross, E.F. Extending the school grounds?—Bullying experiences in cyberspace. *J. Sch. Health* **2008**, *78*, 496–505.

10. Patchin, J.W.; Hinduja, S. Bullies move beyond the schoolyard. A preliminary look at cyberbullying. *Youth Violence Juv. Justice* **2006**, *4*, 148–169.

11. Rigby, K. Consequences of bullying in schools. *Can. J. Psychiatry* **2003**, *48*, 583–590.

12. Varjas, K.; Henrich, C.C.; Meyers, J. Urban middle school students' perceptions of bullying, cyberbullying, and school safety. *J. Sch. Violence* **2009**, *8*, 159–176.

13. Ybarra, M.L. Linkages between depressive symptomatology and internet harassment among young regular internet users. *Cyberpsychol. Behav.* **2004**, *7*, 247–257.

14. Ybarra, M.L.; Diener-West, M.; Leaf, P.J. Examining the overlap in internet harassment and school bullying: Implications for school intervention. *J. Adolesc. Health* **2007**, *41*, S42–S50.

15. Randa, R. The influence of the cyber-social environment on fear of victimization: Cyberbullying and school. *Security J.* **2013**, *26*, 331–348.

16. Randa, R.; Reyns, B. Cyberbullying Victimization and Adaptive Avoidance Behaviors at School. *Vict. Offenders 2014*, **2014**, *9*, 255–275.

17. Dake, J.A.; Price, J.H.; Telljohann, S.K. The nature and extent of bullying at school. *J. Sch. Health* **2003**, *73*, 173–180.

18. Nansel, T.R.; Overpeck, M.D.; Haynie, D.L.; Ruan, W.; Scheidt, P.C. Relationships between bullying and violence among US youth. *Arch. Pediatr. Adolesc. Med.* **2003**, *157*, 348–353.

19. Olweus, D. *Aggression in the Schools: Bullies and Whipping Boys*; Hemisphere: Washington, DC, USA, 1978.

20. Olweus, D. Antisocial Behaviour in the School Setting. In *Psychopathic Behaviour: Approaches to Research*; Hare, R.D., Schalling, D., Eds.; John Wiley & Sons, Ltd.: Chichester, UK, 1978; pp. 319–327.

21. Olweus, D. Bullying at school: Basic facts and effects of a school based intervention program. *J. Child Psychol. Psychiatry* **1994**, *35*, 1171–1190.

22. Seals, D.; Young, J. Bullying and victimization: Prevalence and relationship to gender, grade level, ethnicity, self-esteem, and depression. *Adolescence* **2003**, *38*, 735–747.

23. Pepler, D.J.; Craig, W.M.; Connolly, J.A.; Yuile, A.; McMaster, L.; Jiang, D. A developmental perspective on bullying. *Aggress. Behav.* **2006**, *32*, 376–384.

24. Unnever, J.D.; Cornell, D.G. Middle school victims of bullying: Who reports being bullied? *Aggress. Behav.* **2004**, *30*, 373–388.

25. Cunningham, P.B.; Henggeler, S.W.; Limber, S.P.; Melton, G.B.; Nation, M.A. Patterns and correlates of gun ownership among nonmetropolitan and rural middle school students. *J. Clin. Child Adolesc. Psychol.* **2000**, *29*, 432–442.

26. Gladden, R.M.; Vivolo-Kantor, A.M.; Hamburger, M.E.; Lumpkin, C.D. *Bullying Surveillance Among Youths: Uniform Definitions for Public Health and Recommended Data Elements*; Version 1.0; National Center for Injury Prevention and Control, Centers for Disease Control and Prevention and U.S. Department of Education: Atlanta, GA, USA, 2014.

27. Lagerspetz, K.M.; Björkqvist, K.; Peltonen, T. Is indirect aggression typical of females? Gender differences in aggressiveness in 11- to 12-year-old children. *Aggress. Behav.* **1988**, *14*, 403–414.

28. Galen, B.R.; Underwood, M.K. A developmental investigation of social aggression among children. *Dev. Psychol.* **1997**, *33*, 589–599.

29. Crick, N.R.; Grotpeter, J.K. Relational aggression, gender, and social-psychological adjustment. *Child Dev.* **1995**, *66*, 710–722.

30. Crick, N.R. The role of overt aggression, relational aggression, and prosocial behavior in the prediction of children's future social adjustment. *Child Dev.* **1996**, *67*, 2317–2327.

31. Scheithauer, H.; Hayer, T.; Petermann, F.; Jugert, G. Physical, verbal, and relational forms of bullying among German students: Age trends, gender differences, and correlates. *Aggress. Behav.* **2006**, *32*, 261–275.

32. Nobles, M.R.; Reyns, B.W.; Fox, K.A.; Fisher, B.S. Protection Against Pursuit: A Conceptual and Empirical Comparison of Cyberstalking and Stalking Victimization Among a National Sample. *Justice Q.* **2014**, *31*, 986–1014.

33. Von Marées, N.; Petermann, F. Cyberbullying: An increasing challenge for schools. *Sch. Psychol. Int.* **2012**, *33*, 467–476.

34. Smith, P.K.; Mahdavi, J.; Carvalho, M.; Fisher, S.; Russell, S.; Tippett, N. Cyberbullying: Its nature and impact in secondary school pupils. *J. Child Psychol. Psychiatry* **2008**, *49*, 376–385.

35. Li, Q. Cyberbullying in schools a research of gender differences. *Sch. Psychol. Int.* **2006**, *27*, 157–170.

36. Mishna, F.; Cook, C.; Gadalla, T.; Daciuk, J.; Solomon, S. Cyber bullying behaviors among middle and high school students. *Am. J. Orthopsychiatr.* **2010**, *80*, 362–374.

37. Hinduja, S.; Patchin, J.W. Cyberbullying: An exploratory analysis of factors related to offending and victimization. *Deviant Behav.* **2008**, *29*, 129–156.

38. Erdur-Baker, Ö. Cyberbullying and its correlation to traditional bullying, gender and frequent and risky usage of internet-mediated communication tools. *New Media Soc.* **2010**, *12*, 109–125.

39. Kraft, E.; Wang, J. An exploratory study of the cyberbullying and cyberstalking experiences and factors related to victimization of students at a public liberal arts college. *Int. J. Technoethics (IJT)* **2010**, *1*, 74–91.

40. Rivers, I.; Noret, N. 'I h8 u': Findings from a five-year study of text and email bullying. *Brit. Educ. Res. J.* **2010**, *36*, 643–671.

41. Hinduja, S.; Patchin, J.W. Offline consequences of online victimization: School violence and delinquency. *J. Sch. Violence* **2007**, *6*, 89–112.

42. Kowalski, R.M.; Morgan, C.A.; Limber, S.P. Traditional bullying as a potential warning sign of cyberbullying. *Sch. Psychol. Int.* **2012**, *33*, 505–519.

43. Slonje, R.; Smith, P.K. Cyberbullying: Another main type of bullying? *Scand J Psychol.* **2008**, *49*, 147–154.

44. Vandebosch, H.; Van Cleemput, K. Cyberbullying among youngsters: Profiles of bullies and victims. *New Media Soc.* **2009**, *11*, 1349–1371.

45. Kowalski, R.M.; Limber, S.P. Psychological, physical, and academic correlates of cyberbullying and traditional bullying. *J. Adolesc. Health* **2013**, *53*, S13–S20.

46. Hattie, J. Methodology Review: Assessing unidimensionality of tests and items. *Appl. Psychol. Meas.* **1985**, *9*, 139–164.

Cyberbullying and Primary-School Aged Children: The Psychological Literature and the Challenge for Sociology

Lesley-Anne Ey, Carmel Taddeo and Barbara Spears

Abstract: Cyberbullying is an international issue for schools, young people and their families. Whilst many research domains have explored this phenomenon, and bullying more generally, the majority of reported studies appear in the psychological and educational literatures, where bullying, and more recently, cyberbullying has been examined primarily at the individual level: amongst adolescents and young people, with a focus on the definition, its prevalence, behaviours, and impact. There also is growing evidence that younger children are increasingly accessing technology and engaging with social media, yet there is limited research dedicated to this younger age group. The purpose of this paper is to report on a systematic literature review from the psychological and educational research domains related to this younger age group, to inform future research across the disciplines. Younger children require different methods of engagement. This review highlights the methodological challenges associated with this age group present in the psychological literature, and argues for a greater use of sociological, child-centred approaches to data collection. This review examined studies published in English, between 2009 and 2014, and conducted with children aged 5–12 years, about their experiences with cyberbullying. Searches were conducted on seven key databases using keywords associated with cyberbullying and age of children. A Google Scholar search also examined published and unpublished reports. A total of 966 articles and reports were retrieved. A random peer review process was employed to establish inter-rater reliability and veracity of the review. Findings revealed 38 studies reported specifically on children aged 5–12 years. The dominant focus of these articles was on prevalence of cyberbullying, established through survey methodology. Few studies noted impacts, understanding and behaviours or engaged children's independent voice. This review highlights current gaps in our knowledge about younger children's experiences with this form of bullying, and the importance of employing cross-disciplinary and developmentally appropriate methodologies to inform future research.

Reprinted from *Societies*. Cite as: Ey, L.-A.; Taddeo, C.; Spears, B. Cyberbullying and Primary-School Aged Children: The Psychological Literature and the Challenge for Sociology. *Societies* **2015**, *5*, 492–514.

1. Introduction

Since the advent of readily available, technology-enhanced communications and the ubiquitous diffusion of technology throughout mainstream society, young people have readily embraced a range of devices, platforms and online programs. Research reporting on children's annual online experiences across Europe, between 2007 and 2010, has found that up to 94 per cent of children aged 6–17 years old access the internet [1] and that six per cent of children aged 8–11 years engaged with social networking. Social networking potentially exposes young people to online harassment and cyberbullying which is "arguably the most prevalent online risk faced by children" [1] (p. 29). It is also evident that younger children's ownership and access to these technologies is increasing, and as such, they are exposed to the benefits and risks associated with their use: which until recently, had been reserved for older users [2–4]. Whilst benefits can include broader avenues of communication and new opportunities for learning, one potential risk for children is that of exposure to, and experience of, cyberbullying. The OECD research [1] found that in Europe, up to 31 per cent of children aged 6–14 years had encountered cyberbullying as measured across various time periods, which was dependent on the scale incorporated in the studies. Such research demonstrates a need to investigate cyberbullying issues with young children.

Cyberbullying, like traditional bullying, has been defined in many ways, yet most agree on the substantive elements which need to be present for it to be considered bullying, as distinct from aggression: *viz.*: an imbalance of power, deliberate intent to hurt or harm and repetition in relation to the misuse and abuse of technology [5]. A couple of issues arise here. Bullying as a concept itself, has its own social history, in that it arose as a field of enquiry from studies into mobbing and aggression, which were situated in the psychological domain [6]. Bauman *et al.* [7] raise the issue that cyberbullying behaviours may in fact be more closely associated with cyber-*aggression*, than bullying *per se*, but this discussion (bullying *vs.* aggression) falls outside the parameters of this paper. Certainly the literature is inconsistent in how these traditional criteria are applied [8–13], with repetition being the criterion most often challenged: as the online nature of the setting means that something which is uploaded only once, can be seen and re-posted by many [5,11]. Imbalance of power is also more difficult to ascertain in an online setting, as numbers of protagonists cannot be seen necessarily, nor the ways in which strength/power might be present. Intent is also questionable, when there are no non-verbal cues to ascertain meaning behind the text that might have been sent. Bansel, Davis, Laws and Linnell [14] noted that the largely individualistic approach evident in the psychological literature, is problematic from a sociological standpoint, especially in relation to the definition and how it might actually be identified in actual school settings. Indeed they highlighted that teachers and others would need to:

"establish in relation to one incident, whether or not the act was repeated, whether it intended to hurt and whether it was an acceptable use of power" (p. 60). They argued that a new approach was needed: one where the everyday power relations in children's lives were examined, through analysis of the discourses related to the normalised practices of power relations in schools, and indeed wider society: those of not only power, but race, gender, class and poverty (pp. 60–68). Schott and Søndergard [15] and Spears and Kofoed, [16] also argued for a more diverse approach to examining bullying and cyberbullying, with Spears and Kofoed calling for a shift from privileging quantitative studies in this area, towards encouraging young people to act as knowledge brokers, co-researchers and experts in this domain. They further highlighted that education and sociology are both founded upon the view that people are active agents in their social worlds, constructing meaning, supporting the notion that there are many "truths" and multiple realities, as distinct from psychology: which favours theory testing and emphasises positivism, and objective reality, with directly observable and measurable behaviours.

Behaviours consistently identified as cyberbullying include: threatening or nasty emails, mobile texts or Internet postings; social exclusion from the online community; impersonating another person or forwarding on the cyber victim's private information; posting derogatory or embarrassing pictures or videos; creating websites designed to hurt, intimidate or degrade victims; trolling or stalking; and harassing others in virtual environments or online games [2,10,17–19].

Whilst academic publications about cyberbullying have increased considerably since the earliest papers emerged during first few years of the 21st Century, most of the research to date has focused on adolescents, its prevalence and impact, with much less known about younger children's experiences or understandings [10,20]. This is particularly relevant as younger children are now accessing more devices, earlier and more frequently [2,4,21].

The purpose of this systematic literature review is to therefore examine published psychological research conducted with primary school aged children (5–12 years) concerning children's understanding of cyberbullying: its prevalence, behaviours and impacts, as this comprises the major evidence base available for this age group. The specific aims of this review are to inform future sociological studies by: (a) identifying gaps in current knowledge about this age group and cyberbullying; (b) examining research methods employed to investigate cyberbullying with this age group; (c) provide direction for further research; and (d) propose research methods that best align with the developmental needs of young children aged 5–12 years, for all disciplines.

2. Materials and Methods

2.1. Literature Search and Coding Scheme: Inclusion and Exclusion Criteria

The literature search examined peer reviewed, empirical studies on cyberbullying, published in English in the previous six years (2009–2014), with a specific focus on younger children aged 5–12 years. The decision to apply this timeframe was informed by (a) rapid advances in technology, with younger children increasingly accessing and engaging with technologies, including social media [2,4,22–25]; and (b) a shift in the type of the questions asked of children in Internet related studies: from a more generalised examination of children's Internet practices, to more specific investigations into the nature of children's engagement online, including questions about social media. For example, the Australian Bureau of Statistics' "Children's participation in cultural and leisure activities" study of 2003 did not seek data on children's social networking engagement, but the updated study in 2009 [26] requested such data. To address national and international differences in the way schooling is structured and to facilitate the reporting of findings, children's age as opposed to year or schooling level was considered in the coding scheme.

As the definition of cyberbullying remains contested in the literature, consideration of cyberbullying definitions did not form part of the coding scheme employed. For the purpose of this paper, studies were considered for review if they reported findings from children aged 5–12 years and investigated one or more of the following areas.

- Children's understanding, knowledge and/or perceptions of cyberbullying.
- Cyberbullying behaviours, as identified by children in the studies.
- The prevalence of cyberbullying ascertained through children's reporting of.

  ○ cyberbullying experiences as a cybervictim, cyberbully, cybervictim/cyberbully, bystander or no cyberbullying experiences; or
  ○ the perceived prevalence of cyberbullying.

- Cyberbullying impacts as perceived effects and actual effects of cyberbullying on self and others.

Literature about cyberbullying education, such as education strategies and evaluations of cyberbullying programs, was not included in this review, as it was not deemed relevant to this particular review's aims. Three book chapters were retrieved in the initial search, but ultimately were excluded, as the studies had been published as journal articles and were therefore represented and counted in the pool of articles retrieved.

2.2. Literature Search Method

Seven key data-bases were identified through a scoping exercise, which included consultations with an academic librarian to ascertain the domains where studies on cyberbullying were most commonly published: *viz.*, psychology and education: Education Research Complete; psycINFO; ERIC; Scopus; Psychology Behavioural Science Collection; Sage Premier; and A+ Education. The following key search terms were subsequently identified: Cyberbull*, children, youth, adolesce* and electronic bullying. A supplementary search was also conducted in Google Scholar to locate any additional grey literature such as reports relating to cyberbullying that may not have been captured in the above-mentioned scholarly databases. The coding scheme and search method employed provided an effective and efficient method of obtaining the maximum number of relevant articles across disciplines that most commonly cite research in the area of cyberbullying and children.

2.3. Selection of Relevant Publications

Nine hundred and sixty six (966) articles were identified in the initial search results and subsequently were reviewed by the lead author. The abstract and the results section of each article were individually examined to establish if inclusion criteria had been met. Of these, 928 were subsequently excluded from further consideration. Many of the excluded studies focused on older age groups, or results were not specific to the age ranges identified in the inclusion criteria. Consequently, 38 articles were closely examined in the next stage of the review process.

2.4. Inter-Rater Reliability: Inclusion Criteria

Following identification of the 38 articles by the lead author, the second and third authors independently reviewed a random selection of these studies in order to ensure the inclusion/exclusion criteria had been met. Using a random number generator, 11 articles were subsequently identified for inter-rater review [27]. The number of articles ($n = 11$, 28.9%) considered for the inter-rater reliability process were consistent with the number of articles subjected to rating processes reported in similar studies in the field [28–30].

Table 1 demonstrates the decisions made by each of the coders, establishing an acceptable level of consistency. In three instances, there was some uncertainty regarding whether or not the articles adequately addressed all the required inclusion criteria. Each was discussed further and consensus was reached to include the articles in question.

Table 1. Ratings by coders of acceptability of randomly selected articles.

Article	Coder 1	Coder 2	Coder 3
Article 1	1	1	3
Article 2	1	3	1
Article 3	1	1	1
Article 4	1	3	1
Article 5	1	1	1
Article 6	2	2	2
Article 7	2	2	2
Article 8	2	2	2
Article 9	2	2	2
Article 10	2	2	2
Article 11	2	2	2

1 = Accepted; 2 = Not accepted; 3 = Unsure.

3. Results

3.1. Overview of Methods

Of the 38 empirical studies reviewed, 36 employed survey methodologies and two studies used an open-ended discussion method. Of those that employed survey methodologies, only seven allocated one or more spaces for participants to provide written/qualitative responses. Two were also delivered in a one-on-one/face-to-face interview style, but employed multiple choice response options. Only three studies adapted their language or length of time to accommodate younger children (See Table 2).

3.2. Overview of the Focus of the Studies

Whilst most studies explored more than once aspect of cyberbullying (See Table 2), the greatest research focus, addressed in over 30 studies, concerned prevalence. The impact of cyberbullying was the second highest research focus (11 studies), followed by children's understanding and perspectives of cyberbullying (six studies) and bullying behaviours (six studies). Other themes present in the 38 studies included predictors and influencing factors of cyberbullying, such as characteristics that make children more vulnerable to cyberbullying (10 studies), children's identified responses to cyberbullying (three studies), children's responses to cyberbullying (two studies), reporting behaviours (one study) and children's concerns about cyberbullying (one study). It is also worth noting that the majority of these studies represented older children with only nine studies researching with children under nine years of age.

Table 2. Overview of recent research on cyberbullying prevalence, understandings, behaviours and impacts with children aged 5–12 years.

Author	Year Published	Focus	Sample Age in Years	Sample Number	Methodology	Country/Countries	Year of Research	Setting
[31]	2009	Prevalence of cyberbullying, characteristics of victims and how it effects them	9–15	1330	Self-report survey-multiple choice and Likert scales	Australia	2002–2005	in school except 1 cohort which was mailed
[32]	2009	Prevalence and types of bullying, including cyberbullying and influencing factors	10–15	7182	Self-report questionnaire-multiple choice and Likert scales	US	2005–2006	in school
[33]	2009	Prevalence of cyberbullying, what initiates cyberbullying, reporting practices, cyberbullying opinion and solutions	11–15	365	Self-report survey-182 closed-ended questions e.g., multiple choice, and 10 open-ended questions, Likert scales	Canada	2007	in school
*1 [22]	2009	Prevalence of cyberbullying	8–17	819	Self-report questionnaires-multiple choice, written responses and Likert scales	Australia	2008	online
[17]	2010	Prevalence and behaviours of cyberbullying and associations to suicide	10–16	1963	Self-report survey-multiple choice and summary scale	US	2007	in school
[34]	2010	Prevalence of cyberbullying, demographic or characteristic influences on cyberbullying	10–14	221	Self-report survey-multiple choice and Likert scales	US	2009	in school
[35]	2010	3rd, 4th and 5th grade students perceptions of cyberbullying	8–11	835	Self-report questionnaire-multiple choice, written responses and Likert scales	US	unidentified	in school
[36]	2010	Prevalence and forms of cyberbullying and platforms used and coping strategies	5–25	548	Self-report survey-multiple choice with written responses and Likert scales	Australia	2009	online
[37]	2011	Impacts of cyberbullying	10–11	90	Pen and paper booklets-4 scenarios with Likert scales and self-report paper questionnaire with multiple choice and Likert scales	UK	unidentified	in school

37

Table 2. *Cont.*

Author	Year Published	Focus	Sample Age in Years	Sample Number	Methodology	Country/Countries	Year of Research	Setting
[38]	2011	Prevalence of cyberbullying	12–17	1149	Self-report survey-multiple choice and Likert scales	US	2009	online
[18]	2011	Prevalence of cyberbullying and impact on feelings	11–14	247	Self-report questionnaires-multiple choice and one space for open answer	US	unidentified	in school
*1 [13]	2011	Prevalence of cyberbullying	9–16	25142	Face-to-Face survey-multiple choice and one space for open answer	25 European Countries	2010	in children's homes
*2 [39]	2011	Online habits, including perspectives about cyberbullying	13–17	NA	Six (gender specific) group discussions	Australia	2011	dedicated research venues
			8–12	NA	Six interviews-friendship pairs			in children's homes
			12–15	NA	Six ethnographic immersions-friendship pairs			in children's homes
					Discussion-open ended questions			
[40]	2011	Prevalence of cyberbullying and predictors	8–12	198	Self-report and peer-report of aggression and self-report of cyber-aggression with Likert scales	US	fall	in school
[41]	2011	Prevalence of cyberbullying and predictors. Responses to cyberbullying	11–12	124	Self-report questionnaires-multiple choice and Likert scales	US	unidentified	in school
[5]	2012	Understanding of cyberbullying	11–17	2257	Scenario questionnaires-yes or no responses and ** dimension	6 European	2010	in school
[42]	2012	Prevalence of cyberbullying-bully and cyberbully remorse	9–16	759	Self-report questionnaires-multiple choice	Sweden	2007	in school
*1 [10]	2012	Prevalence of cyberbullying	7–11	220	Self-report questionnaires-multiple choice	UK	2008	in school

Table 2. *Cont.*

Author	Year Published	Focus	Sample Age in Years	Sample Number	Methodology	Country/Countries	Year of Research	Setting
[43]	2012	Prevalence of and role in cyberbullying	12–18	5516	Self-report questionnaires-multiple choice	Finland	2009	online or mailed
[44]	2012	Prevalence of cyberbullying, predictors and impacts	11–17	518	Self-report questionnaires-multiple choice and Likert scales	Germany	2011	in school
[20]	2012	Understanding of cyberbullying and safety strategies	11	5	Self-report questionnaires-multiple choice and one open question	Australia	unidentified	in school
[45]	2012	Prevalence of cyberbullying and predictors	10–12	1127	Self-report questionnaire-multiple choice and Likert scales	Spain	unidentified	in school
[46]	2012	Prevalence and behaviours of cyberbullying and predictors	8–11	389	Self-report questionnaire-multiple choice and Likert scales	Turkey	unidentified	in school
[47]	2012	Prevalence and behaviours of cyberbullying	10–13 y	189	Self-report survey-multiple choice	Europe	unidentified	online
[48]	2012	Prevalence and impacts of cyberbullying	10–17	1530	Self-report pen and paper questionnaire-multiple choice and Likert scales	Australia	Unidentified	In school
[49]	2013	Impacts and responses to cyberbullying	11–12	325	Self-report paper and pen survey-multiple choice and Likert scales	UK	unidentified	in school
[50]	2013	Prevalence of cyberbullying and impacts	10–13	211	Self-report questionnaires-multiple choice and Likert scales	US	unidentified	in school
[19]	2013	Prevalence of cyberbullying	9–19	3112	Self-report survey-multiple choice and Likert scales	Australia	unidentified	in school
[51]	2014	Prevalence of cyberbullying and predictors	11–14	4531	Self-report questionnaires-multiple choice and Likert scales	Korea	unidentified	in school

Table 2. *Cont.*

Author	Year Published	Focus	Sample Age in Years	Sample Number	Methodology	Country/Countries	Year of Research	Setting
[52]	2013	Prevalence of cyberbullying victimization	10–12	1068	Self-report questionnaires-multiple choice and Likert scales	Spain	2012	in school
[53]	2013	Prevalence and cyberbullying behaviours and impact on feelings	10–17	239	Self-report questionnaires-multiple choice and Likert scales	Canada	2007–2008	in school
[54]	2013	Prevalence of cyberbullying	9–14	18412	Self-report questionnaires-multiple choice and Likert scales	Finland	2007–2009	in school
[55]	2013	Prevalence and cyberbullying behaviours	7–15	26420	Self-report questionnaires-multiple choice and Likert scales	Finnish	unidentified	in school
[56]	2013	Understanding, prevalence, behaviours and impacts	11–12	28	face-to-face discussion groups	unidentified	unidentified	in school
[57]	2014	Prevalence of cyberbullying and impact on body-esteem	10–15	1076	Self-report questionnaires-multiple choice and Likert scales	Sweden	2010–2011	in school
[58]	2014	Prevalence of cyberbullying, understanding and concern	8–17	7644	Self-report online survey (18 countries): Face-to-Face self-report survey (7 countries)-multiple choice	25 Countries	2012	online or face-to-face
[11]	2014	Prevalence of cyberbullying	10–14	106	Self-report questionnaire and Likert scales	US	unidentified	in school
[59]	2014	Prevalence of cyberbullying	10–16	529	Pen and paper self-report questionnaires-multiple choice and Likert scales	Italy	unidentified	in school

[*1] Questions adapted for younger age groups; [*2] This study is included because the age categories are reported.

3.3. Contextual Background of the Studies

The majority of the research on younger children and cyberbullying was conducted in North America and Europe. Ten studies were conducted in the United States of America (US) and two in Canada. In Europe: three studies were conducted in the United Kingdom (UK); two in Spain; three which compared two or more European countries; and one each in Germany, Italy and Turkey. Seven studies were conducted in Australia and five studies in Scandinavian countries: three in Finland and two in Sweden. There was one study conducted in Korea; one international study, across 25 countries; and one study did not identify the country (See Table 2).

3.4. Overview of Data Collection Procedures

The majority of the studies (30) collected their data in a school environment. Of these, 27 were conducted using school computers and three used pen and paper. Six studies collected their data using an online survey method in a non-specified environment, with one of these also mailing their surveys to participant's homes, for pen and pencil completion. Two studies were conducted in the children's homes with one of these also using a specific location in the area, as a dedicated research centre, which children and their parents would attend. The majority of surveys conducted in schools were administered by researchers (18), nine were administered by teachers and two studies had researchers and teachers present. Two studies did not identify who administered the surveys (See Table 2).

3.5. Overview of Methodologies Employed

Survey methodologies were employed in 36 of these studies, reflecting the wider bullying and cyberbullying research approaches and their associated advantages and limitations. As such, they represent the most common research methods employed for adolescent research in this field, but this approach may not be the most appropriate for use with younger children, and may pose significant validation concerns when used with younger participants.

Thirty-four of the studies had either small samples, were cross-sectional; omitted vulnerable, marginal or other groups, highlighting some of the limitations associated with survey methodologies [60,61]. Twenty-nine of the studies consisted only of multiple choice and/or Likert scales questions. This method can result in acquiescence bias, where participants are more likely to agree with statements, or indicate positively, and it also limits respondents to choose from the posed responses rather than inviting general statements of opinion or replies [46]. Given the age of the children involved in these studies, the role of using open-ended questions or open dialogue/interviews to determine their knowledge and experiences needs

41

greater consideration, as studies into bullying have revealed that young children often confuse terms and understandings [62].

4. Discussion

4.1. Cyberbullying Research with Primary School Aged Children

Most of the research about cyberbullying and younger children located for this review has focused on the prevalence of this phenomenon and has been driven by the field of psychology, largely as a progression from work done on bullying over the past four decades, and arising from previous studies into aggression. This focus on prevalence is not surprising, given that early efforts to ascertain knowledge about any new phenomenon is largely concerned with how much of it is actually occurring. To do this, prevalence studies require representative survey methodologies. There is limited research evident, however, on younger children's understanding and perspectives of cyberbullying; its impacts; and actual behaviours employed with this age group. This review will act as a foundation to position future work from multiple disciplines, including sociology, concerning this phenomenon and younger children.

Notably, all but one of the studies located for this review were conducted in Western countries, highlighting a need for greater cross-cultural research with younger children, and for greater efforts to widely disseminate findings, so as to inform the research and wider community.

Consistent with survey methodologies employed in studies undertaken with older age-groups (see [63]), many of the studies reviewed provided explanations of cyberbullying to the participants and offered response options relevant to accepted timeframes and frequency cut-offs. Australian Communications and Media Authority [2] was the only study reviewed that provided children with the opportunity to express their perceptions about cyberbullying qualitatively.

Exploring younger children's understanding of cyberbullying without adult input may be critical to obtain an accurate perspective of their understanding, experiences and behaviours. Spears and Kofoed [16] argued for greater use of qualitative methodologies in cyberbullying research, as the construct is unique to the digital age: meaning that adults/researchers would never have experienced this form of bullying in their own childhood. Children's and young people's voice and perspectives are therefore paramount in order to extend and deepen understandings and develop successful interventions that will resonate with young people. They further suggested that a "shared lens across the new sociology of childhood" (p. 217), involving multi-disciplinary methodologies, would enable greater understanding of cyberbullying to emerge through the insights which youth voice can bring. Enabling youth as co-researchers, to co-construct meaning alongside adults, is therefore essential. Younger children's views and understandings then, are clearly needed, especially given they are being exposed to technologies and devices at increasingly earlier ages. Accessing those views, however, almost solely through survey methodologies, may not be the most effective or appropriate approach. By way of support, Spears *et al.* [64] conducted a qualitative exploration of early adolescents' knowledge, understanding and experiences of two forms of bullying: covert and cyberbullying, through use of alternative methodologies such as storytelling and use of Y-Charts. These methods enabled young people to recount examples they knew of, or had experienced, and clarify their own understanding by articulating what cyberbullying "looks, sounds and feels like" to them (p. 191), as distinct from only responding to an adult-provided definition.

This review also identified some studies of younger children that examined the impact of cyberbullying on the following: school connectedness; feelings of loneliness and other emotional responses; conduct and peer issues; school absenteeism; and links to anxiety, depression and suicidal thoughts. In contrast, there were, however, no studies with children aged 12 years or younger located, which explored other cyberbullying impacts, for example, on: self-esteem; sleeping patterns; fears; school attainment; eating disorders; or family relations. Considering that only studies published in English were accessed for this review, other studies in other languages may, however, exist, highlighting again the need for greater cross-cultural dissemination. Given also what is known concerning risk and protective factors in relation to cyberbullying and adolescents, and the need for early intervention [63] these gaps in knowledge about how cyberbullying can potentially impact on younger children's holistic development, highlight opportunities for further research. Conducting longitudinal research from an early age to examine not yet identified and long-term impacts of cyberbullying is needed, particularly as younger children are accessing more technology, earlier, and more frequently than ever before.

In acknowledging the need for further research in this field, it is important to note that researching sensitive topics with children, such as bullying and cyberbullying, is often subjected to close scrutiny from ethics committees, as they balance the need to ensure children have a voice and an opportunity to participate in research, whilst ensuring they are protected from harm [65]. Excluding younger children from research on the basis of suppositious risk may limit adults' understanding of children's experiences and vulnerability, thus our ability to educate and protect them [65]. Furthermore, excluding them on the presumption that cyberbullying is an adolescent problem, fails to recognise the ever-changing role that technology plays in younger children's lives. Concomitant with research that indicates younger children are increasingly engaging with social media, there is an imperative that this age group receives greater attention in this field. It is equally important that such research is constructed to allow researchers to identify age patterns and age appropriate interventions. Given that the majority of the studies reviewed have employed survey methodologies, there is a need to consider: (a) some of the broader implications of relying predominately on this approach for collecting data on cyberbullying with younger children; and (b) opportunities for employing alternative and innovative research methods to engage younger children in this field of research.

4.2. Conceptual Issues for Primary School-Aged Children from a Developmental Perspective

The value of applying and trialling alternative research methodologies with this target age group becomes apparent when some of the challenges in using survey methodologies with younger children are considered. These methods can be problematic with: (a) junior primary children aged 5–7 years, who are just learning to read and write; (b) middle primary children aged 8–10 years who are still developing metalinguistic awareness [66]; and (c) children who have low literacy levels [44]. Given these limitations, developmental theories can assist in determining the most appropriate methodological approaches to employ.

According to Piaget's Cognitive Development theory, children aged 7–11 years are in the concrete-operational stage, and whilst they are likely to focus their attention on key descriptive words [67], they are unlikely to relate the questions to non-concrete descriptions. Because children may have not mastered higher-order abstraction and intangible thinking [67], their ability to conceptualise abstractly is limited. Face-to-face methodologies or those with visual prompts would therefore be more appropriate to this age group than traditional survey methods.

There is also greater likelihood that even younger children: aged 2–7 years, who are in Piaget's pre-operational stage, may misinterpret descriptions of bullying and cyberbullying given their inability to conserve, seriate and classify, and think logically [67].

Monks and Smith [62] in their study of bullying applied such knowledge of child development to their research design. Using a face-to-face interview methodology, with supplementary cartoon visuals, they were able to elicit children's, (aged 4–14 years) understanding of the term bullying. These visual prompts were beneficial in helping children to identify verbal, physical, indirect and relational bullying, as they were unable to recall them freely. Nevertheless, only after the age of eight years were children able to develop a definition of bullying which separated out the different types of bullying.

Monks and Smith [62] study provides valuable insights which have informed subsequent research. Although their research methodologies were age appropriate, younger children were rarely able to differentially conceptualise or identify: bullying and singular incidents, and bullying and aggressive behaviours such as rough and tumble play. These findings suggest that in the first instance, it may be more prudent to examine children's understanding of cyber-aggression before exploring their understanding of cyberbullying.

In examining the 38 studies located, only three adapted their language to accommodate children's developmental levels, and only four ensured a researcher was available to assist with comprehension and answer questions. When researching with younger children it is important to ensure they are supported in being able to comprehend the questions being asked, however, by providing a researcher to answer questions during a survey, children can try to seek "the right" answer. This is particularly so for younger children, who may perceive school administered surveys as a form of "test".

Wachs, Wolf and Pan [44] suggest that some children may see questionnaire style methods as "schoolwork", particularly if administered in a school setting, and may be more concerned about perceived correctness of their responses rather than providing insights into what they honestly think, feel and have experienced. This social desirability bias may be more evident for younger children, than adolescents, but would need to be examined through empirical research processes.

Although some of these issues can be addressed by carefully constructing age-appropriate surveys, with age-appropriate language, there is no guarantee that all children will be able to interpret the questions as intended. Junior and middle primary children and those with low literacy levels will likely need support in item comprehension and in following instructions to fill out questionnaires.

Additionally, culturally relevant and appropriate language and/or scenarios are also important considerations for younger children. According to Vygotsky's Sociocultural theory, language and dialogues are culturally specific [66]. The inconsistency in definitions and language used to describe cyberbullying across cultures, not only have implications with cross-culture comparison research [5], but also have implications when researching with children. Young children from cultures that have no specific word for bullying would indeed have difficulty explaining or understanding cyberbullying, but may find it easier to articulate aggression, or cyber-aggression. Monks and Smith [62] successfully argued that children's cognitive and language development impacts on their comprehension of concepts, such as bullying. Complex or abstract words, words that have multiple meaning or no meaning at all within a child's culture are likely to cause confusion. Microsoft Corporation [58], in their research with 8–17 year old children across 25 countries, recognised the implications of culturally specific language and variations in understanding of cyberbullying, at a cultural and individual level. Their research asked children whether they had been a victim or perpetrator of "mean or unfriendly treatment"; "made fun of or teased"; or "called mean names" online. Although these terms are likely to be translated across cultures quite effectively, they can be open to interpretation, and may not accurately reflect the notion of bullying and/or cyberbullying. For example, if a child had experienced another person sharing a derogatory image of them via a mobile phone, they may not categorise this behaviour as deliberately aggressive, repeated, or have any understanding of the power differential, as it was an image and younger children may not perceive mobile phones as necessarily "online". Paying attention to language, complex constructs and cognitive development, are therefore critical to any exploration of cyberbullying experiences amongst younger children.

Understanding the child's perspective is therefore paramount, and sociological approaches, where the child and his social environment are central, would add considerable value and provide a more holistic understanding of this phenomenon. Co-constructing meaning with young people, particularly the very young, requires a level of reflexivity on the part of the researcher, and sensitivity to their social worlds, which can be enhanced by sociological approaches.

Working collaboratively with younger children throughout all aspects of a study, including the formative stages, to shape the direction of the investigation and the development of the questions, has the potential to contribute to the accuracy and relevancy of findings into cyberbullying and younger children.

4.3. Settings and Administrators of Surveys

In examining appropriate settings for conducting research with younger children, Hill [68] found that children prefer school as a setting for research. However, she emphasised that ideally any data collection conducted in schools should be administered by external parties (field workers, researchers) who meet working with children safety/security requirements, as opposed to teachers or school personnel, in order to help minimise bias.

This review did reveal that schools were the main environments where data were collected and that the majority of surveys conducted in schools were administered by researchers. Nevertheless, when designing research with younger children, bias as a result of adult presence, influence and constraint may be evident in instances where surveys are administered by teachers; mailed to children's homes; or require online participation.

4.4. Using Dialogue to Research with Young Children

Currently, this field has been driven by quantitative methods and psychology and education disciplines, as is evident from our review of the databases: hence, prevalence has been the focus of many studies, but for younger children, sociological methods may be more appropriate. Valuing the rights of the child and placing them at the centre of the research process reflects the new sociology of the child [69]: as an active participant in the creation of knowledge, and not simply a "subject" for research [16].

To obtain an accurate picture of young children's understanding of cyberbullying, this review argues that research methods that align with their developmental levels are necessary. There is a wealth of literature that discusses optimal, developmentally relevant research methodologies for use with younger children; however, these seem to be largely ignored in the research on cyberbullying located for this review. Such methods include: play; use of concrete materials to facilitate comprehension; visual methods; and face-to-face interviews [62,70–72].

The cartoon method used by Monks and Smith [62] to determine children's understanding of the term bullying is one such example of research design that is developmentally suitable for use with younger children. Additionally, qualitative research methods, such as semi-structured face-to-face interviews, or the use of Y charts, narrative and experiential methods which engage youth voice [16,64] may be particularly useful in addressing some of the conceptual challenges encountered when employing survey and questionnaire methods with young children.

Spears and Kofoed [16] articulated the importance of youth voice and qualitative techniques in cyberbullying research, so that young people's experiences do more than simply supplement existing quantitative studies. Rather, youth act as knowledge brokers, and co-researchers, to help adults understand this phenomenon from the perspective of young people themselves. With younger children, this is equally important, as cyberbullying is an adult-conceived term, and it is their understandings that are needed, not adult imposed interpretations of them.

One useful methodology to consider when researching with younger children is that of dialogue, including face-to-face interviews. Using a dialogue method encourages children to discuss their reasoning behind their thinking or actions [65] which fosters children's interpretation and ownership of their own data. In most cultures adults are seen by children as authority figures, thus hold a more powerful position [70,73,74]. Using a dialogue method can reduce power relations between adults and children during data collection and interpretation [75]. According to Graham and Fitzgerald [65] and Harcourt [76] using open-ended research techniques, such as semi-structured interviews, lessen power disparity because children have a certain amount of control over the direction of the discussion. Additionally, a discussion format provides an informality that optimises the likelihood of more equal relationships. The adult-child relationship and minimising any power disparity, which naturally occurs, are critical considerations when researching with younger children, [70,73,77,78].

Although group interviews capitalise on social interaction [79,80], which can be advantageous in prompting one another's memory [60,79–81], the nature of cyberbullying may make children feel uncomfortable sharing their experiences in front of peers. Individual interviews are increasingly being accepted as an appropriate research method to obtain children's perspectives [72,76,82]. Individual interviews allow the researcher to investigate children's experiences confidentially, which is particularly beneficial when "researching sensitive or personal issues" [83], such as cyberbullying. Face-to-face interviews are, however, resource intensive [46], particularly for large studies, where additional staff may need to be employed and trained in interview protocols.

As noted previously, when researching with children, the methods need to be guided by children's developmental levels [74]. For example, from age six, children are sufficiently articulate, have a reasonable vocabulary and a good knowledge of semantic and grammatical rules [66,84,85], which suggests they are cognitively developed enough to participate in interviews. At age 10, however, children are far more advanced in their language, comprehension and social understanding. They are "similar to adults in their recall of historical events" [77] (p. 299) and are beginning to embark on abstract thinking and can appreciate more traditional research methods, such as surveys [66,67,84]. The qualifier to this, however, is that where there are developmental delays, language and cultural contexts, which differ significantly, survey methodologies may not be the most appropriate method for establishing understanding about the construct. Given the considerable difference in developmental levels, researchers need to be meticulous in designing all research with young children, but especially in aligning interview pro-formas to accommodate children's development, and should avoid using traditional survey methods with children under the age of 10 years. Researchers should consider alternative survey structures that utilise visuals and culturally appropriate scenarios, consider survey length and appeal, and whether more than one data collection would be most suitable for their intended audience.

4.5. Using Technology when Researching Cross-Culturally and with Young Children

Technology can be employed to facilitate data collection with young children and in cultures where bullying and cyberbullying are less researched, and can be used to enhance traditional data collection methods, for example, by facilitating record keeping of data and improving efficiency in collection methods. Additionally, young children themselves, including those with poor fine motor skills, can use technology to support them in collecting and recording data. Technology also can provide innovative and alternative approaches to data collection that may positively resonate with young children who are increasingly using a range of technologies both in school and home settings, for example, through PhotoStory and PhotoVoice [86,87]. Yet this field is in its early stage and further investigations are required to establish the merits, if any, of using approaches that utilise technologies for data collection with young children, particularly when researching potentially sensitive topics.

4.6. Limitations of the Systematic Review

This paper has largely argued that children's voice and unique perspective must provide the primary source of data. Whilst the psychological literature gathers data *from* children, there is an imperative to engage children as co-researchers, who are experts in their own experiences. This paper proposes, therefore, that the sociological contribution has a larger role to play in contributing to a holistic representation of cyberbullying, as understood by younger children.

In conducting this review there are some limitations that should be noted. Premised upon the historical development of research into bullying, which grew from the psychological studies of aggression, the academic search consisted of seven databases considered most likely to publish cyberbullying research: those from psychology and education. There would be further cyberbullying publications beyond these databases, in languages other than English, or in other publishing domains, specifically sociology, technology or medicine/public health and this review suggests that these searches be undertaken, so that a multidisciplinary overview of younger children's experiences and knowledge of cyberbullying be established. The search terms were also culturally specific to Western countries, which may have limited the number of publications identified that reported on research conducted in non-Western countries. Additionally, the sample is non-representative of all the cyberbullying research conducted with children aged 12 years or under, as results of some studies did not separate age groups. Nevertheless, this review provides a snapshot of cyberbullying research conducted with children aged 12 years or younger, and provides insights into the research methodologies currently employed with this age group in these domains. In doing so, it highlights the opportunities and the need to conduct cyberbullying research with children in this age range across multiple disciplines.

5. Conclusions

The research field of cyberbullying is relatively young [56] yet there has been an exponential explosion in research published recently [88], with groups who heavily engage with social media receiving the greatest research attention: namely adolescents and young adults. This review has identified that there is limited research about primary school-aged children's understanding and perceptions of cyberbullying, the impacts of cyberbullying and cyberbullying behaviours employed, in both Western and non-Western countries. Given the rise of younger children's engagement with social media and research which shows that cyberbullying is often enacted via social media channels, there is an imperative for children of primary school age to be included as a general rule in cyberbullying research.

However, researching with younger children can pose challenges for researchers, particularly with regard to ensuring that data collected accurately represents their experiences with, and perceptions of, cyberbullying. There is as such a critical need to ensure that developmentally and culturally appropriate research methods are employed in addition to addressing any ethical considerations that may be unique to conducting research with younger age groups. The authors propose that these challenges should not be viewed as a deterrent for conducting research with younger children, but rather should provide the impetus for closely aligning children's developmental needs and stages with research methodologies. The authors suggest there is unlikely to be a "one size fits all" when designing and conducting research with young children. Survey methodologies are less appropriate to use with younger children or those with low literacy levels or from different cultural backgrounds. Qualitative methods, such as, dialogic and visual methods are likely to provide greater validity. Additionally, with advances in technology, including innovative applications and devices, and younger children's increasing engagement with technology, there is a need for further research to examine how these developments can be leveraged to facilitate data collection with younger children. Finally, this review calls for greater input and cross-disciplinary dialogue from all research domains, particularly the field of sociology, so as to holistically inform our understanding of cyberbullying from a child-centred perspective.

Acknowledgments: The authors would like to acknowledge the support of the academic library team at the University of South Australia.

Author Contributions: Lesley-Anne Ey designed the systematic literature review. Lesley-Anne Ey, Carmel Taddeo and Barbara Spears consulted the academic library team of UniSA to identify which databases to search. Given that the concept of bullying arose from the field of psychology and the study of aggression, and the authors' discipline is education, databases relating to these disciplines were researched. Lesley-Anne Ey conducted the literature search across the databases and Google Scholar, retrieving 966 articles. She refined these articles down to 38 articles. Lesley-Anne Ey, Carmel Taddeo and Barbara Spears engaged in the inter-rater reliability coding and analysis process. Lesley-Anne Ey wrote the first draft of the article. Carmel Taddeo refined the Materials and Methods Section and contributed to the discussion section. Barbara Spears refined the Introduction Section and contributed the latest research in the area. She also contributed to the Discussion Section. All three authors contributed to the editing during the refining process.

Conflicts of Interest: The authors declare no conflict of interest.

References

1. Organisation for Economic Co-operation and Development. *The Protection of Children Online: Recommendations of the OECD Council: Report on Risks Faced by Children Online and Policies to Protect Them*; OECD: Paris, France, 2012.
2. Australian Communications and Media Authority. *Like, Post, Share: Young Australians' Experiences of Social Media*; Newspoll Market & Social Research: Melbourne, Australia, 2013.
3. Ofcom. *The Communications Market Report*; Ofcom: London, UK, 2014.

4. Livingstone, S.; Smith, P. Annual research review: Harms experienced by child users of online and mobile technologies: The nature, prevalence and management of sexual and aggressive risks in the digital age. *J. Child Psychol. Psychiatry* **2014**, *55*, 635–654.

5. Menesini, E.; Nocentini, A.; Palladino, B.; Frisen, A.; Berne, S.; Ortega-Ruiz, R.; Calmaestra, J.; Scheithauer, H.; Schultze-Krumbholz, A.; Luik, P.; *et al.* Cyberbullying definition among adolescents: A comparison across six European countries. *Cyberpsychol. Behav. Soc. Netw.* **2012**, *15*, 455–462.

6. Heinemann, P. Apartheid. *Liber. Debatt* **1969**, *3*, 3–14.

7. Bauman, S.; Underwood, M.; Card, N. Definitions: Another perspective and a proposal for a beginning with cyberagression. In *Principles of Cyberbullying Research: Definitions, Measures, and Methodology*; Bauman, S., Cross, D., Walker, J., Eds.; Routledge: London, UK, 2012; pp. 41–46.

8. Vazsonyi, A.T.; Machackova, H.; Sevcikova, A.; Smahel, D.; Cerna, A. Cyberbullying in context: Direct and indirect effects by low self-control across 25 European countries. *Eur. J. Dev. Psychol.* **2012**, *9*, 210–227.

9. Van den Eijnden, R.; Vermulst, A.; van Rooij, A.J.; Scholte, R.; van de Mheen, D. The bidirectional relationships between online victimization and psychosocial problems in adolescents: A comparison with real-life victimization. *J. Youth Adolesc.* **2014**, *43*, 790–802.

10. Monks, C.; Robinson, S.; Worlidge, P. The emergence of cyberbullying: A survey of primary school pupils' perceptions and experiences. *Sch. Psychol. Int.* **2012**, *33*, 477–491.

11. Brown, C.F.; Demaray, M.K.; Secord, S.M. Cyber victimization in middle school and relations to social emotional outcomes. *Comput. Hum. Behav.* **2014**, *35*, 12–21.

12. Campbell, M.; Spears, B.; Cross, D.; Slee, P. Cyberbullying in Australia. In *Cyberbullying in Australia: A Cross-National Comparison*; Mora-Merchan, J., Thomas, J., Eds.; Verlag Empirische Padagogik: Landau, Germany, 2010; pp. 232–245.

13. Livingstone, S.; Haddon, L.; Gorzig, A.; Olafsson, K. *Risks and Safety on the Internet: The Perspective of European Children. Full Findings*; The London School of Economics and Political Science: London, UK, 2011.

14. Bansel, P.; Davies, B.; Laws, C.; Linnell, S. Bullies, bullying and power in the contexts of schooling. *Br. J. Sociol. Educ.* **2009**, *30*, 59–69.

15. Schott, R.M.; Søndergaard, D.M. *School Bullying: New Theories in Context*; Cambridge University Press: Cambridge, MA, USA, 2014.

16. Spears, B.; Kofoed, J. Transgressing research binaries: Youth as knowledge brokers in cyberbulying research. In *Cyberbullying through the New Media: Findings from an International Network*; Smith, P., Steffgen, G., Eds.; Psychology Press: London, UK, 2013; pp. 201–221.

17. Hinduja, S.; Patchin, J. Bullying, cyberbullying, and suicide. *Arch. Suicide Res.* **2010**, *14*, 206–221.

18. Mark, L.; Ratliffe, K. Cyber worlds: New playgrounds for bullying. *Comput. Sch.: Interdiscipl. J. Pract. Theory Appl. Res.* **2011**, *28*, 92–116.

19. Campbell, M.; Slee, P.; Spears, B.; Bultler, D.; Kift, S. Do cyberbullies suffer too? Cyberbullies' perceptions of the harm they cause to others and to their own mental health. *Sch. Psychol. Int.* **2013**, *34*, 613–629.

20. Toshack, T.; Colmar, S. A cyberbullying intervention with primary-aged students. *Austr. J. Guid. Couns.* **2012**, *22*, 268–278.

21. Ofcom. *Children's Online Behaviour: Issues of Risk and Trust-Qualitative Research Findings*; London School of Economics and Political Science (LSE): London, UK, 2014; pp. 1–96.

22. Australian Communications and Media Authority. *Click and Connect: Young Australians Use of Online Social Media*; GfK Bluemoon: Melbourne, Australia, 2009; pp. 1–118.

23. Australian Communications and Media Authority. *Trends in Media Use by Children and Young People: Insights from the Kaiser Family Foundation's Generation m2 2009 (USA), and Results from the Acma's Media and Communications in Australian Families 2007*; Australian Communications and Media Authority: Melbourne, Australia, 2010.

24. Rideout, V.J.; Foehr, U.G.; Roberts, D.F. *Generation m2: Media in the Lives of 8–18 Year Olds*; Kaiser Family Foundation: Menlo Park, CA, USA, 2010; pp. 1–85.

25. Ofcom. *Uk Children's Media Literacy*; Ofcom: London, UK, 2010; pp. 1–81.

26. Australian Bureau of Statistics. *Children's Participation in Cultural and Leisure Activities, Australia, April 2009*; Australian Bureau of Statistics: Canberra, Australia, 2009.

27. Krippendorff, K. Agreement and information in the reliability of coding. *Commun. Methods Meas.* **2011**, *5*, 93–112.

28. Perren, S.; Corcoran, L.; Cowie, H.; Dehue, F.; Garcia, D.; Mc Guckin, C.; Sevcikova, A.; Tsatsou, P.; Vollink, T. Coping with Cyberbullying: A Systematic Literature Review. In International Conference on Cyberbullying, Paris, France, 28–29 June 2012; Universitat Zurich: Paris, France, 2012.

29. Garcia, C. Conceptualization and measurement of coping during adolescence: A review of the literature. *J. Nurs. Scholarsh.* **2010**, *52*, 166–185.

30. Berne, S.; Frisen, A.; Scheltze-Krumbholz, A.; Scheithauer, H.; Naruskov, K.; Luik, P.; Katzer, C.; Erentaite, R.; Ziukauskiene, R. Cyberbullying assessment instruments: A systematic review. *Aggr. Violent Behav.* **2013**, *18*, 320–334.

31. Cross, D.; Shaw, T.; Hearn, L.; Epstein, M.; Monks, H.; Lester, L.; Thomas, L. *Australian Covert Bullying Prevalence Study*; Edith Cowan University: Perth, Australia, 2009.

32. Wang, J.; Iannotti, R.J.; Nansel, T.R. School bullying among adolescents in the United States: Physical, verbal, relational, and cyber. *J. Adolesc. Health* **2009**, *45*, 368–375.

33. Cassidy, W.; Jackson, M.; Brown, K.N. Sticks and stones can break my bones, but how can pixels hurt me? Students' experiences with cyber-bullying. *Sch. Psychol. Int.* **2009**, *30*, 383–402.

34. Bauman, S. Cyberbullying in a rural intermediate school: An exploratory study. *J. Early Adolesc.* **2010**, *30*, 803–833.

35. D'Antona, R.; Kevorkian, M.; Russom, A. Sexting, texting, cyberbullying and keeping youth safe online. *J. Soc. Sci.* **2010**, *6*, 523–528.

36. Price, M.; Dalgleish, J. Cyberbullying: Experiences, impacts and coping strategies as described by Australian young people. *Youth Stud. Austr.* **2010**, *29*, 51.

37. Jones, S.E.; Manstead, A.S.; Livingstone, A.G. Ganging up or sticking together? Group processes and children's responses to text-message bullying. *Br. J. Psychol.* **2011**, *102*, 71–96.

38. Ybarra, M.L.; Mitchell, K.J.; Korchmaros, J.D. National trends in exposure to and experiences of violence on the internet among children. *Pediatrics* **2011**, *128*, e1376–e1386.

39. Australian Communications and Media Authority. *Like, Post, Share: Young Australians' Experience of Social Media*; GfK bluemoon: Melbourne, Australia, 2011.

40. Schoffstall, C.L.; Cohen, R. Cyber aggression: The relation between online offenders and offline social competence. *Soc. Dev.* **2011**, *20*, 587–604.

41. Accordino, D.B.; Accordino, M.P. An exploratory study of face-to-face and cyberbullying in sixth grade students. *Am. Second. Educ.* **2011**, *40*, 14–30.

42. Slonje, R.; Smith, P.K.; Frisen, A. Processes of cyberbullying, and feelings of remorse by bullies: A pilot study. *Eur. J. Dev. Psychol.* **2012**, *9*, 244–259.

43. Lindfors, P.L.; Kaltiala-Heino, R.; Rimpelä, A.H. Cyberbullying among Finnish adolescents—A population-based study. *BMC Public Health* **2012**, *12*, 1027.

44. Wachs, S.; Wolf, K.D.; Pan, C.-C. Cybergrooming: Risk factors, coping strategies and associations with cyberbullying. *Psicothema* **2012**, *24*, 628–633.

45. Navarro, R.; Yubero, S.; Larrañaga, E.; Martínez, V. Children's cyberbullying victimization: Associations with social anxiety and social competence in a Spanish sample. *Child Indic. Res.* **2012**, *5*, 281–295.

46. Arslan, S.; Savaser, S.; Hallett, V.; Balci, S. Cyberbullying among primary school students in Turkey: Self-reported prevalence and associations with home and school life. *Cyberpsychol. Behav. Soc. Netw.* **2012**, *15*, 527–533.

47. Blakeney, K. An instrument to measure traditional and cyber bullying in overseas schools. *Int. Sch. J.* **2012**, *32*, 45.

48. Sakellariou, T.; Carroll, A.; Houghton, S. Rates of cyber victimization and bullying among male Australian primary and high school students. *Sch. Psychol. Int.* **2012**, *33*, 533–549.

49. Völlink, T.; Bolman, C.A.; Dehue, F.; Jacobs, N.C. Coping with cyberbullying: Differences between victims, bully-victims and children not involved in bullying. *J. Commun. Appl. Soc. Psychol.* **2013**, *23*, 7–24.

50. Price, M.; Chin, M. Prevalence and internalizing problems of ethnoracially diverse victims of traditional and cyber bullying. *Sch. Ment. Health* **2013**, *5*, 183–191.

51. Jung, Y.-E.; Leventhal, B.; Kim, Y.S.; Park, T.W.; Lee, S.-H.; Lee, M.; Park, S.H.; Yang, J.-C.; Chung, Y.-C.; Chung, S.-K. Cyberbullying, problematic internet use, and psychopathologic symptoms among Korean youth. *Yonsei Med. J.* **2014**, *55*, 826–830.

52. Navarro, R.; Serna, C.; Martínez, V.; Ruiz-Oliva, R. The role of internet use and parental mediation on cyberbullying victimization among spanish children from rural public schools. *Eur. J. Psychol. Educ.* **2013**, *28*, 725–745.

53. Nordahl, J.; Beran, T.; Dittrick, C.J. Psychological impact of cyber-bullying: Implications for school counsellors. *Can. J. Couns. Psychother.* **2013**, *47*, 383–402.

54. Christian Elledge, L.; Williford, A.; Boulton, A.J.; dePaolis, K.J.; Little, T.D.; Salmivalli, C. Individual and contextual predictors of cyberbullying: The influence of children's provictim attitudes and teachers' ability to intervene. *J. Youth Adolesc.* **2013**, *42*, 698–710.

55. Yang, A.; Salmivalli, C. Different forms of bullying and victimization: Bully-victims versus bullies and victims. *Eur. J. Dev. Psychol.* **2013**, *10*, 723–738.

56. Baas, N.; de Jong, M.D.; Drossaert, C.H. Children's perspectives on cyberbullying: Insights based on participatory research. *Cyberpsychol. Behav. Soc. Netw.* **2013**, *16*, 248–253.

57. Frisen, A.; Berne, S.; Lunde, C. Cybervictimization and body esteem: Experiences of Swedish children and adolescents. *Eur. J. Dev. Psychol.* **2014**, *11*, 331–343.

58. Microsoft Corporation. *Online Bullying among Youth 8–17 Years Old-Australia*; Cross-Tab Marketing Services & Telecommunications Research Group: Redmond, WA, USA, 2014.

59. Ciucci, E.; Baroncelli, A. The emotional core of bullying: Further evidences of the role of callous–unemotional traits and empathy. *Personal. Indiv. Differ.* **2014**, *67*, 69–74.

60. Graziano, A.M.; Raulin, M.L. *Research Methods: A Process of Inquiry*, 7th ed.; Allyn & Bacon: Boston, MA, USA, 2010.

61. Walter, M. Surveys. In *Social Research Methods*; Walter, M., Ed.; Oxford University Press: Victoria, Australia, 2013; pp. 121–146.

62. Monks, C.; Smith, P. Definitions of bullying: Age differences in understanding of the term, and the role of experience. *Br. Psychol. Soc.* **2006**, *24*, 801–821.

63. Kowalski, R.; Guiumetti, G.; Schroeder, A.; Lattanner, M. Bullying in the digital age: A critical review and meta-analysis of cyberbullying research among youth. *Psychol. Bull.* **2014**, *140*, 1073–1137.

64. Spears, B.; Slee, P.; Owens, L.; Johnson, B. Behind the scenes and screens: Insights into the human dimension of covert and cyberbullying. *Zeitschrift fur Psychologie/J. Psychol.* **2009**, *217*, 189–196.

65. Graham, A.; Fitzgerald, R. Children's participation in research: Some possibilities and constraints in the current Australian research environment. *J. Sociol.* **2010**, *46*, 133–147.

66. Berk, L. *Infants, Children, and Adolescents*, 7th ed.; Pearson Education: Boston, MA, USA, 2012.

67. Peterson, C. *Looking Forward through the Lifespan: Developmental Psychology*, 5th ed.; Pearson Australia: Frenchs Forest, Australia, 2010.

68. Hill, M. Children's voices on ways of having a voice: Children's and young peoples' perspectives on methods used in research and consultation. *Childhood* **2006**, *13*, 69–89.

69. UNICEF. *A Summary of the Rights under the Convention on the Rights of the Child*; UNICEF: New York, NY, USA, 2011.

70. Einarsdottir, E. Research with children: Methodological and ethical challenges. *Eur. Early Childh. Educ. Res. J.* **2007**, *15*, 197–211.

71. Formosinho, J.; Araujo, S.B. Listening to children as a way to reconstruct knowledge about children: Some methodological implications. *Eur. Early Childh. Educ. Res. J.* **2006**, *14*, 21–31.

72. Irwin, G.; Johnson, J. Interviewing young children: Explicating our practices and dilemmas. *Qual. Health Res.* **2005**, *15*, 821–831.

73. Punch, S. Research with children: The same or different from research with adults? *Childhood* **2002**, *9*, 321–341.

74. Mahon, A.; Glendinning, C. Researching children: Methods and ethics. *Child. Soc.* **1996**, *10*, 145–154.

75. Morrow, V.; Richards, M. The ethics of social research with children: An overview. *Child. Soc.* **1996**, *10*, 90–105.

76. Harcourt, D. An encounter with children: Seeking meaning and understanding about childhood. *Eur. Early Childh. Educ. Res. J.* **2011**, *19*, 331–343.

77. Curtin, C. Eliciting children's voices in qualitative research. *Am. J. Occup. Ther.* **2000**, *55*, 295–302.

78. Griffin, K.M.; Lahman, M.; Opitz, M. Shoulder-to-shoulder research with children: Methodological and ethical consdierations. *J. Early Childh. Res.* **2014**.

79. Parkinson, D. Securing trustworthy data from an interview situation with young children: Six integrated interview strategies. *Child Study J.* **2001**, *31*, 137–155.

80. Bell, J. *Doing Your Research Project: A Guide for First Time Researchers in Education, Health and Social Science*, 5th ed.; McGraw Hill: New York, NY, USA, 2010.

81. Burns, R.B. *Introduction to Research Methods*, 4th ed.; Longman Array Frenchs Forest: London, UK, 2000.

82. Danby, S.; Ewing, L.; Thorpe, K. The novice researcher: Interviewing young children. *Qual. Inquiry* **2011**, *17*, 74–84.

83. Morgan, M.; Gibbs, S.; Maxwell, K.; Britten, N. Hearing children's voices: Methodological isues in conducting focus groups with children aged 7–11 years. *Qual. Res.* **2002**, *2*, 5–20.

84. Hoffnung, M.; Hoffnung, R.J.; Seifert, K.L.; Burton Smith, R.; Hine, A. *Childhood*; John Wiley & Sons Australia, Ltd: Milton, ON, Canada, 2010.

85. Berk, L. *Child Development*, 9th ed.; Pearson: Boston, MA, USA, 2013.

86. Skrzypiec, G.; Harvey-Murray, R.; Kreig, S. The photostory method as a legitimate research tool in evaluations: More than a nice story *J. Early Childh. Res.* **2013**, *38*, 25.

87. Hill, S. The millennium generation: Teacher-researchers exploring new forms of literacy. *J. Early Childh. Liter.* **2010**, *10*, 314–340.

88. Smith, P. *Understanding School Bullying: Its Nature and Prevention Strategies*; SAGE Publications Ltd: London, UK, 2014.

Characterizing Cyberbullying among College Students: Hacking, Dirty Laundry, and Mocking

Rajitha Kota, Shari Schoohs, Meghan Benson and Megan A. Moreno

Abstract: Bullying behaviors occur across the lifespan and have increasingly migrated to online platforms where they are known as cyberbullying. The purpose of this study was to explore the phenomenon of cyberbullying among college students. Participants were recruited for focus groups through purposeful sampling, including recruitment from groups traditionally at risk for bullying. Focus groups discussed views and perceptions of cyberbullying on campuses. Groups were led by a trained facilitator and were audio recorded and manually transcribed. The constant comparative approach was used to identify themes and representative quotations. The 42 participants had an average age of 19.2 (SD = 1.2), 55% were female, 83% were Caucasian. Three themes emerged from the data: (1) lack of agreement on a definition of cyberbullying, but consensus on three representative scenarios: hacking, dirty laundry and mocking; (2) concerns with translating definitions of traditional bullying to cyberbullying; (3) opinions that cyberbullying may manifest differently in college compared to younger adolescents, including increased potential for long-term effects. College students were not in agreement about a theoretical definition, but they could agree upon specific representative instances of cyberbullying. Future studies could consider using common case examples or vignettes of cyberbullying, or creation of developmentally representative definitions by age group.

Reprinted from *Societies*. Cite as: Kota, R.; Schoohs, S.; Benson, M.; Moreno, M.A. Characterizing Cyberbullying among College Students: Hacking, Dirty Laundry, and Mocking. *Societies* **2014**, *4*, 549–560.

1. Introduction

Bullying occurs throughout the world and can happen at many stages in the life course—from childhood, to adolescence, even to adulthood. Though traditional "schoolyard" bullying still exists, in recent years the Internet has provided a new platform for bullying. There are many online platforms in which bullying may take place, including e-mail, blogs, social networking websites (e.g., Facebook, Twitter), online games and text messaging. This phenomenon has been called cyberbullying, electronic aggression or online harassment [1]. Several definitions of cyberbullying exist; most are predicated on accepted definitions for traditional bullying. One commonly used definition defines cyberbullying as "an aggressive, intentional act or behavior that is carried out by a group or an individual, using electronic forms of contact, repeatedly and over time against a victim who cannot easily defend him or herself [2]".

Previous studies have examined the substantial psychological effects that cyberbullying can have on its victims [3]. Adolescents who have been cyberbullied report higher levels of depression and lower self-esteem [4]. Victims are also more likely to exhibit externalized hostility and delinquency [5]. Finally, cyberbullying victims report lower grades and other academic problems as a result of the experience [6].

Assessing the prevalence of cyberbullying remains a challenge because the field lacks an accepted operational definition of the term. One study of younger Canadian adolescents defined cyberbullying as "harassing using technology such as email, computer, cell phone, video cameras, etc." In this study the prevalence rate of cyberbullying victimization was 25% [7]. A second study of adolescents defined cyberbullying broadly as "mean things" or "anything that someone does that upsets or offends someone else" and found that 72% considered themselves victims of cyberbullying [8]. A third study defined cyberbullying more narrowly as "bullying through text messaging, email, mobile phone calls or picture/video clip." This study found the prevalence of reported victimization to be 17.6% [3]. Using varied definitions of cyberbullying may lead individuals to report it differently based on how broadly or narrowly the term is defined. This range of reported prevalence across studies creates challenges in determining the magnitude of this problem and in developing appropriate prevention and intervention tools. The importance of achieving consensus on an approach to bullying was recently highlighted by the Centers for Disease Control's recent report on bullying [9].

Although much attention has been paid to bullying behaviors of younger teens, less is known about young adult college students. College students may be a population at risk for cyberbullying as they are among the highest users of the Internet and other forms of communication technology [10], and have greatly reduced parental oversight compared to younger adolescents. Current data suggest that up to 20% of college students have experienced cyberbullying, though the specific nature and perspectives of college students regarding this behavior remains unclear [11,12]. At present, efforts are ongoing by numerous scholars and groups toward understanding how to define cyberbullying, and whether cyberbullying falls completely within the purview of traditional bullying that affects younger adolescent populations. Our goals for this study were to understand key issues from the perspectives of college students that merit consideration in efforts to achieve a definition and age-appropriate understanding of this emerging phenomenon. Obtaining this information would provide a deeper understanding of how cyberbullying may change over the stages of adolescence; utilizing participant voices may provide a more resonant characterization of cyberbullying in this age group.

2. Methods

2.1. Setting and Participants

Focus group participants were recruited through purposeful sampling at a large Midwestern university between September 2011 and October 2012. Eligible subjects were current undergraduate students between the ages of 18 and 22 years. The University of Wisconsin-Madison and Seattle Children's Hospital Institutional Review Boards approved this study.

To enhance the depth and breadth of representation of campus groups, participants were purposefully recruited from a wide range of campus activities and groups. Recruitment methods included canvassing the annual student organization fair and attending student group meetings to generate interest in the study. Effort was made to sample students in groups that are traditionally more likely to be bullied such as lesbian, gay, bisexual, transgender and questioning (LGTBQ) students and racial/ethnic minorities [8,13]. We contacted interested participants to schedule them for a focus group ahead of time based on their availability, including offering focus group opportunities in evenings when students were unlikely to be in class. Students were offered opportunities to attend a group at the time of their choice to maximize convenience for study participants.

2.2. Focus Groups

A trained facilitator conducted semi-structured focus groups. Focus groups allow for interaction between participants as well as opportunities for participants to build on each other's thoughts [14,15]. Participants were asked open-ended as well as probing questions and encouraged to share their thoughts on how they viewed and defined cyberbullying in the college setting. Near the end of the focus group, participants were provided a common definition of cyberbullying based in traditional bullying. Participants were asked for their views on this definition in the context of the previous discussions. The definition of cyberbullying provided during groups was "an aggressive, intentional act or behavior that is carried out by a group or an individual, using electronic forms of contact, repeatedly and over time against a victim who cannot easily defend him or herself [2]".

2.3. Study Procedure

Before the start of each focus group, participants completed an anonymous demographic survey, which included questions about age, year in school, and race/ethnicity. Students also indicated what kind of campus organizations they were involved with and their major in school, in order to assess that we were including views from students with a wide range of backgrounds. The facilitator then explained the purpose of the focus group. Each focus group lasted between 45 and 90 minutes.

2.4. Analysis

All audio recordings were transcribed verbatim with the exception of any identifying data such as names. Audio recordings were completed within seven–10 days of completion of the focus group. Data saturation was monitored during the focus group data collection by review of transcripts at scheduled intervals. It became clear that data saturation had been reached due to the commonality of ideas that emerged across groups.

Analysis was conducted using an open coding approach and the constant comparative method [16]. The constant comparative method is a qualitative methodology that requires the researcher to collect data prior to forming hypotheses. Once the data are collected, key points are coded and then arranged into groups or themes with similar conceptual meanings through several rounds of coding and meeting.

Analyses were conducted by three investigators (RK, SS, MM). All transcripts were initially read separately by the three investigators using an open coding approach. The three investigators then met to discuss coding schemes and outline common themes. After a second review of the transcripts, investigators discussed common themes and concepts using the constant comparative method [16]. At the final analysis meeting, the investigators discussed and reached consensus among major themes in the data and also determined illustrative quotations. Both themes and illustrative quotations required consensus by all three investigators in order to be included in the final results.

3. Results

3.1. Participants

A total of 42 students participated in six focus groups that ranged in size from three to 12 participants. Participants' average age was 19.2 (SD = 1.2), 55% were female and 83% were Caucasian. All participants contributed to the discussion and completed the demographic survey. Participants represented a wide range of majors and campus activities (Table 1).

3.2. Themes

Three major themes emerged from our data. First, there was a lack of agreement on a specific definition of cyberbullying but agreement upon three specific cases as representative. Second, participants noted key differences between traditional bullying and cyberbullying. Third, developmental differences in young adult cyberbullying, compared to adolescent cyberbullying, were highlighted by participants.

Table 1. Demographic information and campus involvement for college student focus group participants (n = 42)

Demographic Characteristics (n = 42)	% of participants
Gender	
Female	54.8
Male	45.2
Ethnicity	
Caucasian	83
Asian/Pacific Islander	11.9
Hispanic/Latino	4.8
Year in School	
Freshmen	42.8
Sophomores	23.8
Juniors	23.8
Seniors	9.5
Major	
Basic Sciences (e.g. Biology, Pre-Med, Math)	16.6
Social Sciences (e.g. Psychology, Sociology)	26.2
Humanities (e.g. History, English, Art)	9.5
Engineering	11.9
Business	23.8
Journalism	4.8
Undecided	7.1
Student Organizations	
Academic Groups	14.3
Pre-Health Groups	9.5
Student Life	19.0
LGBTQ Groups	9.6
Cultural and Ethnic Groups	4.8
Greek Community	26.1
Sports and Athletics	4.8
None	9.5

3.2.1. Theme 1: No Agreement on Definition, but Consensus on Representative Cases

Participants tried to achieve a definition of cyberbullying, but struggled to agree upon one. There were diverse opinions both within and across groups. Despite the fact that participants could not agree upon a definition statement, an interesting pattern emerged in each focus group in which specific examples of behaviors that were considered cyberbullying were discussed. These discussions often led to specific examples that were agreed upon as representative of cyberbullying among college students. These 3 scenarios that were commonly discussed and achieved consensus included:

(1). Hacking social media profiles: A commonly described behavior that was considered cyberbullying was "hacking" into a social media profile, such as Facebook, and posting inappropriate information. Hacking was described as Facebook user gaining access to another user's profile and posting information on that profile without permission. This phenomenon was often described as a scenario between roommates or former romantic partners. One example was described below:

> "The worst thing I can think of is actually a girlfriend and a boyfriend. They broke up and the girlfriend knew the password to his Facebook and his e-mail and she changed his password and got the confirmation e-mail on his e-mail account and she had control of his account for like two weeks or something, and she was like, harassing other girls, [making comments] like, 'you were sleeping with him, you were dating him, weren't you'. She ... like, legitimately took control of his Facebook and was using it for her own means and to embarrass him; she was posting like statuses and secrets."

Another type of hacking described by participants was related to representing another student's sexual identity. Participants emphasized that this representation was not necessarily always targeted at a victim's actual sexual orientation. An example is described below:

> "I remember I knew a guy ... someone hacked his account and like changed everything to like rainbows and calling him gay and he was really upset about it. Like, the entire page and all of his pictures were like that. I would definitely consider that cyberbullying."

Participants who identified as LGTBQ pointed out that they had seen this phenomenon on Facebook but did not know of any specific hacking incidents within their personal community of LGTBQ students. However, some participants remarked that incidents of hacking into a Facebook profile to change a student's sexual orientation representation to gay or bisexual still had potential to reflect negatively on the LGTBQ community.

(2). Posting information about social discord publicly: Another commonly discussed type of cyberbullying was situations that involved social discord between roommates, romantic partners, or a campus group, and one member posting about it on a social media profile. This public documentation of an otherwise personal issue, or "airing dirty laundry" was considered cyberbullying. One example included:

"The only bad one I've heard of is a good friend of mine who in her first year here, her roommate and her weren't getting along. So she didn't even find out about it until her roommate posted on Facebook that 'I have the worst roommate ever.' And at first, it was taken as a joke but then she realized that there were some really bad tensions and I guess that was like a really indirect way of finding out that there was a big problem . . . so now a lot of people won't room with her next year because they're hesitant if she's a good person."

(3). Public shaming from posted content: A final agreed upon cyberbullying technique was to publicly mock, tease or put down others related to their own posted content. Examples of this phenomenon included mocking a photograph another student had chosen to post, or purposefully posting a photograph that would embarrass another student. One participant described:

"Umm, one example I can think of is when someone posts that just awful like drunk picture of someone, you know what I mean, where they just look terrible, and then all these people comment and like it and say 'ha ha ha' and it just puts that person down. And like why even post it, do you know what I mean, there has to be some intention [to bully] . . . "

3.2.2. Theme 2: Differences between Traditional Bullying and Cyberbullying

In discussing how to define cyberbullying, participants often began by reflecting on definitions and terms used in describing traditional bullying from the definition read to them during the group. Participants expressed concerns with several of these traditional bullying terms applied to cyberbullying.

Aggression

Participants suggested that including the word "aggressive" in a definition of bullying was appropriate for traditional bullying but not for cyberbullying, as they felt these terms were strongly associated with physical violence. Participants argued that cyberbullying did not need to involve aggression to be hurtful; an example comment is below:

"[Cyberbullying] could be a much more passive bullying than what it would be in real life. In real life it would be a lot more active and aggressive, and through cyberbullying it could be really passive and still hurt."

Intention

The concept of "intention" to describe a bully's approach to a victim was frequently discussed among participants. Intention is a hallmark of traditional bullying but its relevance to cyberbullying was debated. Many participants felt that cyberbullying can occur without intention. An example scenario was friends who take a joke too far online and post comments that are misinterpreted by a particular student. One participant noted:

> "Who is doing the bullying? Is it a friend, because then apparently it's not bullying, it's not ill-intention, but if it's someone that you don't like [it is bullying] . . . ."

Participants also felt that cyberbullies may not be aware of the potential seriousness of their behavior or its impact on the person. For example, though a cyberbully's intention may have been to mildly embarrass the victim, the bully may not realize they have greatly hurt or harmed the victim.

Repetition

Participants discussed that the concept of repetition of behavior, often associated with traditional bullying, may not apply to cyberbullying. Participants described that even one negative comment, picture, or video sent via texting or posted online could easily be circulated to many people via the Internet, so repetition could be viral rather than purposeful.

3.2.3. Theme 3: Differences in Cyberbullying across Developmental Stages of Adolescence

Participants engaged in lively discussions about their views on differences in cyberbullying across the stages of adolescence. Most participants agreed that in younger adolescence, such as during middle or high school, cyberbullying usually involved insulting someone's appearance or other superficial characteristics. In contrast, many students stated that college cyberbullying often involves offensively challenging others' ideas. Many students described how debates about politics, sexuality, and other social issues often take place online and then "devolve into heated arguments" that become personal attacks instead of civil disagreements. An example quotation from a research participant included:

> "I think that [cyberbullying] is not as prevalent for college students, but still . . . especially politically, things can get heated and malicious pretty quickly and once it starts to get like personal attacks that definitely I think counts as cyberbullying and it happens."

Participants also expressed their views that bullying in college could have a more profound impact on students' reputations or career prospects because of the personal nature of the attacks. One participant explained:

"I'd say, in high school, [cyberbullying] is much less serious, but it happens more often. Something that happens in high school probably won't ruin your life, but as a scandal in real life, if someone's spreading rumors about you when you're an adult, that's a much bigger deal. You could ruin someone's entire livelihood. And their career."

A common idea repeated in nearly every focus group was that adolescents reach a new level of maturity in college compared to high school. Participants who discussed the maturity of college students were also likely to downplay the possibility that cyberbullying was a problem in college; and behaviors that would be considered as cyberbullying in a middle or high school setting were only seen as humorous in college. Though a few participants emphasized their newfound maturity in college, these same participants commonly admitted to having engaged in the bullying behaviors that they had defined as immature. The following quotes were stated by the same participant and suggest a disconnect between perceived maturity and actual behaviors.

"I'd like to think college is more of a bully-free environment than high school or middle school . . . in general, people don't care as much about who you are, what you like . . . "

"[Hacking people's Facebook profiles], that happens all the time. It's like, probably like every other day that your newsfeed is filled with like, 'I'm gay, I'm gay' . . . it's just kind of funny . . . "

In one group there was a discussion about behaviors that were immature and unlikely to be done by college students. After this discussion one participant admitted to engaging in the behaviors that the focus group had previously identified as immature:

"Full disclosure here, my friend left his page up one time and I like sent a request to a girl he was kind of seeing, like a relationship request, and he didn't like that girl at all, he was just kind of hooking up with her and that like ended the relationship. Just cut off from her. I thought it was hilarious, but that's pretty bad."

4. Conclusions

We conducted focus groups with college students towards characterizing the nature of cyberbullying in that population and defining key issues that may impact future efforts to define, understand and prevent cyberbullying. Consensus on a definition of cyberbullying remained elusive. This finding illustrates how challenging it can be to achieve consensus on an applicable definition of a societal concept, mirroring struggles that professional groups may have encountered in developing a clear definition of cyberbullying. These mixed views of what constitutes cyberbullying may explain why previous studies present a variety of prevalence rates [6,7,11,17].

While a consensus on a definition of cyberbullying remained elusive, there was consensus reached across groups on representative cases of cyberbullying including hacking, airing dirty laundry and mocking. The inclusion of airing dirty laundry as a representative case raises key questions regarding how society should approach defining cyberbullying and whose input should be prioritized. College administrators and scholars in related fields may question whether "airing dirty laundry" meets criteria as bullying, or whether it represents behavior that, while unpleasant, should not be considered cyberbullying. It remains unclear whether a definition of cyberbullying should prioritize views of age-appropriate groups involved who experience cyberbullying themselves, or whether a definition should prioritize views and experiences from adult scholars or experts in bullying. While our study cannot answer this question, our findings raise key issues that merit consideration in how to create a definition of cyberbullying that has relevance across different age groups and professional societies.

Many of our participants engaged in discussions about differences between traditional and online bullying. Participants were quick to identify ways in which cyberbullying differed from traditional bullying, including a reduced emphasis on aggression, intention and repetition. It is possible that placing cyberbullying in the context of traditional bullying may hinder our ability to comprehensively define this new concept. Studying cyberbullying by applying existing concepts from another form of bullying may limit the ability to approach cyberbullying with fresh ideas and new constructs. However, separating cyberbullying from the overall context of bullying may limit our understanding of how bullying risks, actions and consequences may vary across the life course. Rather than developing a single definition of bullying, future efforts may wish to consider developing a repertoire of case examples of bullying, or a conceptual model that describes concepts that are critical to bullying across different settings or age ranges.

Participants generally agreed that bullying behaviors among older adolescents could include attacking victims at the level of their beliefs or character. This finding may be concerning as college presents a unique time period where bullying may have harmful effects. Many students are living away from their homes, families, and familiar environments for the first time and are newly independent [18]. While navigating these developmental challenges, older adolescents are also progressing through a stressful, vulnerable period of identity formation [19]. Therefore, attacks during this period may have a significant impact. Further, if left unchecked, these bullies may continue their behavior into adulthood and the workplace. Workplace bullies have been characterized as manipulating others to gain power or privilege, often through subtle techniques that do not involve being directly hostile [20]. These techniques share similarities with participants' descriptions of cyberbullying. Thus, the college years may represent the last opportunity to identify or intervene with bullies, as well as victims, before patterns and consequences are established that may impact the years ahead.

Another finding from our study is that participants' comments suggested that most college students had exposure to a case or had personal experiences with cyberbullying in college. These comments may suggest that cyberbullying is more common that previously thought in college, or they may reflect our study design of focus groups and that many participants wanted to contribute to discussions. Likely it suggests that college students are aware of cyberbullying as an issue on college campuses, and are willing and enthusiastic to discuss their views. This suggests that future studies on this topic using qualitative methods such as participant interviews or focus groups may be well received by this population.

This study is not without limitations. Although the sample was largely ethnically homogenous, we included students from a variety of college communities. The demographics of our study participants reflect the demographic makeup of the school involved in the study, which meant that not all ethnic groups were represented. For this reason, future studies should attempt to capture the perspectives of students from a wider range of groups. Second, there may be recruitment bias as people who have had either more or less experience with cyberbullying may have been more or less attracted to participate in the study. Last, we did not elicit personal experiences from participants with the intention of providing students with a comfortable environment to discuss these issues, but it is possible that asking individual students directly about real life examples may have been more informative in characterizing cyberbullying behaviors.

Despite these limitations, our findings have important implications. Without a widely known and accepted definition of cyberbullying, it may be difficult to both identify cases and design interventions to combat this problem. However, future work can use our findings through participant viewpoints and voices in several ways. First, researchers conducting studies of cyberbullying in older adolescents can consider novel approaches to assess these behaviors. Rather than selecting one of many proposed definitions of cyberbullying, future studies could examine the prevalence of cyberbullying by providing specific examples of behaviors to adolescents such as "hacking into another person's Facebook profile". Providing examples to illustrate types of cyberbullying may lead to accurate prevalence assessments and an understanding of which behaviors are most salient during particular stages of adolescence. Alternatively, researchers may benefit from an interdisciplinary approach to develop a conceptual model that takes into account different bullying actions across life stages. Second, findings suggest a small but vocal group of students who argued that college students were too mature to engage in cyberbullying, and those specific cases suggested as bullying behaviors were "just kind of funny." This group may merit further investigation as to motivations for engaging in behaviors that are considered bullying by others. Third, for clinicians and educators, future work is needed to consider cyberbullying screening across the full span of adolescence. Novel prevention approaches using social media to disseminate interventions or raise awareness of the negative consequences of bullying may help reach college students. Since cyberbullying takes place online, placing prevention or intervention messages in the online space may allow broach reach and dissemination of effective programs.

Acknowledgments: This study was funded by support from the University of Wisconsin Department of Pediatrics. The authors would like to acknowledge Lyn Turkstra for her assistance with this project.

Author Contributions: Rajitha Kota developed study proposal, collected data, analyzed data, wrote and edited manuscript. Shari Schoohs collected data, contributed to analysis, contributed to editing manuscript. Meghan Benson advised on study proposal, contributed to analysis, and edited the manuscript. Megan A. Moreno advised on study proposal, contributed to analysis, and edited the manuscript.

Conflicts of Interest: The authors declare no conflict of interest.

References and Notes

1. U.S. Department of Justice. Research and Evaluation on Children Exposed to Violence. Available online: https://ncjrs.gov/pdffiles1/nij/sl001042.pdf (accessed on 27 January 2014).
2. Smith, P.K.; Mahdavi, J.; Carvalho, M.; Fisher, S.; Russell, S.; Tippett, N. Cyberbullying: Its nature and impact in secondary school pupils. *J. Child Psychol. Psychiatr.* **2008**, *49*, 376–385.
3. Slonje, R.; Smith, P.K. Cyberbullying: Another main type of bullying? *Scand. J. Psychol.* **2008**, *49*, 147–154.
4. Ybarra, M.L.; Mitchell, K.J.; Wolak, J.; Finkelhor, D. Examining Characteristics and Associated Distress Related to Internet Harassment: Findings from the Second Youth Internet Safety Survey. *Pediatrics* **2006**, *118*, e1169–e1177.
5. Patchin, J.W.; Hinduja, S. Bullies move beyond the schoolyard a preliminary look at cyberbullying. *Youth Violence Juv. Justice* **2006**, *4*, 148–169.
6. Beran, T.; Li, Q. The relationship between cyberbullying and school bullying. *J. Stud. Wellbeing* **2007**, *1*, 15–33.
7. Li, Q. A cross-cultural comparison of adolescents' experience related to cyberbullying. *Educ. Res.* **2008**, *50*, 223–234.
8. Juvonen, J.; Gross, E.F. Extending the school grounds?—Bullying experiences in cyberspace. *J. Sch. Health* **2008**, *78*, 496–505.

9. Center for Disease Control and Prevention. Featured Topic: Bullying Research. Available online: http://www.cdc.gov/violenceprevention/youthviolence/bullyingresearch/index.html (accessed on 20 January 2014).

10. Lenhart, A.; Purcell, K.; Smith, A.; Zickhur, K. *Social Media and Young Adults*; Pew Internet and American Life Project: Washington, DC, USA, 2010.

11. MacDonald, C.D.; Roberts-Pittman, B. Cyberbullying among college students: Prevalence and demographic differences. *Soc. Behav. Sci.* **2010**, *9*, 2003–2009.

12. Molluzzo, J.C.; Lawler, J. A Study of the Perceptions of College Students on Cyberbullying. *Inf. Syst. Educ. J.* **2012**, *10*, 84–109.

13. Kosciw, J.; Greytak, E.A.; Bartkiewicz, M.J.; Boesen, M.J.; Palmer, N.A. *The 2007 National School Climate Survey: The Experiences of Lesbian, Gay, Bisexual and Transgender Youth in Our Nation's Schools*; Gay Lesbian and Straight Education Network (GLSEN): New York, NY, USA, 2008.

14. Krueger, R.A.; Casey, M.A. *Focus Groups: A Practical Guide for Applied Research*, 4th ed.; SAGE Publications: Thousand Oaks, CA, USA, 2009.

15. Glesne, C. *Becoming Qualitative Researchers*, 2nd ed.; Addison Wesley Longman: Reading, MA, USA, 1999.

16. Glaser, B.G.; Strauss, A. *The Discovery of Grounded Theory: Strategies for Qualitative Research*; Aldine Transaction: Hawthorne, New York, NY, USA, 1967.

17. Varjas, K.; Henrich, C.C.; Meyers, J. Urban middle school students' perceptions of bullying, cyberbullying, and school safety. *J. Sch. Violence* **2009**, *2*, 159–176.

18. Ross, S.E.; Niebling, B.C.; Heckert, T.M. Sources of stress among college students. *Coll. Student J.* **1999**, *3*, 312–317.

19. Orlofsky, J.L. Sex-role orientation, identity formation and self-esteem in college men and women. *Sex Roles* **1977**, *3*, 561–575.

20. Zapf, D.; Escartín, J.; Einarsen, S.; Hoel, H.; Vartia, M. *Empirical Findings on Bullying in the Workplace in Bullying and Emotional Abuse in the Workplace: International Perspectives on Research and Practice*; Taylor and Francis: London, UK, 2003.

Traditional, Cyber and Combined Bullying Roles: Differences in Risky Online and Offline Activities

Sebastian Wachs, Marianne Junger and Ruthaychonee Sittichai

Abstract: This study (1) reports frequency rates of mutually exclusive traditional, cyber and combined (both traditional and cyber) bullying roles; and (2) investigates whether adolescents belonging to particular bullying roles show higher levels of involvement in risky online activities (Compulsive Internet Use (CIU), online grooming victimization, and sexting) and risky offline activities (bad behavior in school, drinking alcohol and truancy) than non-involved adolescents. The sample comprised self-reports of 1928 German, Dutch and Thai adolescents (Age = 12–18; M = 14.52; SD = 1.6). The results revealed age, sex and country differences in bullying frequency rates. CIU, sending of sexts and risky offline activities were most strongly associated with combined bully-victims. The receiving of sexts was most strongly associated with combined bullies; and online grooming victimization was most strongly related to cyber bully-victims. Another important finding is that the associations between risky offline activities and combined bullying are stronger than for traditional and cyber bullying. The findings contribute to better understanding of the associations between varying bullying roles and risky online and offline activities among adolescents. In sum, the results underscore the need to promote life skills rather than adopting more conventional approaches, which focus almost exclusively on reduction of risks.

Reprinted from *Societies*. Cite as: Wachs, S.; Junger, M.; Sittichai, R. Traditional, Cyber and Combined Bullying Roles: Differences in Risky Online and Offline Activities. *Societies* **2015**, *5*, 109–135.

1. Introduction

Bullying is a multifaceted phenomenon that describes a variety of physically, verbally and relationally aggressive behaviors that occur repetitively in the long-term against a defenseless victim [1]. Identifying various roles of those adolescents who are involved in traditional bullying has been a crucial aspect of previous research. The results identified three main roles: bullies, victims, and bully-victims. The person who initiates and caries out the major role in bullying is called the bully, the target person who suffers from bullying is called the victim. Bully-victims who are both bullies and victims seem to be a special risk group who display the psychological characteristics of both victims and bullies and often show worse emotional, social and psychological difficulties than pure victims or pure bullies [2–5].

A much more recent manifestation of bullying is cyberbullying, which can be defined as "any behavior performed through electronic or digital media by individuals or groups that repeatedly communicates hostile or aggressive messages intended to inflict harm or discomfort on others" [6] (p. 278). As in traditional bullying (bullying without the use of ICT), roles like cyberbully, cybervictim and cyberbully-victim were identified in cyberbullying. With the increasing research on cyberbullying, new participant roles that combine traditional and cyber bullying roles like victim-cybervictims (hereafter combined victims), bully-cyberbullies (hereafter combined bullies) or bully-victim-cyberbully-cybervictims (hereafter combined bully-victims) have been debunked [7–9].

To date, there has been a lively discussion in bullying research whether involvement in either cyber or traditional bullying or even in both has a bigger impact on adolescents [7,10]. Most research suggests that those adolescents involved in traditional bullying share nearly the same level of engagement in similar risky and problematic behaviors as those engaged in cyberbullying [11–14]. However, research concerning combined bullying seems to be limited and contradictory. While some studies report that combined bullies, victims and bully-victims display worse engagement in risky and problematic behaviors in comparison with pure cyber or traditional bullying roles [8,15]; other studies state that if one adolescent is already involved in traditional bullying, the additional involvement in cyberbullying does not increase negative outcomes [11,13,16]. These inconsistent findings suggest a strong argument for including combined bullying roles in further analysis.

Involvement in bullying might be associated with engagement in risky activities among adolescents. In psychology, *Problem Behavior Theory* (PBT) developed by Jessor and Jessor [17] states that the presence of one form of problem or risky activity increases the likelihood of the occurrence of another. At present, several studies found problem behaviors such as substance abuse, aggressive behavior, delinquency, vandalism, sexual risk behavior, injury and suicidal ideation to be intertwined, and to co-vary which increases the risk for a negative development [18–23]. Further, adolescents who are engaged in several forms of risky behavior also show higher risks of becoming a part of a deviant peer group, where these behaviors might be more accepted and prevalent that often culminates in further conflicts with the environment [18].

For bullying roles, the involvement in risky online activities (*i.e.*, compulsive Internet use, sexting and online grooming victimization) and risky offline activities (*i.e.*, problems with teachers, truancy and drinking alcohol) might differ greatly within and between traditional, cyber and combined bullying typologies. To enhance our understanding about similarities and differences between traditional and cyber bullying, it is important to understand whether differing roles share the same pattern of potentially risky online and offline activities.

1.1. Risky Online Activities

1.1.1. Compulsive Internet Use

Compulsive Internet Use (CIU) is also known as Internet Addiction or Excessive Internet behavior. It is usually defined by four characteristics: (1) a loss of sense of time or a neglect of basic drives and needs; (2) withdrawal, involving feelings of anger, anxiety, and/or depression when the Internet is not accessible; (3) an increasing need for more hours of use; and (4) negative psychological and social consequences, e.g., disputes, lying, lower school achievement, social isolation [24,25]. Associations between CIU and bullying involvement can be explained as followed: On one side, some victims/cybervictims could try to cope with negative experiences by compulsive use of ICTs. Hence, the victims could try to search for a safer place online where they cannot be assaulted directly (*i.e.*, hit physically) and where they can try to be another person and meet new people who are not aware of their victim status. In addition, victims/cybervictims could lose the sense of an appropriate use of ICT and self-control while searching the Internet for new compromising material spread by the perpetrators or to assure that there is no new defaming material posted and shared. This insecurity could lead to a loss of appropriate use of ICTs and might increase the risk for CIU. On the other side, bullies/cyberbullies could also show a higher risk for CIU, since both phenomena share common risk factors like high impulsivity and low self-control [26–28]. Some research observed elevated scores of aggression and a greater irritability as a consequence of CIU involvement [25,29], which could raise the risk for problems with peers and result in bullying as a coping strategy. Within this line of thinking, CIU might be related to intrapersonal conflicts (in regard to the own feelings and well-being) and to interpersonal conflicts (in regard to social relationships) [28].

Previous empirical findings concerning the associations between CIU and involvement in bullying and cyberbullying are mixed and focus on cyberbullying and not traditional bullying. While one study found CIU to be associated with cybervictimization but not cyberbullying [30], another study stated the opposite: CIU was not associated with cybervictimization but was related to cyberbullying [31]. In a comparison of the associations between CIU and various cyberbullying roles, cyber bully-victims presented a higher level of engagement than pure cyberbullies and cybervictims [30]. Whether CIU is associated with other roles like traditional bully-victims and combined bullying roles remains contemplated and unanswered yet. In the current study, we will pay attention in more detail to the intra- und interpersonal conflicts due to CIU associated with varying bullying roles.

1.1.2. Online Grooming

Online grooming (or cybergrooming) can be defined as a process of manipulation, rapport building, deception and misuse of trust by which a significantly older offender prepares sexual abuse of a minor by the means of ICTs [32,33]. Until now, only very few studies investigated the associations between bullying and online grooming. However, some research was conducted on the associations between unhealthy romantic relationships, sexual harassment and traditional bullying involvement.

Previous research indicates that bullies might be at higher risk of falling victim to online grooming. For instance, in one study, with a sample of 1758 students in Grades 5 through 8, bullies reported to start dating earlier, appeared to be highly relationship oriented and reported more advanced pubertal development [34]. These characteristics may be similar in the online context, *i.e.,* talking with strangers about sexual topics, the willingness to have sexual contacts and form relationships online. Especially, the relationship orientation of the bullies might favor the frequently applied strategy of online groomers who build rapport with their victims prior to sexual abuse [33]. However, being a bully could not only be seen as a risk factor for online grooming victimization but also a consequence. Some bullies might choose to bully others as an inappropriate coping strategy to overcome experiences of abuse [35].

Research shows that victims of traditional and cyber bullying are more likely to become a victim of online grooming [36,37]. This can be explained by several factors: First, victims of bullying face serious social problems (*i.e.,* lack of good peer relationships, more frequently rejected by their peers and more often excluded from peer-to-peer activities) [14,38]. Online groomers might take advantage of this poor social situation of bullying victims by faking friendships and exploiting the natural need for attention and affection [33]. Consistent with this, some research found that cybervictims more often flirt online with unknown people [39]. Second, victims of bullying/cyberbullying might share certain risk factors with victims of online grooming which might partially explain the co-occurrence of both phenomena. Both victims of bullying and victims of online grooming have relatively low self-esteem, high impulsivity, increased sexual risk behavior and risky online behavior (disclosing private information about phone number, instant messenger id *etc.*) in comparison with non-victims [32,33,39].

Some research suggests that bully-victims show even more risk for sexual harassment. For instance, in a study with 684 middle and high school students, bully-victims reported more physical dating violence victimization than pure bullies, pure victims or uninvolved students and more emotional abuse in dating relationships than uninvolved students or pure victims. Bully-victims and victims also reported the highest amount of sexual peer harassment [2].

However, no study investigated the associations of online grooming with varying bullying roles like bully-victims or combined roles yet. Particularly, combined roles who are facing peer problems online and offline might show higher risk of falling victim to online grooming as cyber or traditional roles.

1.1.3. Sexting

Receiving and sending of sexually explicit messages or nude, semi-nude selfies (digital images of one's self), videos or texts via ICTs, is usually defined as sexting [40,41]. There are a variety of reasons why adolescents engage in sexting. Some adolescents want to show off in front of their friends by forwarding nude pictures of their girlfriends or boyfriends. Others share nude pictures to prove commitment as a part of or instead of face-to-face sexual activities and yet others try to entice a prospective girlfriend or boyfriend by sending so-called sexts [41].

However, sometimes sexts are also used to embarrass or humiliate someone and can lead to social isolation. Dake and colleagues [40] described the associations between cyberbullying and sexting as two phenomena with blurred lines. The authors emphasize the voluntariness of the act and the intent to harm as main distinguishing characteristics between sexting and cyberbullying. While sexts are generally sent voluntarily, they might be misused in cyberbullying to cause harm to the sender by being forwarded to persons who were not supposed to receive them. Indeed, Dake and colleagues [40] found traditional and cyber victims more likely to be engaged in sexting. However, until now, no study has investigated whether different bullying roles tend to send or receive sexual messages via ICT more likely.

1.2. Risky Offline Activities

Involvement in both traditional and cyber bullying seems to be associated with a variety of risky offline activities. Traditional bullies, victims and bully-victims were found to show an increased risk of school-related behavioral problems like frequent truancy and trouble with teachers [42,43]. A number of studies also inferred that bullies and victims were more likely to frequently engage in drinking alcohol than non-involved adolescents [44–46]. Olweus [1] stated that both bullies and bully-victims, once grown-up, showed clearly higher risks of engaging in alcohol abuse. Other studies showed that cyberbullies as well as cybervictims showed increased levels of several risky offline activities including *i.e.*, truancy, fighting, and the consumption of alcohol [47]. More recently, a longitudinal study indicated that substance use predicted cybervictimization and that cyber bully-victims show higher risk for substance abuse as cyberbullies or cybervictims [30]. However, the associations between risky offline activities and combined bullying roles were not thoroughly investigated until now.

1.3. Socio-Demographics

Although age and sex are commonly investigated covariates in traditional and cyber bullying, research on the associations is not conclusive. While some studies report that there are no age differences in traditional and cyber bullying [48,49], other studies indicate that both decline with increasing age. Tokunaga [6] argues, on the basis of a literature review, that the occurrence of both traditional and cyber bullying seems to follow a curvilinear development whereby cyberbullying seems to peak during the 7th and 8th grade while traditional bullying is expected to peak slightly earlier. In accordance with this, Khoury-Kassabri [50] states that with increasing age certain forms of aggressive behaviors (e.g., traditional bullying) decrease whereas other forms that might occur outside of school (e.g., cyberbullying) might increase with older age adolescents.

In traditional bullying, bullies and bully-victims tend to be male, particularly in physical bullying, whereas victims tend to be more often female [16,44,51]. The role sex plays in cyberbullying has varied considerably between studies and still remains unclear. In some studies, no significant sex differences in cyberbullies, cybervictims and/or cyber bully-victims were found [49,52]; other studies reported that more boys were found to be involved as cyberbullies [44,51], or indicated that girls are more often found to be involved as cybervictims [16,44,53], or *vice versa* [54]. In cyber bully-victims, the results are also mixed. Some studies reported that boys were significantly more often cyber bully-victims [16,44,53,54] and other studies found girls to be more often cyber bully-victims [55]. Only very few studies have focused on sex differences in combined roles (traditional and cyber). While some studies did not find any sex differences [9], other reported that boys tend to be more often combined bullies [8,11], and yet others found combined victims and combined bully-victims more frequently to be girls [16].

The vast majority of studies on traditional and cyber bullying were carried out in Western countries, especially Europe, North America, and Australia. Fewer studies were conducted in Japan, South Korea and China [56]. Studies about traditional and cyber bullying in Southeast Asian countries like Thailand are very scarce. Sittichai and Smith [56] stated in a literature review on bullying in Thailand that studies were mainly qualitative, and did not consistently distinguish bullying from general aggression. Consequently, there is a need for studies that investigate traditional and cyber bullying among Thai adolescents and a need for cross-national comparison between Western and Southeast Asian countries.

In sum, the inconsistent findings on sex differences and gaps in bullying research among Thai adolescents suggest strong arguments for including socio-demographics as control variables in further analysis.

2. The Present Study

Various risky online and offline activities with regards to traditional and cyber bullying roles were investigated, but the same is not true for risky online activities like CIU, online grooming and sexting. Further, most bullying studies focused on comparison between traditional and cyber roles, but fewer have included cyber or traditional bully-victims and even less included combined bullying roles. Building on the findings of previous research, this study aimed to make a comparative analysis of online and offline correlates in traditional, cyber and combined bullying roles in order to understand bullying involvement in a broader context of problem behavior both online and offline.

In the present study, we investigated two research questions: First, how many adolescents can be categorized as involved in traditional, cyber and combined bullying in the present sample? Second, are risky online and offline activities associated with involvement in traditional, cyber and combined bullying roles?

3. Method

3.1. Participants

A total of 2004 adolescents from three secondary schools in Germany, three secondary schools from the Netherlands and one school from Thailand were recruited as a convenience sample. Questionnaires were screened for containing several illogic responses, extremely one-sided response patterns, consistently filling in the extremes or with many questions unanswered. Overall, 76 questionnaires were identified based on those criteria; this corresponds to 3.7% of the data. We decided to remove those questionnaires, because according to Tabachnick and Fidell [57], if missing data represent less than 5% of the total sample "almost any procedure for handling missing values yields similar results" (p. 63). The final sample consisted of 1928 adolescents aged between 11 and 18 years (M = 14.52; SD = 1.6). The sex distribution was 866 (44.9%) boys and 1062 (55.1%) girls. Distribution across countries was Germany 849 (44.3%), the Netherlands 379 (19.8%) and Thailand 700 (35.8%). Table 1 shows the distribution of participants by age, sex and country.

Table 1. Frequencies by age, sex and country (*N* = 1925 *).

Age	Sex	German		Dutch		Thai		Total	
		n	%	n	%	n	%	n	%
11 + 12	Boys	39	2.0	19	1.0	36	1.8	94	4.8
	Girls	43	2.2	13	1.4	64	3.3	120	6.9
13	Boys	94	4.8	51	2.6	34	1.7	179	9.1
	Girls	93	4.8	30	1.5	66	3.4	189	9.7
14	Boys	104	5.4	30	1.5	34	1.7	168	8.6
	Girls	123	6.3	26	1.3	66	3.4	215	11.0
15	Boys	121	6.2	63	3.2	35	1.8	219	11.2
	Girls	112	5.8	51	2.6	65	3.3	228	11.7
16	Boys	44	2.2	28	1.4	40	2.0	112	5.6
	Girls	44	2.2	28	1.4	60	3.1	132	6.7
17 + 18	Boys	12	1.6	23	1.1	46	2.3	81	5.0
	Girls	17	0.8	17	0.8	154	8,0	188	9.6
Total		846	44.3	379	19.8	700	35.8	1925	100

* Discrepancy between total and sample size is due to missing data (*n* = 3) for age in the German sample.

3.2. Procedure

The study was conducted in schools in Germany and the Netherlands in the summer of 2013 and in Thailand in the autumn of 2013, during normal school time. In Germany and the Netherlands, the data were collected by an online survey that transcribes the results into a file that can be exported to SPSS. Due to technical considerations in Thailand, the data was collected by paper-pencil-questionnaires.

The data protection officer and educational authority of the federal state of Lower Saxony, Germany, approved this procedure (OS 1 R.24-0541/2 N). As the adolescents were underage, parents had to sign a written consent form allowing them to participate.

In all countries, adolescents were explained why the present study was being conducted and how they could contribute. Adolescents were told that partaking in the study was optional, questions could be skipped and participation in the survey could be stopped at any time, without the need for giving a reason and without fear of negative consequences. The average time needed to complete the questionnaire was about 30 min. About 95% of eligible pupils participated in the study.

3.3. Measures

3.3.1. Traditional and Cyber Bullying

The Mobbing Questionnaire for Students by Jäger, Fischer and Riebel [58] was applied to measure bullying and cyberbullying involvement, using a reference period of within the last 12 months. The questionnaire starts with a definition of traditional bullying which includes the three central characteristics (imbalance of power, repetition of the acts and intention to hurt) mentioned by Olweus [13]. Traditional bullying was measured with each one global item for traditional bullying and traditional victimization in reference to Olweus [1]. Regarding the victim, the following question was asked: "How many times have you been bullied in the last twelve months?" and for the perpetrators' side "How many times have you bullied others in the last twelve months?"

Then cyberbullying was explained in the same way like traditional bullying but including the use of ICTs. Cyberbullying was measured with two global items by asking about victimization "How many times have you been cyberbullied in the last twelve months?" and about perpetration "How many times have you cyberbullied others in the last twelve months?" The answers, for both traditional and cyberbullying, could be given on a five-point ordinal scale (1–5), ("Never", "Once or twice", "Twice or thrice a month", "About once a week" or "Several times a week").

3.3.2. Compulsive Internet Use

To assess CIU, the Internet-Related Experiences Questionnaire developed by Beranuy, Chamarro, Graner, and Carbonell-Sánchez [59] was used. This scale consists of 10 items and comprises two subscales with each five items. The first subscale reflects intrapersonal conflicts caused by compulsive use of ICT including items like "When you are not connected to the Internet do you feel nervous or worried?" "Do you get angry or irritated when someone distracts you while you are connected?" and "How often do you stop your regular activities to spend more time on the Internet?" The second subscale addresses interpersonal conflicts caused by compulsive use of ICT and include items like "Do you find it easier or more comfortable to relate to people via Internet than face-to-face?" and "How often do you make new friends online?" All items using a four-point ordinal scale (1–4), with response options of "never", "rarely", "sometimes", "often". Casas *et al.* [60] validated the Internet-Related Experiences Questionnaire with a sample of Spanish adolescents. The authors confirmed a two factors structure. An intrapersonal factor (CIU INTRA) measures psychological or emotional ICT-related problems while the interpersonal factor (CIU INTER) reflects ICT-related social problems. They obtained for the total scale reliabilities of $\alpha = 0.79$, with $\alpha = 0.72$ for the Intrapersonal Factor and $\alpha = 0.64$ for the Interpersonal Factor. In this study, acceptable reliabilities were found for the total scale $\alpha = 0.81$, the Intrapersonal Factor $\alpha = 0.75$, and the Interpersonal Factor $\alpha = 0.67$.

3.3.3. Online Grooming

In order to improve the validity of responses, adolescents were given a definition of online grooming. This definition was based on a literature review and was already applied in a previous study [36]:

> "A cybergroomer is a person who is at least 7 years older than you and whom you have known for a long period exclusively through online communication. At the beginning, the cybergroomer seems to be interested in your daily life problems, but after a certain time s/he appears to be interested in sexual topics and in the exchange of sexual fantasies and/or nude material (pictures or video chats)".

There is no validated scale for the assessment of online grooming. In the present study, one single item was used. Adolescents were asked "How many times did you have contact with a cybergroomer in the last twelve months?" by utilizing a five-point ordinal scale with the same answer options as in bullying.

3.3.4. Sexting

Sexting was assessed with two single items in reference to Hinduja and Patchin [61] by asking "How often did you receive naked or semi-naked pictures via ICTs from others in the last 12 months?" and "How often did you send naked or semi-naked pictures of yourself to others via ICTs in the last 12 months?", with response options of "never", "once or twice", "monthly", "weekly", and "daily".

3.3.5. Risky Offline Activities

To assess facets of risky offline activities, three items were used (adapted from Currie et al. [62]). Adolescents should state how many times they made experiences with potential risky offline activities: "Been in trouble with my teacher for bad behavior", "Missed school lessons without my parents knowing", and "Had so much alcohol that you got really drunk" with answer options from never to several times a week (1–5). The reliability for the scale was acceptable [57,63] with $\alpha = 0.735$. In order to disprove unequal weighting of these three items a Principal Component Analysis (PCA) was carried out. All items loaded well on one component (0.806; 0.823; 0.808) (eigenvalue 1). That is, an unequal weighting of the individual items was not indicated. It was mentioned explicitly to the participants that the item "Been in trouble with my teacher for bad behavior" was not about online behavior.

3.3.6. Demographics

Questions regarding age, sex, and country of the adolescents assessed socio-demographics.

3.4. Translation Procedure

The translation procedure was uniformly regulated, using the following steps recommended by Sousa and Rojjanasrirat [64]: First, the authors translated the original items into each of the required languages, and then a bilingual person who had not seen the original items before reviewed the translation. The Cronbachs' Alpha measures showed good to adequate internal reliability compared by country (see Table 2).

Table 2. Internal consistencies in cross-national comparison (N = 1925).

Instrument	Number of Items	GER	DUT	THAI
CIU (total)	10	0.842	0.805	0.797
CIU INTRA	5	0.745	0.737	0.641
CIU INTER	5	0.706	0.624	0.754
Risky offline activities	3	0.670	0.801	0.777

3.5. Analytical Approach

Analyses consisted of two steps: descriptive statistics and multinomial logistic regressions. Descriptive statistics were used to determine the frequency rates of bullying roles in the present sample. Pearson's correlational analysis was applied to describe bivariate associations between the study variables. Pearson's Chi-squared test was used to assess the bivariate associations between the bullying typologies and sex and country. Cramer's V was used to calculate the effect size.

In order to continue former bullying research that used the categorical approach [7,8,11,14,16], embrace the skewed distributions, and allow comparison of distinct risk factors of several bullying roles, we treated the bullying items as categorical and applied logistic regressions. In this way, we accepted loss of statistical power but avoided biased parameter estimates due to non-normal deviated outcomes [57,63].

Logistic regression models were used to compare different typologies (traditional, cyber and combined) in relation to risky online activities and risky offline activities. We collapsed the bullying/victimization and cyberbullying/ cybervictimization variables into polynomial variables with mutually distinctive categories, in order to enable the identification of group differences concerning several independent variables. As a lower-bound cutoff point for classifying adolescents as involved in bullying, we used "two or three times a month" which was recommended by previous research to identify real group differences, considering that bullying occurs repeatedly [13,65]. Consequently, adolescents who scored less than "two or three times a month" (1–2) were classified as not involved, while adolescents who scored about "two or three times a month" or more often (3–5) were classified as bullies or victims and adolescents who reported on both (bullying and victimization) higher than "two or three times a month" were labeled as bully-victims. Under this procedure, we built the following three typologies basing on previous findings in bullying research [8,9,11,53]: Traditional typology: bully, victim, bully-victim, non-involved; cyber typology: cyberbully, cybervictim, cyber bully-victim, non-involved; combined typology: combined bully, combined victim, combined bully-victim and non-involved.

We chose multinomial regression analysis since this procedure allows more than two discrete outcomes. For each of the bullying typologies, one multinomial logistic regression was performed with one bullying typology as the outcome (non-involved as the reference category), and with CIU, online grooming victimization, sexting, and risky offline activities as independent variables and socio-demographics (age, sex and country) as control variables.

Before applying multinomial regression analysis, we checked the data for two essential assumptions: outliers and multicollinearity [57,63,66]. Univariate outliers in all ordinal independent variables were winsorized by replacing values beyond the 5th and 95th percentile by exactly these values in order to reduce the effect of possibly spurious outliers. If they were just dropped, the calculations would lose too much of the potentially valuable information. Since multicollinearity between predictors reduces the probability to assess the individual importance of a predictor, correlations among the winsorized predictors were estimated and evaluated in order to examine multicollinearity before conducting the multinomial logistic regression analysis (see Table 3). The correlation matrix indicated that the data were suitable for consideration as independent variables in a multinomial regression analysis since no high correlations (>0.07) could be detected [63,66]. Further, Table 3 shows the four dependent bullying variables.

Table 3. Correlation matrix of all variables used in this study ($N = 1925$).

	2.	3.	4.	5.	6.	7.	8.	9.	10.	11.	12.	13.
1. CIU INTRA	0.508 **	0.199 **	0.132 **	0.151 **	0.215 **	0.090 **	0.116 **	0.090 **	0.172 **	0.151 **	0.215 **	0.198 **
2. CIU INTER	1	0.169 **	0.066 **	0.256 **	0.123 **	0.130 **	0.192 **	0.393 **	0.190 **	0.204 **	0.235 **	0.284 **
3. Receiving of sexts		1	0.290 **	0.169 **	0.375 **	-0.120 **	0.132 **	-0.029	0.258 **	0.027	0.273 **	0.102 **
4. Sending of sexts			1	0.162 **	0.194 **	-0.092 **	0.027	-0.030	0.155 **	0.045 *	0.200 **	0.103 **
5. Online grooming				1	0.101 **	0.085 **	0.068 **	0.308 **	0.100 **	0.172 **	0.207 **	0.308 **
6. Risky offline activities					1	-0.127 **	0.208 **	-0.136 **	0.349 **	0.084 **	0.278 **	0.111 **
7. Sex						1	0.075 **	0.190 **	-0.133 **	0.071 **	-0.059 *	0.059 **
8. Age							1	0.139 **	-0.022	-0.074 **	0.059 **	-0.039
9. Country								1	0.011	0.207 **	-0.080 **	0.283 **
10. Bullying									1	0.285 **	0.469 **	0.165 **
11. Victimization										1	0.167 **	0.375 **
12. Cyberbullying											1	0.370 **
13. Cybervictimization												1

Note: * $p < 0.05$, ** $p < 0.01$.

81

3.6. Control Variables

In all regression analyses, age, sex and country were included as control variables.

4. Results

4.1. Frequency Rates of Traditional, Cyber and Combined Bullying

To address our first research question regarding the frequency of traditional, cyber and combined bullying in the sample, Table 4 provides frequency rates of bullies, victims, bully-victims and non-involved categorized by lenient cut off (at least "two or three times a month") in total, by country and by sex. The frequency rates compared by country revealed some statistically significant differences. In traditional bullying, fewer Thai adolescents were non-involved, more German adolescents were bullies, more Thai adolescents were victims and bully-victims, χ^2 (6, 1900) = 68.1, $p < 0.0001$, Cramer's $V = 0.134$. In cyberbullying, less Thais were non-involved, more Thais were cyber-victims and cyber bully-victims χ^2 (6, 1925) = 145.4, $p < 0.0001$, Cramer's $V = 0.194$. In combined bullying, Thai adolescents were rather frequently non-involved and more likely combined victims and combined bully-victims, χ^2 (6, 1604) = 89.2, $p < 0.0001$, Cramer's $V = 0.167$.

Differences in the sex composition of the traditional bullying roles were statistically significant, χ^2 (3, 1900) = 31.0, $p < 0.0001$, Cramer's $V = 0.128$, suggesting that boys were more likely than girls to be bullies and girls more likely than boys victims. Significant sex differences were also observed for cyberbullying roles, χ^2 (3, 1925) = 19.3, $p < 0.0001$, Cramer's $V = 0.100$, suggesting that boys were more likely than girls to be cyberbullies and girls were more likely than boys to be cybervictims. Significant sex differences were also found for combined bullying roles, χ^2 (3, 1604) = 18.0, $p < 0.0001$, Cramer's $V = 0.106$, suggesting that boys were more likely than girls to be combined bullies and girls were more likely to be combined victims.

4.2. Associations between Bullying and Risky Online and Offline Activities

To investigate our second research question, whether risky online activities (CIU, online grooming victimization and sexting) and risky offline activities (problems with teachers, truancy and alcohol drinking) are associated with involvement in traditional, cyber and combined bullying roles, multinomial logistic regressions were performed for each of the three bullying typologies: traditional (Table 5), cyber (Table 6), and combined bullying (Table 7). In each of the three multinomial logistic regressions, the bullying typology was the outcome variable, with the non-involved as the reference category, and with risky online and risky offline activities as independent variables and age, sex and country as control variables.

Table 4. Frequency rates of bullies, victims, bully-victims, and non-involved in each typology by country and sex.

Category	Total		German		Dutch		Thai		Male		Female	
	N	%	N	%	N	%	N	%	N	%	N	%
Traditional Typology												
Bully	97	5.1	56	6.7 ***	15	4.1	26	3.7	66	7.8 ***	31	1.6
Victim	184	9.7	55	6.6	22	6.0	107	15.4 ***	62	7.3	122	11.6 ***
Bully-Victim	63	3.3	14	1.7	14	1.7	39	5.6 ***	31	3.7	32	3.0
Non-involved	1556	81.9	711	85.0	320	88.2	525	75.3 ***	689	81.2	867	83.8
Cyber Typology												
Cyberbully	63	3.3	37	4.4	10	2.6	16	2.3	39	4.5 ***	24	2.3
Cybervictim	146	7.6	29	3.4	12	3.2	105	15.1 ***	47	5.4	99	9.3 ***
Cyber bully-victim	60	2.4	9	1.1	4	1.1	47	6.7	33	3.8	27	2.5
Non-involved	1656	86.7	774	91.1	353	93.1	529	75.9 ***	745	86.3	911	85.9
Combined Typology												
Combined bully	38	2.4	20	2.1	7	1.9	11	2.0	28	3.9 ***	10	1.1
Combined victim	91	5.7	17	1.8	6	1.6	68	12.2 ***	30	4.2	61	6.9 ***
Combined Bully-Victim	29	1.8	4	1.5	5	1.1	20	3.6 ***	15	2.1	14	1.6
Non-involved	1446	90.1	678	94.5	329	96.2	556	82.4 ***	642	89.8	804	90.4

Note: Roles were classified by cut-off value from at least "twice or thrice a month". *** $p < 0.001$.

Table 5. Multinomial logistic regression analysis for variables predicting involvement in traditional bullying.

	B	O.R.	C.I. $_{95\%}$
Pure Bully			
CIU INTRA	0.149	1.1	0.779–1.7
CIU INTER	0.684 **	1.9	1.3–2.9
Online Grooming	0.137	1.1	1.0–1.4
Receiving of Sexts	0.212 **	1.3	1.0–1.4
Sending of Sexts	−0.310	0.733	0.397–1.3
Risky offline activities	1.0 **	2.9	2.0–3.9
Age [a]	−0.208 **	0.813	0.695–0.950
Sex (male) [a,b]	0.925 **	2.5	1.5–4.0
Dutch Adolescents [a,c]	−0.148	0.717	0.387–1.9
German Adolescents [a,c]	0.454	1.5	0.848–2.9
Pure Victim			
CIU INTRA	0.312 **	1.3	1.1–1.7
CIU INTER	0.269	1.1	1.2–2.4
Online Grooming	0.200	1.2	0.958–1.5
Receiving of Sexts	−0.090	0.914	0.773–1.0
Sending of Sexts	−0.127	0.881	0.474–1.6
Risky offline activities	0.483 **	1.6	1.2–2.1
Age [a]	−0.265 **	0.767	0.694–0.848
Sex (male) [a,b]	−0.885 **	0.413	0.215–0.791
Dutch Adolescents [a,c]	−0.919 **	0.399	0.232–0.687
German Adolescents [a,c]	−0.929 **	0.395	0.263–0.593
Pure Bully-Victim			
CIU INTRA	0.510 **	1.6	1.0–2.7
CIU INTER	0.577 **	1.7	1.1–2.8
Online Grooming	0.184	1.2	0.828–1.7
Receiving of Sexts	0.072	1.0	0.856–1.3
Sending of Sexts	0.357	1.4	0.623–3.2
Risky offline activities	0.997 ***	2.7	1.8–4.0
Age [a]	−0.353 **	0.703	0.593–0.833
Sex (male) [a,b]	0.230	1.2	0.100–0.459
Dutch Adolescents [a,c]	−1.4 **	0.225	0.105–0.482
German Adolescents [a,c]	−0.844 *	0.430	0.183–1.0

* $p < 0.05$, ** $p < 0.01$, *** $p < 0.001$; [a] control variable; [b] reference category: female sex; [c] reference category: Thai adolescents.

Table 6. Multinomial logistic regression analysis for variables predicting involvement in cyberbullying.

	B	O.R.	C.I. $_{95\%}$
Pure Cyberbully			
CIU INTRA	0.059	1.0	0.649–1.7
CIU INTER	0.821 ***	2.2	1.4–3.6
Online grooming	−0.050	0.951	0.598–1.5
Receiving of Sexts	0.317 **	1.3	1.1–1.6
Sending of Sexts	0.867 **	2.3	1.1–4.7
Risky offline activities	0.794 **	2.2	1.4–3.2
Age [a]	0.020	0.980	0.810–1.1
Sex (male) [a,b]	0.634 *	1.8	1.0–3.3
Dutch Adolescents [a,c]	0.395	1.4	0.690–3.1
German Adolescents [a,c]	−0.176	0.839	0.309–2.2
Pure Cybervictim			
CIU INTRA	0.455 **	1.5	1.1–2.2
CIU INTER	0.333 **	1.3	1.0–1.8
Online grooming	0.264 **	1.3	1.0–1.6
Receiving of Sexts	0.036	1.0	0.872–1.3
Sending of Sexts	0.691 *	1.9	1.0–3.7
Risky offline activities	0.620 **	1.8	1.3–2.5
Age [a]	−0.312 ***	0.732	0.656–0.817
Sex (male) [a,b]	−0.303	0.738	0.497–1.0
Dutch Adolescents [a,c]	−1.7 ***	0.173	0.105–0.284
German Adolescents [a,c]	−1.6 ***	0.188	0.094–0.374
Pure Cyber bully-victim			
CIU INTRA	0.645 **	1.9	1.1–3.3
CIU INTER	1.2 ***	3.3	2.0–5.6
Online grooming	0.649 ***	1.9	1.3–2.7
Receiving of Sexts	0.077	1.0	0.850–1.3
Sending of Sexts	0.698	2.0	0.862–4.6
Risky offline activities	1.1 ***	2.7	1.7–4.2
Age [a]	−0.257 **	0.773	0.648–0.922
Sex (male) [a,b]	0.662 **	1.9	1.0–3.5
Dutch Adolescents [a,c]	−1.7 ***	0.176	0.073–0.425
German Adolescents [a,c]	−1.9 **	0.148	0.039–0.565

* $p < 0.05$, ** $p < 0.01$, *** $p < 0.001$; [a] control variable; [b] reference category: female sex; [c] reference category: Thai adolescents.

Table 7. Multinomial logistic regression analysis for variables predicting involvement in combined bullying.

	B	O.R.	C.I. $_{95\%}$
Pure Combined Bully			
CIU INTRA	0.182	1.1	0.634–2.2
CIU INTER	1.4 ***	4.1	2.1–7.9
Online grooming	0.370	1.4	0.834–2.5
Receiving of Sexts	0.833 **	2.2	0.930–5.6
Sending of Sexts	0.330	1.6	1.0–1.8
Risky offline activities	1.1 ***	3.5	1.8–5.3
Age [a]	−0.269 **	0.764	0.594–7.8
Sex (male) [a,b]	1.2 **	3.4	1.5–6.3
Dutch Adolescents [a,c]	0.418	1.5	0.551–4.1
German Adolescents [a,c]	0.275	1.3	0.350–4.9
Pure Combined Victim			
CIU INTRA	0.449 **	1.5	1.0– 2.3
CIU INTER	0.510 **	1.6	1.1–2.4
Online grooming	0.309 *	1.3	0.996–1.8
Receiving of Sexts	0.077	1.0	0.874–1.3
Sending of Sexts	0.587	1.7	0.776–4.1
Risky offline activities	1.1 ***	2.7	1.8–4.0
Age [a]	−0.427 **	0.652	0.564–0.755
Sex (male) [a,b]	−0.300	0.741	0.449–1.2
Dutch Adolescents [a,c]	−1.8 ***	0.154	0.081–0.292
German Adolescents [a,c]	−1.9 ***	0.143	0.055–0.371
Pure Combined bully-victim			
CIU INTRA	0.966 **	2.6	1.1–6.1
CIU INTER	1.5 ***	4.8	2.0–11.1
Online grooming	0.206	1.2	0.686–2.2
Receiving of Sexts	−0.094	0.910	0.610–1.3
Sending of Sexts	1.4 **	4.2	1.1–15.9
Risky offline activities	1.4 ***	4.2	1.1–8.6
Age [a]	−0.429 **	0.651	0.487–0.870
Sex (male) [a,b]	0.099	1.1	0.422–2.8
Dutch Adolescents [a,c]	−2.2 **	0.102	0.024–0.438
German Adolescents [a,c]	−1.2	0.286	0.048–0.438

$* p < 0.05, ** p < 0.01, *** p < 0.001;$ [a] control variable; [b] reference category: female sex; [c] reference category: Thai adolescents.

Model 1 (traditional typology) was significant, Log likelihood (null) = 2139.319; LR (full) = 1824.38; LR χ^2 = 314.80, df = 30, $p < 0.001$, Nagelkerke's R^2 = 0.210. Table 5 shows that adolescents who scored high on the intrapersonal factor of CIU had an increased risk of being a victim or bully-victim and that adolescents who reported higher scores on the interpersonal factor of CIU showed a higher likelihood of being a bully or bully-victim. Further, adolescents who reported receiving sexts were more likely to be bullies. Risky offline activities were associated with being a bully, victim and bully-victim. With increasing age, the occurrence of being a bully, victim and bully-victim seems to decrease. Boys demonstrated a higher likelihood to be a bully and girls displayed an increased risk to be a victim. Dutch and German adolescents compared with Thai adolescents showed lower odds ratios to be a traditional victim or bully-victim.

Model 2 (cyber typology) was significant, Log likelihood (null) = 1844.16; LR (full) = 1422.36; LR χ^2 = 421.80, df = 30, $p < 0.001$, and Nagelkerke's R^2 = 0.301. As Table 6 illustrates, adolescents who reported higher scores on the intrapersonal factor of CIU showed an increased likelihood to be a cybervictim and cyber bully-victim. Additionally, adolescents who reported higher scores on the interpersonal factor of CIU were more likely to be a cyberbully and cybervictim. Adolescents who reported receiving sexts displayed a higher risk to be a cyberbully. Adolescents who reported sending sexts demonstrated an increased likelihood to be a cyberbully and cybervictim. Adolescents who reported of victimization through online grooming showed higher odds ratios of being a cybervictim and cyber bully-victim. Risky offline activities were associated with playing all three cyber roles. With increasing age, the occurrence of cybervictims and cyber bully-victims seems to decrease. Boys were more likely to be a cyberbully or cyber bully-victim. German and Dutch adolescents showed a lower risk to be a cybervictim and cyber bully-victim compared with Thai adolescents.

Model 3 (combined typology) was significant, Log likelihood (null) = 1180.06; LR (full) = 854.72; LR χ^2 = 325.34, df = 30, $p < 0.000$, and Nagelkerke's R^2 = 0.336. Table 7 shows that adolescents who reported higher scores on the intrapersonal factor of CIU showed higher odds ratios to be a combined bully-victim. Adolescents who reported higher scores on the interpersonal factor of CIU were more likely to be a combined bully and combined bully-victim. Adolescents who reported receiving sexts demonstrated an increased risk of being a combined bully and adolescents who reported sending sexts showed an increased likelihood to be a combined bully-victim. Online grooming victimization was associated with combined victimization only. Risky offline activities were related significantly to engagement as combined bully, victim and bully-victim. With increasing age the risk for being a combined bully, victim or bully-victim decreased. Boys were more likely to be a combined bully. Dutch and German adolescents showed a lower risk to be combined victims compared with Thai adolescents. Dutch adolescents showed lower odds ratios to be combined bully-victims compared with Thai adolescents.

5. Discussion

The purpose of this study was to report the occurrence of bullying roles in the present sample and to provide evidence on the associations between traditional, cyber and combined bullying and risky online activities (CIU, online grooming victimization, sexting), risky offline activities (problems with teachers, truancy, drinking alcohol). We used logistic multinomial regression analysis as a categorical approach for multivariate statistical analyses with bullying roles as outcome variables and risky online and offline activities as independent variables taking into account age, sex and country as control variables.

Concerning our first aim, to report the occurrence of traditional, cyber and combined bullying, we found 18.1% of adolescents were involved in traditional bullying, 13.3% of adolescents were involved in cyberbullying and 9.9% were involved in combined bullying. Comparing the results with Beckmann and colleagues [7], who used also global items for the assessment of bullying and cyber-bullying, we found clearly lower frequency rates in our study. One possible explanation for this might be that in the present study, a more strict lower-bound cutoff point for the categorization as in bullying involved was used ("Twice or thrice a month" *vs.* "Once or twice"). In line with Beckmann and colleagues [7], we found the group of victims in cyber and combined bullying to be the largest group, followed by bullies and bully-victims. While we found the same composition in traditional bullying, Beckmann and colleagues [7] found more traditional bullies than victims. In contrast to previous research, we obtained clearly lower rates of combined bully-victims in the present study [7,11].

The present study supports the idea that traditional bullying still occurs more frequently than cyberbullying [6–8,11,13]. However, the difference between traditional and cyber bullying found in the present study was smaller than as described by Smith [67]—A ratio of 4:1 or 3:1. One possible explanation for this might be that those statements are more applicable for Western than for Asian countries, probably because the vast majority of previous research on bullying has been carried out within Western populations [56]. Indeed, we found Thai adolescents were nearly as much involved in traditional bullying (24.7%) as in cyberbullying (24.1%). After controlling for age and sex, German and Dutch adolescents showed, in comparison with Thai adolescents, a lower risk being cybervictims, cyber bully-victims, combined victims and combined bully-victims. This is somewhat surprising, because Thai adolescents seem to have less access to ICT and use ICT less intensively compared with German and Dutch adolescents [68].

Besides country differences, the current study revealed differences by age and sex in the frequency rates of bullying. In accordance with previous studies (*i.e.*, [6]), we found bullying to decrease with increasing age. The only exceptions were cyberbullies: for this role no significant age differences were found. Also, in line with several authors, we observed associations between bullying and sex: In accordance with Gradinger *et al.* [8], we identified male sex—after controlling for age and country—as an important risk factor for involvement as bully, cyberbully and combined bully. Further, we found boys more likely to be cyber bully-victims and less likely to be traditional victims, which is also in line with some other research [16,44,53,54]. Although the present sample could not be considered as representative, this study constitutes in the literature one of the first comparative data sets about traditional, cyber and combined bullying among German, Dutch and Thai adolescents.

The second aim of the current study was to analyze whether risky online activities and risky offline activities were associated with involvement in traditional, cyber and combined bullying roles. We hypothesized those adolescents who report higher scores in risky online and offline activities display an increased likelihood to be involved in bullying. A comparison of the three regression models (traditional, cyber and combined bullying roles) revealed that the amount of variance explained by logistic regression models were acceptable for all three models (from 21% to 33%) [63]. However, the explained variance was slightly better for the cyber and combined typology. This means that the investigated variables are somewhat more useful in predicting involvement in cyber or combined bullying than traditional bullying.

Concerning risky online activities, the present study demonstrated that CIU was associated with all bullying roles. However, the association differed between either psychological (intrapersonal) or social conflicts (interpersonal) due to CIU or even both. Adolescents who were only facing psychological conflicts caused by CIU were more likely to be traditional victims. Adolescents who reported only of social conflicts due to CIU were more likely to be traditional, cyber or combined bullies. This suggests that it might be worth investigating common underlying risk factors (*i.e.*, high impulsivity, low self-control or greater irritability; elevated scores of aggressions), which might be an explanation for the co-occurrence of social conflicts caused by CIU and bullying perpetration. Adolescents who were facing both psychological and social conflicts caused by CIU were more likely to be traditional, cyber and combined bully-victims. This supports the statement from Olweus [1] that bully-victims unite social and psychological problem profiles. However, adolescents who were facing both were also more likely to be cyber and combined victims.

Casas and colleagues [31], who used the same instrument to measure CIU, also observed associations between CIU and cyberbullying. However, in contrast to Casas and colleagues [31] and in line with Gámez-Guadix *et al.* [30], this study revealed significant association between CIU and cybervictimization. Further, we observed associations between CIU and cyber bully-victims to be stronger compared with cybervictims, which is also consistent with previous research [30]. We add to the literature associations between CIU and combined bullying roles and found that combined bully-victims displayed, compared with all other roles, the strongest associations with both psychological and social conflicts caused by CIU, suggesting that combined bully-victims might be a special risk group.

Another risky online activity we investigated was online grooming victimization. The current study suggests no associations between online grooming victimization and traditional bullying. However, consistent with previous research, we found associations with cybervictimization [36,37] and add to the literature associations with combined victimization. Interestingly, victims of online grooming did not appear to be at higher risk of being traditional victims but showed a higher risk to be cybervictims and combined victims. This difference might be caused by common underlying ICT-related risk factors that might explain multiple online victimization. These might be a specific online behavior, *i.e.*, disclosing of private information on social networking sites, or disclosing of contact details like phone number, instant messenger id, or the willingness to flirt online and get in contact online with strangers. In line with previous research [2] that found bully-victims as a particular risk group for sexual harassment offline and physical dating violence victimization, we add to the literature that cyber bully-victims displayed higher risk of falling victim to online grooming. The finding that some adolescents experiencing victimization in both peer and sexual violence raises important questions, as well as concerns. Future studies should focus on these poly-victimized adolescents, how to make them more resilient, what harm is caused by the multiple exposures and which individual pathways of victimization could be identified.

A further risky online activity we addressed was sexting. With it, we found the receiving of sexts to be associated with being a traditional, cyber and combined bully only. Two possible explanations are offered. Firstly, it is hypothesized that bullies try to receive sexts from others to embarrass and humiliate the sender, *i.e.*, by forwarding the sexts to others who are not supposed to see the pictures. Secondly, bullies might use sexts more frequently for establishing relationships, to show off, to flirt and to become sexually aroused [41]. In support of the second explanation, previous research showed that, bullies often start dating earlier and being highly relationship oriented [34]. However, the associations between sending of sexts and bullying roles differed; adolescents who reported more often sending of sexts were more likely to be a cyberbully, cybervictim and combined bully-victim. The sending of sexts was most strongly related to combined bully-victims and the receiving of sexts with combined bullies. The results support previous research that adolescents who were engaged in sexting were more likely to be involved in bullying [40] and extent the literature on associations between sexting and combined bullying. The findings point out the need to address sexting in anti-bullying prevention measurements as a tool of aggression and a risk for victimization.

Finally, we examined facets of risky offline activities (problems with teachers, truancy and alcohol drinking). The study demonstrates that risky offline activities have clear relevance to all kinds of bullying roles. There is a large literature that supports the thesis that various forms of risky and problem behaviors are interrelated [17,20,30,45,46]. More specific, we found risky offline activities were more strongly associated with combined bullying roles than with cyber or traditional roles. This result might indicate that the simultaneous involvement in both traditional and cyber bullying might have a bigger impact on engagement in risky offline activities than only the involvement in either cyber or traditional bullying which also has been reported by some earlier research [8,15].

5.1. Practical Implications

The finding that various risky online and offline activities appeared to be inter-correlated with traditional, cyber and combined bullying roles has some relevance for further prevention work. This result supports the need for more holistic prevention programs that aim to promote a positive youth development and contradict engagement in risky activities in a broader view. An example of a broad approach is "Life skills". Life skills might play an important role here and help mitigate risks by focusing on resiliency against a wide variety of risky online and offline activities. The World Health Organization defines life-skills as "abilities for adaptive and positive behavior that enable individuals to deal effectively with the demands and challenges of everyday life" [69] (p. 1). Life-skills are loosely classified into three broad categories of skills: cognitive skills for analyzing and using information, personal skills for developing personal agency and managing oneself, and inter-personal skills for communicating and interacting effectively with others [70]. Thus, Life-Skills-Programs (LSPs) promote core life-skills (*i.e.*, participation, democracy beliefs, responsibility, self-esteem, empathy, coping strategies) instead of focusing only on reducing specific risks [71]. Consequently, LSP go beyond a harm-avoidance approach and strive to generate positive youth development.

Schools might possess the right learning environment to implement LSPs due to the variety of social interactions, the possibility to learn peer-to-peer, the crucial role of teachers as socialization agents for children and adolescents, and the compulsory school attendance that facilitates reaching most children and adolescents. These programs based on interactive processes (role play, theatre play, group work, relaxing and physical exercises) in the context of a resource-orientated curriculum [72]. Some of already implied and evaluated LSPs are Lions Quest [73] and Information + Psychosocial Competence = Protection (IPSY) [74]. Compared with prevention programs that only aim to reduce risk, LSPs have been found to be the most effective programs to reduce problem behaviors among adolescents [70,72].

5.2. Limitations and Strengths

There were several limitations to this study. The cross-sectional nature of the survey limits the ability to make causal conclusions, so it is not possible to understand whether the correlates were antecedents or consequences. Longitudinal studies are needed to confirm the predictive effects of risky online and offline activities on involvement in traditional and cyber bullying, or *vice versa*. Further, all data relied exclusively on self-reports. Therefore, the correlates might be inflated through shared method variance. A multi-informant approach is recommended for future studies in order to overcome mono-method problems. In addition, we relied on single item measurement for the assessment of traditional and cyber bullying. Although there is some evidence for validity of the items for measuring bullying [13,65], future studies should try to include validated scales for both traditional and cyber bullying to overcome problems with single-items measurements (*i.e.*, degree of validity, accuracy, and reliability).

There is still controversy among researchers on whether bullying is best considered as categorical variable or continuous dimension. While some researchers apply the categorical approach by using specific cut-off points to classify between involved in bullying and not involved, others researchers are using continuous dimensions allowing several degrees of involvement [75]. Reasons for using the categorical approach are that bullying variables mostly do not meet assumptions of normality and are positively skewed [75,76]. In addition, cyberbullying does not occur very frequently in many studies, which makes dimensional approaches more problematic [75]. Due to various reasons (continuing former research, conceptual argument, skewed distributions of the outcomes, comparison of distinct risk factors) we treated the bullying variables as categorical in a multinomial regression analysis. However, more research is needed to find the most appropriate way to examine bullying [75,76]. Future research should replicate the results found in the current study by using a continuous approach and alternative units of analysis (latent-class analyses, mixed Rasch modeling or structural equation modeling) to come up to the multivariate association of bullying and risky online and offline activities.

Nevertheless, this study also has strength and extends the body of research in several ways. Firstly, we put forward conceptual and traditional arguments as to why adolescents become involved in bullying and gave an accurate definition of bullying participants. In addition, we used mutually exclusive roles of bullying that enabled establishing clear patterns of involvement and assessing the real correlates for involvement in various bullying roles, and, thus, this may enhance our knowledge in the planning of preventative work for specific target groups. Secondly, in contrast to this study, many studies on the correlates of cyberbullying have failed to account for groups like combined bullying roles. Finally, most of the research on bullying has been confined to Western populations. A major future issue might be to extend research to more non-Western populations and to undertake systematic, cross-national comparisons in order to capture what is general as well as what is cultural and idiosyncratic in adolescents' behavior and development and in their determinants. This aspect might be especially important in regard to development of prevention and intervention programs and the inter-cultural validity of such programs.

6. Conclusions

In summary, this study is one of the first comparing traditional, cyber and combined bullying in Western and South-East Asian countries. With it, we found Thai adolescents to be more frequently cybervictims, cyber bully-victims, combined victims and combined bully-victims and Thai adolescents nearly just as much involved in traditional bullying as in cyberbullying. We found also some sex differences; male adolescents tended to be more often traditional, cyber and combined bullies. This warrants that attention be paid to sex specific risk factors in bullying perpetration. We found also support for our hypothesis that risky online and offline activities are associated with involvement in traditional, cyber and combined bullying. CIU, sending of sexts and risky offline activities were most strongly associated with combined bully-victims. The receiving of sexts was most strongly associated with combined bullies and online grooming victimization was most strongly associated with cyber bully-victims. In addition, we found risky offline activities to be more strongly associated with combined bullying roles compared with traditional and cyber bullying roles. This result indicates how important it is to consider both traditional and cyber bullying roles simultaneously to identify special risk groups. Overall, the findings stress the need to move away from prevention programs that are designed to reduce specific risk behaviors and develop more integrated approaches that might help to develop life-skills in adolescents in order to be able to cope with a wide variety of risky online and offline activities.

Acknowledgments: The work of the first author and the data collection in Thailand was partly funded by a research grant from the University of Bremen.

Author Contributions: Sebastian Wachs and Marianne Junger designed the study. Marianne Junger, Ruthaychonee Sittichai and Sebastian Wachs recruited participants and collected data. Sebastian Wachs performed the statistical analyses and drafted the manuscript. Marianne Junger and Ruthaychonee Sittichai provided constructive feedback on drafts of the manuscript. Sebastian Wachs processed all feedback from the other authors and reviewers. All authors read and approved of the final manuscript.

Conflicts of Interest: The authors declare no conflict of interest.

References

1. Olweus, D. Bullying at school: Basic facts and effects of a school based intervention program. *J. Child Psychol. Psychiatry* **1994**, *35*, 1171–1190.

2. Espelage, D.L.; Holt, M.K. Dating violence & sexual harassment across the bully-victim continuum among middle and high school students. *J. Youth Adolesc.* **2007**, *36*, 799–811.

3. Lester, L.; Cross, D.; Shaw, T.; Dooley, J. Adolescent bully-victims: Social health and the transition to secondary school. *Camb. J. Educ.* **2012**, *42*, 213–233.

4. Espelage, D.L.; Holt, M.K. Suicidal ideation and school bullying experiences after controlling for depression and delinquency. *J. Adolesc. Health* **2013**, *53*, S27–S31.

5. Yang, A.; Salmivalli, C. Different forms of bullying and victimization: Bully-victims *versus* bullies and victims. *Eur. J. Dev. Psychol.* **2013**, *10*, 1–16.

6. Tokunaga, R.S. Following you home from school: A critical review and synthesis of research on cyberbullying victimization. *Comput. Hum. Behav.* **2010**, *26*, 277–287.

7. Beckman, L.; Hagquist, C.; Hellström, L. Discrepant gender patterns for cyberbullying and traditional bullying—An analysis of Swedish adolescent data. *Comput. Hum. Behav.* **2013**, *29*, 1896–1903.

8. Gradinger, P.; Strohmeier, D.; Spiel, C. Traditional bullying and cyberbullying: Identification of risk groups for adjustment problems. *J. Psychol.* **2009**, *217*, 205–213.

9. Wachs, S.; Brosowski, T. Gemeinsames Auftreten von Bullying und Cyberbullying im Merkmalsraum: Eine multivariate Typologie. *Schulpädagogik Heute.* 2013, 7, pp. 1–17. Available online: http://www.schulpaedagogik-heute.de/index.php/archiv (accessed on 29 October 2014).

10. Sticca, F.; Perren, S. Is cyberbullying worse than traditional bullying? Examining the differential roles of medium, publicity, and anonymity for the perceived severity of bullying. *J. Youth Adolesc.* **2013**, *42*, 739–750.

11. Beckman, L.; Hagquist, C.; Hellström, L. Does the association with psychosomatic health problems differ between cyberbullying and traditional bullying? *Emot. Behav. Diffic.* **2012**, *17*, 421–434.

12. Corcoran, L.; Connolly, I.; O'Moore, M. Cyberbullying in Irish schools: An investigation of personality and self-concept. *Irish J. Psychol.* **2012**, *33*, 153–165.

13. Olweus, D. Cyberbullying. An overrated phenomenon? *Eur. J. Dev. Psychol.* **2012**, *9*, 520–538.

14. Wachs, S. Moral disengagement and emotional and social difficulties in bullying and cyberbullying: Differences by participant role. *Emot. Behav. Diffic.* **2012**, *17*, 347–360.

15. Perren, S.; Dooley, J.; Shaw, T.; Cross, D. Bullying in school and cyberspace: Associations with depressive symptoms in Swiss and Australian adolescents. *Child Adolesc. Psychiatry Ment. Health* **2010**, *4*, 1–10.

16. Campbell, M.; Spears, B.; Slee, P.; Butler, D.; Kift, S. Victims' perceptions of traditional and cyberbullying, and the psychosocial correlates of their victimisation. *Emot. Behav. Diffic.* **2012**, *17*, 389–401.

17. Jessor, R.; Jessor, S.L. *Problem Behavior and Psychosocial Development: A Longitudinal Study of Youth*; Academic Press: New York, NY, USA, 1977.

18. Raithel, J. *Jugendliches Risikoverhalten: Eine Einführung*, 2nd ed.; Springer: Wiesbaden, Germany, 2011.

19. Junger, M.; Dekovic, M. Crime as a risk-taking: Co-occurrence of delinquent behavior, health endangering behaviors. In *Advances in Criminological Theory*; Gottfredson, M., Britt, C., Eds.; Transaction Publishers: New Brunswick, NJ, USA, 2003; pp. 213–248.

20. Jessor, R. Problem-behavior theory, psychosocial development, and adolescent problem drinking. *Br. J. Addict.* **1987**, *82*, 331–342.

21. Armitage, C.J.; Conner, M. Efficacy of the theory of planned behaviour: A meta-analytic review. *Br. J. Soc. Psychol.* **2001**, *40*, 471–499.

22. Vazsonyi, A.T.; Chen, P.; Jenkins, D.D.; Burcu, E.; Torrente, G.; Sheu, C.J. Jessor's problem behavior theory: Cross-national evidence from Hungary, the Netherlands, Slovenia, Spain, Switzerland, Taiwan, Turkey, and the United States. *Dev. Psychol.* **2010**, *46*, 1779.

23. Donovan, J.E.; Jessor, R. Structure of problem behavior in adolescence and young adulthood. *J. Consult. Clin. Psychol.* **1985**, *53*, 890.

24. Block, J. Issues for DSM-V: Internet addiction. *Am. J. Psychiatry* **2008**, *165*, 306–307.

25. Hahn, A.; Jerusalem, M. Internetsucht: Jugendliche gefangen im Netz. In *Risikoverhaltensweisen Jugendlicher*; Raithel, J., Ed.; VS Verlag für Sozialwissenschaften: Wiesbaden, Germany, 2001; pp. 279–293.

26. Renati, R.; Berrone, C.; Zanetti, M.A. Morally disengaged and unempathic: Do cyberbullies fit these definitions? An exploratory study. *Cyberpsychol. Behav. Soc. Netw.* **2012**, *15*, 391–398.

27. Çankaya, İ.H.; Tan, Ç. Effect of cyber bullying on the distrust levels of preservice teachers: Considering internet addiction as a mediating Variable. *Procedia Comput. Sci.* **2011**, *3*, 1353–1360.

28. Meixner, S. Exzessive Internetnutzung im Jugendalter. *Kinder und Jugendschutz in Wissenschaft und Praxis* **2010**, *55*, 3–7.

29. Kammerl, R.; Hirschhäuser, L.; Rosenkranz, M.; Schwinge, C.; Hein, S.; Wartberg, L.; Petersen, K.U. EXIF–Exzessive Internetnutzung in Familien. In *Zusammenhänge Zwischen der Exzessiven Computer-und Internetnutzung und dem (Medien-) Erzieherischen Handeln in den Familien*; Pabst Science Publishers: Lengerich, Germany, 2012.

30. Gámez-Guadix, M.; Orue, I.; Smith, P.K.; Calvete, E. Longitudinal and Reciprocal Relations of Cyberbullying with Depression, Substance Use, and Problematic Internet Use among Adolescents. *J. Adoles. Health* **2013**, *53*, 446–452.

31. Casas, J.A.; del Rey, R.; Ortega-Ruiz, R. Bullying and cyberbullying: Convergent and divergent predictor variables. *Comput. Hum. Behav.* **2013**, *29*, 580–587.

32. Wachs, S. Cybergrooming–Erste Bestandsaufnahme einer neuen Form sexueller Onlineviktimisierung. In *Enzyklopädie Erziehungswissenschaft Online*; Fachgebiet/ Unterüberschrift: Medienpädagogik, Aktuelle Diskurse; Meister, D., von Gross, F., Sander, U., Eds.; BELTZ Juventa: Weinheim, Germany; Basel, Switzerland, 2014; doi:10.3262/EEO18140331.

33. Whittle, H.; Hamilton-Giachritsis, C.; Beech, A.; Collings, G. A review of online grooming: Characteristics and concerns. *Aggress. Violent Behav.* **2013**, *18*, 62–70.

34. Connolly, J.; Pepler, D.; Craig, W.; Taradash, A. Dating experiences of bullies in early adolescence. *Child Maltreatment* **2000**, *5*, 299–310.

35. Mörchen, V. "Ich war doch schon immer der Fußabtreter für alle ... "—Mehrfachbetroffenheit männlicher Opfer sexualisierter Gewalt. In *Sexualisierte Gewalt Gegen Jungen: Prävention und Intervention*; Mosser, P., Hans-Joachim, L., Eds.; Springer Fachmedien: Wiesbaden, Germany, 2014; pp. 183–209.

36. Wachs, S.; Wolf, K.D.; Pan, C.C. Cybergrooming: Risk factors, coping strategies and associations with cyberbullying. *Psicothema* **2012**, *24*, 628–633.

37. Brottsförebyggande rådet (Brå). *The Online Sexual Solicitation of Children by Adults in Sweden*; English Summary of Brå-report 2007. Swedish National Council for Crime Prevention: Stockholm, Sweden. Available online: http://www.bra.se/bra/bra-in-english/home/publications/archive/publications/2007-07-25-the-online-sexual-solicitation-of-children-by-adults-in-sweden.html (accessed on 28 October 2014).

38. Wolke, D.; Copeland, W.E.; Angold, A.; Costello, E.J. Impact of bullying in childhood on adult health, wealth, crime, and social outcomes. *Psychol. Sci.* **2013**, *24*, 1958–1970.

39. Sengupta, A.; Chaudhuri, A. Are social networking sites a source of online harassment for teens? Evidence from survey data. *Child. Youth Serv. Rev.* **2011**, *33*, 284–290.

40. Dake, J.A.; Price, J.H.; Maziarz, L.; Ward, B. Prevalence and correlates of sexting behavior in adolescents. *Am. J. Sex. Educ.* **2012**, *7*, 1–15.

41. Döring, N. Erotischer Fotoaustausch unter Jugendlichen: Verbreitung, Funktionen und Folgen des Sexting. *Z. Sex.* **2012**, *25*, 4–25.

42. Forero, R.; McLellan, L.; Rissel, C.; Bauman, A. Bullying behaviour and psychosocial health among school students in New South Wales, Australia: Cross sectional survey. *BMJ* **1999**, *319*, 344–348.

43. Ponzo, M. Does bullying reduce educational achievement? An evaluation using matching estimators. *J. Policy Model.* **2013**, *35*, 1057–1078.

44. Sourander, A.; Brunstein Klomek, A.; Ikonen, M.; Lindroos, J.; Luntamo, T.; Koskelainen, M.; Helenius, H. Psychosocial risk factors associated with cyberbullying among adolescents: A population-based study. *Arch. Gen. Psychiatry* **2010**, *67*, 720–728.

45. Tharp-Taylor, S.; Haviland, A.; D'Amico, E.J. Victimization from mental and physical bullying and substance use in early adolescence. *Addict. Behav.* **2009**, *34*, 561–567.

46. Ybarra, M.; Mitchell, K. Youth engaging in online harassment: Associations with caregiver-child relationships, Internet use, and personal characteristics. *J. Adolesc.* **2004**, *27*, 319–336.

47. Hinduja, S.; Patchin, J.W. Cyberbullying: An exploratory analysis of factors related to offending and victimization. *Deviant Behav.* **2008**, *29*, 129–156.

48. Patchin, J.; Hinduja, S. Bullies move beyond the schoolyard: A preliminary look at cyberbullying. *Youth Violence Juv. Justice* **2006**, *4*, 148–169.

49. Wachs, S.; Wolf, K.D. Über den Zusammenhang von Bullying und Cyberbullying, Erste Ergebnisse einer Selbstberichtsstudie. *Praxis der Kinderpsychologie und Kinderpsychiatrie* **2011**, *60*, 735–744.

50. Khoury-Kassabri, M. The relationship between staff maltreatment of students and students' violent behavior. *Child Abuse Negl.* **2009**, *33*, 914–923.

51. Erdur-Baker, Ö. Cyberbullying and its correlation to traditional bullying, gender and frequent and risky usage of internet-mediated communication tools. *New Media Soc.* **2010**, *12*, 109–125.

52. Slonje, R.; Smith, P.K. Cyberbullying: Another main type of bullying? *Scand. J. Psychol.* **2008**, *49*, 147–154.

53. Wang, J.; Iannotti, R.J.; Nansel, T.R. School bullying among adolescents in the United States: Physical, verbal, relational, and cyber. *J. Adolesc. Health* **2009**, *45*, 368–375.

54. Aricak, T.; Siyahhan, S.; Uzunhasanoglu, A.; Saribeyoglu, S.; Ciplak, S.; Yilmaz, N.; Memmedov, C. Cyberbullying among Turkish adolescents. *CyberPsychol. Behav.* **2008**, *11*, 253–261.

55. Mishna, F.; Khoury-Kassabri, M.; Gadalla, T.; Daciuk, J. Risk factors for involvement in cyber bullying: Victims, bullies and bully-victims. *Child. Youth Serv. Rev.* **2012**, *34*, 63–70.

56. Sittichai, R.; Smith, P.K. Bullying and cyberbullying in Thailand: A review. *Int. J. Cyber Soc. Educ.* **2013**, *6*, 31–44.

57. Tabachnick, B.G.; Fidell, L.S. *Using Multivariate Statistics*, International Edition ed; Pearson: Boston, MA, USA, 2011.

58. Jäger, R.; Fischer, U.; Riebel, J. Mobbing bei Schülerinnen und Schülern in der Bundesrepublik Deutschland. In *Eine Empirische Untersuchung auf der Grundlage einer Online Befragung im Jahre 2007*; Zentrum für empirische pädagogische Forschung (zepf): Landau, Germany, 2007.

59. Beranuy, F.M.; Chamarro, L.A.; Graner, J.C.; Carbonell, S.X. Validation of two brief scales for Internet addiction and mobile phone problem use. *Psicothema* **2009**, *21*, 480–485.

60. Casas, J.A.; Olivares, R.R.; Ruiz, R.O. Validation of the Internet and Social Networking Experiences Questionnaire in Spanish Adolescents. *Int. J. Clin. Health Psychol.* **2013**, *13*, 40–48.

61. Hinduja, S.; Patchin, J.W. *School Climate 2.0: Preventing Cyberbullying and Sexting one Classroom at a Time*; Sage Publications: Thousand Oaks, CA, USA, 2012.

62. Currie, C.; Gabhainn, S.N.; Godeau, E.; Roberts, C.; Smith, R.; Currie, D.; Picket, W.; Richter, M.; Morgan, A.; Barnekow, V. (Eds.) *Inequalities in Young People's Health: Health Behaviour in School-Aged Children (HBSC) International Report from the 2005/2006 Survey*; WHO Regional Office for Europe: Copenhagen, Denmark, 2008. Available online: http://www.childhealthresearch.eu/riche/research/add-knowledge/HBSC%20international%20report%202005-06%20survey.pdf (accessed on 28 October 2014).

63. Backhaus, K.; Erichson, B.; Plinke, W.; Weiber, R. *Multivariate Analysemethoden: Eine Anwendungsorientierte Einführung*, 11th ed.; Springer: Berlin, Germany, 2006.

64. Sousa, V.D.; Rojjanasrirat, W. Translation, adaptation and validation of instruments or scales for use in cross-cultural health care research: A clear and user-friendly guideline. *J. Eval. Clin. Pract.* **2011**, *17*, 268–274.

65. Solberg, M.E.; Olweus, D. Prevalence estimation of school bullying with the Olweus Bully/Victim Questionnaire. *Aggress. Behav.* **2003**, *29*, 239–268.

66. Field, A. *Discovering Statistics Using IBM SPSS Statistics*, 4th ed.; Sage Publications: Thousand Oaks, CA, USA, 2013.

67. Smith, P.K. Cyberbullying and cyber aggression. In *Handbook of School Violence and School Safety: International Research and Practice*, 2nd ed.; Jimerson, S.R., Nickerson, A.B., Mayer, M.J., Furlong, M.J., Eds.; Routledge: New York, NY, USA, 2012; pp. 93–103.

68. International Telecommunication Union. Use of Information and Communication Technology by the World's Children and Youth a Statistical Compilation. Available online: http://www.itu.int/ITU-D/ict/material/Youth_2008.pdf (accessed on 16 December 2014).

69. World Health Organization (WHO). *Life Skills Education in Schools*; WHO: Geneva, Switzerland, 1997. Available online: http://whqlibdoc.who.int/hq/1994/who_mnh_psf_93.7a_rev.2.pdf (accessed on 28 October 2014).

70. Jerusalem, M.; Meixner, S. Lebenskompetenzen. In *Psychologische Förder- und Interventionsprogramme für das Kindes- und Jugendalter*; Lohaus, A., Domsch, H., Eds.; Springer: Heidelberg, Germany, 2009; pp. 141–157.

71. Lerner, R.M.; Brentano, C.; Dowling, E.M.; Anderson, P.M. Positive youth development: Thriving as the basis of personhood and civil society. *New Dir. Youth Dev.* **2002**, *95*, 11–33.

72. Weichold, K.; Silbereisen, R.K. Positive Jugendentwicklung und Prävention. In *Prävention und Gesundheitsförderung. Bd. III: Kinder und Jugendliche Tübingen*; Röhrle, B., Ed.; DGVT-Verlag: Tübingen, Germany, 2007; pp. 103–125.

73. 5Wilms, H.; Wilms, E. *Erwachsen Werden Life-Skills-Programm für Schülerinnen und Schüler der Sekundarstufe I. Handbuch für Lehrerinnen und Lehrer*; Lions Club International: Wiesbaden, Germany, 2004.

74. Weichold, K. Alkoholprävention durch Lebenskompetenzprogramme. In *Alkoholprävention in Erziehung und Unterricht*; Tossmann, P., Weber, N.H., Eds.; Centaurus-Verlag: Herbholzheim, Germany, 2008; pp. 102–114.

75. Underwood, M.K.; Card, N.A. Moving beyond tradition and convenience. In *Principles of Cyberbullying Research: Definitions, Measures, and Methodology*; Bauman, S., Cross, D., Walker, J., Eds.; Routledge: New York, NY, USA, 2013; pp. 125–140.

76. Kyriakides, L.; Kaloyirou, C.; Lindsay, G. An analysis of the Revised Olweus Bully/Victim Questionnaire using the Rasch measurement model. *Br. J. Educ. Psychol.* **2006**, *76*, 781–801.

Peer Attachment and Cyber Aggression Involvement among Chinese, Indian, and Japanese Adolescents

Michelle F. Wright, Ikuko Aoyama, Shanmukh V. Kamble, Zheng Li, Shruti Soudi, Li Lei and Chang Shu

Abstract: Significant advancements have been made in cyber aggression literature, with many studies revealing the consequences associated with adolescents' involvement in these behaviors. Few studies have focused on cyber aggression involvement in China, India, and Japan. The present study examined differences in cyber aggression perpetration and victimization among 1637 adolescents living in China, India, and Japan, while controlling for face-to-face bullying involvement, individualism, and collectivism. Another aim of the present study was to examine country of origin and cyber aggression involvement (*i.e.*, the uninvolved, cyberaggressor-cybervictims, cyberaggressors, and cybervictims) differences in peer attachment. Findings revealed that adolescents from India had the highest levels of cyber aggression involvement when compared to adolescents from China or Japan. Chinese adolescents engaged in more cyber aggression perpetration and were victimized more by cyber aggression when compared to Japanese adolescents. No country of origin differences were found for peer attachment. However, uninvolved adolescents reported higher levels of peer attachment when compared to the other groups. Cyberaggressor-cybervictims had the lowest levels of peer attachment, followed by cybervictims and cyberaggressors. These results suggest that there should be concern about cyber aggression involvement among adolescents in these countries, especially in India, where cyber aggression research has been slow to develop.

Reprinted from *Societies*. Cite as: Wright, M.F.; Aoyama, I.; Kamble, S.V.; Li, Z.; Soudi, S.; Lei, L.; Shu, C. Peer Attachment and Cyber Aggression Involvement among Chinese, Indian, and Japanese Adolescents. *Societies* **2015**, *5*, 339–353.

1. Introduction

Most adolescents have spent their lives completely enmeshed in a digital world, with various opportunities and information at their fingertips. Technology usage has many benefits for adolescents, allowing them to quickly communicate with friends and family and to access a wealth of information quickly. Despite such benefits, adolescents also experience risks associated with their technology usage. Cyber aggression is one risk, and it has received attention from researchers, educators, parents, and the general public. Research on cyber aggression is increasing, but research focused on these behaviors in other countries has been slower to develop, particularly in China, India, and Japan. Although the literature has been advancing on cyber aggression, moving from frequency rates to the behavioral characteristics and consequences, little attention has been given to the role of peer relationships in these behaviors. Of this literature, research indicates that perpetrators of cyber aggression are often peers at adolescents' schools and that peer rejection is related to cyber aggression, perpetration, and victimization [1,2]. Furthermore, poor peer attachment is related positively to cyber aggression involvement. However, little attention has been given to examining country of origin and cyber aggression involvement differences in peer attachment. To address this gap in the literature, the present study examined differences in cyber aggression perpetration and victimization among Chinese, Indian, and Japanese adolescents as well as the roles of country of origin and cyber aggression involvement in adolescents' perceptions of their peer attachment.

2. Cyber Aggression Involvement and Culture

This study utilizes the terminology of cyber aggression, which is a broader form of cyberbullying. Cyber aggression includes intentionally harmful behaviors, such as hacking someone's online accounts, sending degrading messages, spreading rumors, and calling others mean names [3]. These behaviors are directed toward others who find such behaviors offensive and unwanted, and such behaviors can occur through email, chat programs, text messages, gaming consoles, social networking sites, blogs, and discussion boards. Unlike cyberbullying, Grigg [3] argues that aggressive cyber behaviors do not always include repetition. This component is central to the traditional bullying and cyberbullying definitions. Therefore, measures of cyberbullying focus on repetition while cyber aggression measures do not include the repetition component. This literature review uses both terminologies in order to accurately describe the terminology and methodology of the studies. In addition, cyber aggressive behaviors also include those behaviors that do not have a face-to-face equivalent, like hacking someone's Facebook account. Hacking, as a form of cyber aggression, is carried out with malicious intent, with the desire to damage someone's reputation and/or their relationships.

Extensive research has focused on the factors which predict adolescents' involvement in cyber aggression and cyberbullying. In this literature, face-to-face aggression, face-to-face victimization, and cyber victimization are all found to be associated positively with cyber aggression and cyberbullying perpetration [2,4–8]. Other research implicates peer rejection, a lack of empathy, beliefs about anonymity, and narcissism as predictors of cyber aggression and cyberbullying perpetration [2,9–11]. Research aimed at understanding cyber aggression and cyberbullying involvement is important, as these behaviors relate to adjustment difficulties, specifically depression, anxiety, and loneliness [12–14]. In addition, cyber aggression and cyberbullying involvement is linked to poor academic performance, increased absences, and more truancy [1,15–17]. Researchers have classified aggression involvement into different categories including the uninvolved (neither perpetrator nor victim), cybervictims, cyberbullies, and cyberbully-cybervictims (both perpetrator and victim) [13].

Cyber aggression and cyberbullying research is even more important as research indicates that this phenomenon is not only found in one country, though much of the research has been conducted in the United States. The available research suggests that cyber aggression is a global concern. Of these studies, researchers have identified cyber aggression and cyberbullying involvement in Australia [12], Belgian [18], Germany [19], Ireland [20], Italy [21], Spain [22], Sweden [23,24], and Turkey [25].

Research on cyber aggression and cyberbullying involvement has been slower to develop in Asia, with findings revealing that perpetration and victimization occurs in some countries and areas, including China [26], Korea [27], Singapore [28], and Taiwan [16]. Examining cyber aggression involvement in Asia is imperative as the top four countries according to internet usage include China, India, and Japan, as well as the United States [29]. China ranks as number one, followed by the United States, India, and Japan. Understanding where a country ranks in terms of internet usage is important as access to the internet and the more time spent online are both risk factors associated with cyberbullying perpetration and victimization [30,31].

Given the high levels of internet consumption in China, India, and Japan, more research attention should focus on adolescents' involvement in cyber aggression in these countries. Although some research has examined cyberbullying involvement in China, this research has focused on frequency rates, demographic variables, and lower academic achievement as factors linked to the perpetration of these behaviors [26,32]. Few empirical investigations exist concerning cyberbullying perpetration and victimization in India and Japan. In one study, Japanese adolescents reported cyberbullying, but their levels of involvement were lower than adolescents from the United States and Austria [33,34]. Studies conducted in India focus on cyber gender harassment, a form of cyber harassment involving similar behaviors as cyberbullying, except that this behavior occurs among adults instead of children and adolescents [35]. Taken together, research from China, India, and Japan indicate that cyber aggression and cyberbullying occur among adolescents in these countries, and that their high levels of internet consumption warrant further investigation.

Furthermore, cultural values, including collectivism and individualism, impact adolescents' involvement in aggressive behaviors [36–39]. Collectivistic countries, like China and Japan, promote, prime, and reinforce individuals for behaving consistently with an interdependent self-construal [40]. Individualistic countries, like the United States, reinforce independent self-construal. India is considered both a collectivistic and an individualistic country, which might place these adolescents at an elevated risk of cyber aggression involvement when compared to adolescents from China and Japan. In the literature, collectivism is related negatively to aggression involvement, while individualism is associated positively with aggression perpetration and victimization [34,40]. Few studies have examined whether cultural values influence adolescents' perpetration and victimization by cyber aggression. Barlett and colleagues [33] examined interdependent self-construal as a moderator in the relationship between country of origin (*i.e.*, United States, Japan) and cyberbullying perpetration. The results revealed that cyberbullying was highest for young adults from the United States when they endorsed low levels of interdependent self-construal. These results were not found for Japanese young adults. However, it isn't clear whether independent self-construal would impact cyber aggression perpetration. Based on the previous research on face-to-face aggression perpetration, it might be likely that independent self-construal increases the risk of engaging in cyber aggression [34,40].

Gender differences in cyber aggression involvement in the United States and in European countries are mixed [2,9,41–43]. The literature on gender differences in cyber aggression perpetration and victimization is not as mixed in Asian countries. In this research, Chinese boys perpetrate and are victimized by cyberbullying more often than Chinese girls [26,32,44]. Similar patterns were found in Japan as well, with Japanese young adult males perpetrating these behaviors at higher rates than Japanese young adult females [33]. It is unclear whether Japanese males would experience more or less victimization than Japanese females as there has been no research conducted on this topic. In addition, research has not been conducted on gender differences in cyber aggression involvement among Indian adolescents. Given that research on cyber gender harassment conducted in India focuses solely on men harassing women through digital technologies, it might be likely that girls are more at risk for cyber victimization while boys might perpetrate cyber aggression more often than girls [35].

3. Peer Attachment and Aggression

High peer attachment involves adolescents' internationalization of the knowledge that their peers will be available and responsive when needed [36]. Problems within peer relationships can place adolescents at a higher risk of being involved in conflicts with their peers [37]. Thus, it is not surprising that adolescents with higher rates of victimization and those with behavioral problems are likely to rate their peer relationships as poor, due to these adolescents being less socially integrated in the peer group [45,46]. These adolescents also show less empathy toward their peers and this lack of empathy combined with behavioral problems might exacerbate their aggression directed toward their peers. Furthermore, social integration is directly related to adolescents' peer relationships, and when such integration is low, these adolescents are unable to manage and deal with relationships effectively [46]. When ostracized by the peer group, adolescents often act reactively by using aggression, developing favorable attitudes toward these behaviors [47]. In the literature, higher peer attachment relates to more sympathetic attitudes toward peers, and less delinquency and aggressive behaviors [48]. Peer attachment is also related negatively to face-to-face bullying and cyberbullying as well as victimization by both types of bullying. Some attention has focused on the relationship between peer attachment and cyberbullying categories. One of the few studies conducted on these associations found that cyberbully-cybervictims have lower levels of peer attachment than uninvolved adolescents [49]. No other research exists concerning differences in peer attachment among cyberbullies and cybervictims. Gender has also been investigated as a factor relating to peer attachment. Research suggests that girls are more attached to their peers than boys, though it isn't clear how cyber aggression classification type might alter these associations [50].

Little attention has been given to examining peer attachment among adolescents in China, India, and Japan. The literature suggests that members of collectivistic cultures are attached to their peers, due to the reinforcement of interdependence and maintaining relationships with others in their society [51]. Therefore, considering that countries, like China, India, and Japan, have collectivistic focuses, it is likely that these adolescents are also attached to their peers. Given that individualism is endorsed in India as well, these adolescents might experience different levels of peer attachment than adolescents from China and Japan. In the literature, adolescents from the United States had higher levels of peer attachment than adolescents from India [52]. On the other hand, other research indicates that Chinese adolescents who immigrated to Italy have higher rates of peer attachment than Italian adolescents [53]. Considering these contrasting findings, it is difficult to conclude whether Indian adolescents experience higher or lower levels of peer attachment when compared to adolescents from China and India. In one of the few studies to investigate peer attachment in relation to aggression, Yang and colleagues [54] found that poor peer attachment related positively to Chinese adolescents' aggression and delinquency. These patterns are similar to those found in the United States, though it isn't clear whether similar patterns would be found in India and Japan. In addition, there is no literature revealing the role of cyber aggression categories (*i.e.*, the uninvolved, cybervictims, cyberaggressors, cyberaggressors-cybervictims) and country of origin in adolescents' attachment to their peers.

4. Present Study

Few investigations have been conducted on cyber aggression involvement among adolescents in China, India, and Japan, especially studies conducted to compare rates across these countries. In addition, it is unknown whether peer attachment relates to cyber aggression perpetration and victimization. To this end, the first aim of the present study compared rates of cyber aggression involvement in China, India, and Japan, while controlling for face-to-face bullying perpetration and victimization, individualism, and collectivism. It was hypothesized that Indian adolescents would report higher levels of cyber aggression involvement when compared to Chinese and Japanese adolescents, given the emphasis on both collectivism and individualism in India [35]. Although China and Japan are both collectivistic societies, China is a little less collectivistic and has higher rates of internet consumption, which might contribute to adolescents in this country being more at risk for cyber aggression involvement [29]. Therefore, it was hypothesized that Chinese adolescents would report higher levels of cyber aggression involvement than Japanese adolescents. Another aim was to examine the role of gender in adolescents' cyber aggression perpetration and victimization based on country of origin. Chinese and Japanese boys were expected to engage in more cyber aggression perpetrators than girls from these countries. In addition, Chinese boys were also expected to experience more cyber victimization when compared to Chinese girls. Due to the research on cyber gender harassment in India, it was expected the girls would experience more cyber victimization, whereas boys would be more likely to be the perpetrators of cyber aggression [35].

The second aim of the present study was to examine differences in cyber aggression involvement categories (*i.e.*, the uninvolved, cybervictims, cyberaggressors, cyberaggressors-cybervictims) for peer attachment among Chinese, Indian, and Japanese adolescents. Therefore, three-way interactions were examined among gender, country of origin, and cyber aggression involvement. Since Indian adolescents were hypothesized to have higher levels of cyber aggression involvement, it was also hypothesized that cyberaggressors-cybervictims from India would have the lowest levels of peer attachment when compared to cyberaggressors-cybervictims from China and Japan. Uninvolved adolescents were expected to have the highest peer attachment, despite their country of origin. No other hypotheses were made regarding the interaction of cyber aggression involvement classifications and gender.

5. Methods

5.1. Participants

Participants were 1637 adolescents (age range 11–15 years old; 48.3% girls) from China (*n* = 683; 46.7% girls), India (*n* = 480; 46.5% girls), and Japan (*n* = 474; 52.6% girls). In China, data was collected from two schools, with one located in Beijing and the other in the An Hui Province. Adolescents from India were from six schools in the Karnataka state of India. Japanese adolescents were recruited from two schools

104

located in a suburb of Tokyo. All data was collected in the Fall of 2013, except for Japanese adolescents. Japanese schools begin in April, and data was collected in July 2014.

5.2. Procedures and Measures

Emails were sent to principals from target schools, describing the purpose of the study, how the school could participate, and what adolescents would be expected to do. When principals expressed an interest in the study, a meeting was setup with principals and teachers in order to receive their permission for their students to participate in the study. All principals and teachers agreed to allow students to participant in the study. Consent documents were sent home with adolescents, and then returned to their teachers, except in Japan where consent was obtained from school principals only. On the day of data collection, adolescents provided their assent to participate in the study before completing the surveys. No adolescents refused to participate. This study is part of a larger study on the psychosocial development of adolescents from various countries around the world, with a major focus on understanding the contextual factors which influence their involvement in cyber aggression. For this study, the following questionnaires were administered, including individualism and collectivism, face-to-face aggression involvement, cyber aggression involvement, and peer attachment. All consent, assent, and questionnaires were translated into the primary language of adolescents' country of origin, and then back-translated by researchers fluent in both English and the language of the country of origin.

5.2.1. Individualism and Collectivism

This questionnaire assessed adolescents' endorsement of individualism and collectivism [55]. Li and colleagues [55] adapted the Horizontal and Vertical Individualism and Collectivism measure [56] by changing some items to be suitable for adolescents (e.g., "It is important that I do my work better than others" was changed to "It is important that I do my schoolwork better than others"). There were sixteen items included in this measure, with eight for individualism (e.g., Winning is everything) and eight for collectivism (e.g., Family members should stick together, no matter what sacrifices are required). Participants rated the items on a scale of 1 (*Absolutely disagree*) to 9 (*Absolutely agree*). Both subscales demonstrated adequate reliability ($\alpha = 0.92$ for individualism; $\alpha = 0.79$ for collectivism).

5.2.2. Face-to-Face Aggression Involvement

To examine face-to-face aggression involvement, adolescents completed a questionnaire concerning how often they perpetrated face-to-face aggression (e.g., How often do you tell a peer that you will not like him or her unless he or she does what you want?) and were victimized by face-to-face aggression (e.g., How often does a peer say they won't like you unless you do what he or she wants you to do?) [57]. The items were described as occurring within the current school year. Adolescents rated the eighteen items (nine per subscale) on a scale of 1 (*Never*) to 5 (*All of the Time*). Face-to-face aggression perpetration had a Cronbach's alpha of 0.79 and 0.81 for face-to-face victimization.

5.2.3. Cyber Aggression Involvement

Adolescents indicated how often they perpetrated cyber aggression (e.g., How often do you spread bad rumors about another peer online or through text messages?) and were victimized by cyber aggression (e.g., How often does a peer spread bad rumors about you online or through text messages?) [11]. Eighteen items were included on this measure, with nine items per subscale. The items were described as occurring within the current school year. They rated all items on a scale of 1 (*Never*) to 5 (*All of the Time*). Cronbach's alphas were acceptable for both cyber aggression perpetration ($\alpha = 0.90$) and cyber aggression involvement ($\alpha = 0.90$).

5.2.4. Peer Attachment

The peer attachment subscale of the Inventory of Parent and Peer attachment was used to assess adolescents' perceptions of the positive and negative dimensions of their relationship with their peers [58]. There were 25 items used, each rated on a scale of 1 (*Almost Never or Never True*) to 5 (*Almost Always or Always True*). Cronbach's alpha was 0.89 for this measure.

6. Results

To examine the hypotheses for this study, two separate sets of analyses were performed. The first analysis examined differences among adolescents from the three countries regarding their cyber aggression perpetration and victimization. The second analysis investigated the role of cyber aggression involvement in peer attachment, and the differences across the three countries. Bonferroni corrections were utilized for all post-hoc follow-up analyses. Multi-group factor analysis was performed in *Mplus* for all four measures. Measurement invariance was not found among any of the groups. In addition, the MANOVAs and ANOVAs were performed without the cultural values, but the models with cultural values were better. Therefore, the models included cultural values. Interested readers should contact the first author for more information about these additional analyses.

6.1. Differences in Cyber Aggression Involvement

A MANOVA was conducted with cyber aggression perpetration and victimization as the dependent variables, country and gender as the independent variables, and face-to-face aggression involvement (perpetration and victimization) and cultural values (individualism and collectivism) as covariates. An interaction was included between country and gender. Main effects of country (Wilks' $\Lambda = 0.85$, $F(4, 3130) = 65.83$, $p < 0.001$) and gender (Wilks' $\Lambda = 0.97$, $F(2, 1565) = 11.34$, $p < 0.001$) were found. The interaction was also significant (Wilks' $\Lambda = 0.99$, $F(4, 3130) = 4.75$, $p < 0.001$).

Table 1. Correlation among all variables for Chinese, Indian, and Japanese adolescents.

	1	2	3	4	5	6	7
1. IND							
2. COLL	0.52 ***/ 0.73 ***/ 0.29 ***						
3. PA	0.18 **/ 0.35 ***/ 0.08	0.44 ***/ 0.31 ***/ 0.52 ***					
4. CAP	0.03/ 0.24 ***/ 0.03	−0.16 ***/ −0.16 ***/ −0.01	−0.08 */ −0.23 ***/ −0.02				
5. CV	0.06/ 0.13 **/ 0.09	−0.08 */ −0.19 ***/ −0.03	−0.04/ −0.24 ***/ −0.05	0.71 ***/ 0.67 ***/ 0.52 ***			
6. FAP	0.06/ 0.21 ***/ 0.01	−0.20 ***/ −0.03/ −0.23 **	−0.34 ***/ −0.20 ***/ −0.37 ***	0.27 ***/ 0.11 */ 0.20 ***	0.17 ***/ 0.23 ***/ 0.15 ***		
7. FV	0.13 ***/ 0.14 ***/ 0.01	−0.20 ***/ −0.09 */ −0.29 ***	−0.31 ***/ −0.31 ***/ −0.48 ***	0.14 ***/ 0.14 **/ 0.25 ***	0.18 ***/ 0.13 **/ 0.32 ***	0.48 ***/ 0.31 ***/ 0.65 ***	—

Note: IND = individualism; COLL = collectivism; PA = peer attachment; CAP = cyber aggression perpetration; CV = cyber victimization; FAP = face-to-face aggression perpetration; FV = face-to-face victimization. The first number is the correlation for Chinese adolescents. The second number is the correlation for Indian adolescents. The third number is the correlation for Japanese adolescents. * $p < 0.05$; ** $p < 0.01$; *** $p < 0.001$.

Next, follow-up ANOVAs for cyber aggression perpetration and victimization were conducted with the same variables used in the MANOVA (see Table 1 for correlations and Table 2 for means and standard deviations). Similar main effects were found for cyber aggression perpetration (country: $F(2, 1565) = 129.21$, $p < 0.001$; gender: $F(1, 1565) = 21.55$, $p < 0.001$) and cyber aggression victimization (country: $F(2, 1565) = 56.72$, $p < 0.001$; gender: $F(1, 1565) = 15.07$, $p < 0.001$). Interactions were also significant for cyber aggression involvement (perpetration: $F(2, 1565) = 8.70$, $p < 0.001$; victimization: $F(2, 1565) = 6.41$, $p < 0.01$). Indian adolescents (perpetration: $M = 1.86$; $SD = 0.74$; victimization: $M = 1.79$; $SD = 0.86$) reported greater cyber aggression perpetration and cyber aggression victimization than adolescents from China (perpetration: $M = 1.47$; $SD = 0.59$; victimization: $M = 1.58$; $SD = 0.72$) and

Japan (perpetration: $M = 1.19$; $SD = 0.26$; victimization: $M = 1.26$; $SD = 0.41$). Cyber aggression involvement was also higher among Chinese adolescents than Japanese adolescents. Boys reported more cyber aggression involvement than girls in China and India. There were no gender differences in cyber aggression perpetration and victimization among Japanese adolescents.

Table 2. Means and standard deviations of cyber aggression perpetration and victimization for China, India, and Japan.

Country	Cyber Aggression Perpetration			Cyber Victimization		
	Full Sample M (SD)	Girls M (SD)	Boys M (SD)	Full Sample M (SD)	Girls M (SD)	Boys M (SD)
China	1.47 (0.59)$_{ab}$	1.40 (0.43)	1.55 (0.61)	1.58 (0.72)$_{ab}$	1.50 (0.67)	1.67 (0.79)
India	1.86 (0.74)$_a$	1.71 (0.63)	1.99 (0.78)	1.79 (0.86)a	1.65 (0.80)	1.92 (0.91)
Japan	1.19 (0.26)$_{ab}$	1.20 (0.26)	1.12 (0.24)	1.26 (0.41)$_{ab}$	1.28 (0.42)	1.24 (0.41)

Note: Covariates include face-to-face aggression perpetration, face-to-face victimization, individualism and collectivism. Means within a column sharing the same subscript letter were found to be significantly different.

6.2. Peer Attachment and Cyber Aggression Involvement

Before conducting the analysis, adolescents were split into the following groups based on the means of cyber aggression perpetration ($M = 1.51$, $SD = 0.66$) and cyber aggression victimization ($M = 1.56$, $SD = 0.75$). The following is the breakdown of the groups: cyberaggressors-cyber victims (Group 1; $n = 433$), cyberaggressors (Group 2; $n = 127$), cybervictims (Group 3; $n = 150$), and the uninvolved (Group 4; $n = 866$). An ANOVA was conducted with parental attachment as the dependent variable, and country, gender, and group as the independent variables. Face-to-face aggression involvement, individualism, and collectivism were included as covariates. Three two-way interactions were included between country and groups, country and gender, and gender and groups. A three-way interaction was also included among country, gender, and groups. Main effects of gender ($F(1, 1565) = 32.82$, $p < 0.001$) and groups ($F(3, 1565) = 14.78$, $p < 0.001$) were found. The main effect of country and the interactions were not significant. Girls ($M = 3.78$, $SD = 0.04$) reported more peer attachment when compared to boys ($M = 3.45$, $SD = 0.04$). Uninvolved adolescents ($M = 3.88$, $SD = 0.03$) had greater peer attachment when compared to the other groups (cyberaggressors-cybervictims: $M = 3.30$, $SD = 0.05$; cyberaggressors: $M = 3.69$, $SD = 0.06$; cybervictims: $M = 3.53$, $SD = 0.06$). Cybervictims had lower levels of peer attachment than cyberaggressors and uninvolved adolescents. Cyberaggressors-cybervictims had the lowest peer attachment when compared to cybervictims, cyberaggressors, and uninvolved adolescents.

7. Discussion

The purposes of this study were twofold. The first aim was to investigate the conjoint influence of country of origin and gender on cyber aggression involvement among Chinese, Indian, and Japanese adolescents. The second aim was to examine the combined effects of country of origin, gender, and the cyber aggression involvement classifications on peer attachment. Results from the present study provide further evidence that cyber aggression is an issue impacting adolescents across the world. The findings of the present study contribute greatly to the body of literature on cyber aggression involvement because cultural values and face-to-face aggression involvement were included as covariates.

Providing support for one of the study's hypotheses, Indian adolescents reported greater cyber aggression perpetration and victimization than adolescents from either China or Japan. Such findings might be supported by the literature, suggesting that Indian culture promotes and rewards both individualistic and collectivistic behaviors [40]. Given their stronger tendency toward individualism than adolescents in China or Japan, adolescents from India might be more at risk for cyber aggression involvement, which is further supported from the literature linking more face-to-face bullying and victimization among adolescents from individualistic countries (e.g., the United States) than collectivistic countries (e.g., China, Japan) [37–39]. Furthermore, Chinese adolescents reported higher cyber aggression involvement when compared to Japanese adolescents, which supported the study's hypotheses. This finding is difficult to reconcile with the literature, considering that both countries highly value collectivism and that collectivism is usually associated with less bullying involvement [40]. Another possibility is that China's greater internet consumption might indicate that Chinese adolescents also spend more time using the internet than Japanese adolescents. Access to the internet and frequency of usage is a risk factor associated with cyber aggression involvement, which might indicate that Chinese adolescents are more at risk than Japanese adolescents [30,31]. Such findings are also aligned with other work in Japan, revealing that Japanese adolescents rarely reported being involved in cyberbullying [34].

Understanding cyber aggression involvement in Asia is better understood by focusing on country of origin and gender differences, which reveal complex patterns. The significant two-way interaction between country of origin and gender suggests that boys reported more cyber aggression involvement in China and India than girls in these countries. Finding that Chinese boys perpetrated and were victimized by cyber aggression more often than Chinese girls is consistent with the literature on gender differences in Chinese adolescents' involvement in cyberbullying [26,32,39]. The findings from India are difficult to compare with the literature since no research has been conducted on cyber aggression involvement in this country. No gender differences were found for cyber aggression perpetration and victimization among

Japanese adolescents. This result is not consistent with the literature. For instance, Barlett *et al.* [33] found that Japanese males had higher levels of cyberbullying perpetration than Japanese females. One possibility for this inconsistent finding is that Barlett and colleagues' study included young adults, whereas the present study included adolescents. Such differences might reflect developmental differences in the samples.

Concerning peer attachment, country of origin was not significant. Thus, adolescents in China, India, and Japan did not differ in their levels of peer attachment. Such findings might reflect the focus on collectivistic values within their countries, which emphasize interdependence and possibly positive peer relationships [40]. Gender was significant, indicating that girls reported more peer attachment when compared to boys, no matter their country of origin. This finding is consistent with a recent meta-analysis on gender differences in peer attachment [50]. In addition, uninvolved adolescents reported greater peer attachment when compared to cyberaggressors-cybervictims, cybervictims, and cyberaggressors, which is supported by the literature [53]. Furthermore, cyberaggressors-cybervictims had the worst levels of peer attachment when compared to cybervictims and cyberaggressors. The findings regarding cyber aggression involvement supported the study's hypotheses. Unlike Burton and colleagues [53], the present study also found that cybervictims had lower levels of peer attachment than cyberbullies. However, this finding is supported by the literature on face-to-face bullying involvement [59–61]. The interaction among country of origin, gender, and cyber aggression involvement was not significant. This was not expected since it was hypothesized that Indian adolescents' greater involvement in cyber aggression would worsen their peer attachment. Such a finding might suggest that collectivism serves some type of protective function. In their review of the ecological contexts of bullying, Huang and colleagues [37] suggested that the macrosystem, particularly the emphasis on collectivism *versus* individualism, might mitigate the negative effects associated with face-to-face bullying involvement among Chinese children and adolescents.

Limitations and Future Directions

Even though the present study provided much needed information concerning cyber aggression perpetration and victimization in China, India, and Japan, there are a few limitations that should be noted and addressed in future research. First, this study relied on self-reports to assess face-to-face and cyber aggression perpetration and victimization. A multiple informant approach is needed in this research as it reduces the biases associated with self-reports. In addition, recent research has demonstrated the strength of utilizing peer-nominations to assess peer-based cyber aggression involvement [2,11]. Second, this study utilized a concurrent research design to assess cyber aggression perpetration and victimization.

Thus, it is impossible to understand the temporal ordering of peer attachment and cyber aggression involvement, and future research should focus on utilizing longitudinal designs.

8. Conclusions

The present study provided a much needed examination of the differences in cyber aggression perpetration and victimization among Chinese, Indian, and Japanese adolescents as well as the differences in the cyber aggression involvement classifications for peer attachment. It is also among a few studies to control for face-to-face aggression involvement and cultural values when examining these differences, which is a methodological improvement and an important direction for researchers interested in the role of culture in cyber aggression perpetration and victimization. Despite the differences found in the study, these findings suggest that more research should be conducted on cyber aggression involvement among adolescents in China, India, and Japan. This is incredibly important for cyber aggression perpetration and victimization in India as Indian adolescents had the highest levels of these behaviors and victimization when compared to Chinese and Japanese adolescents. This study may inform school personnel in these countries concerned with identifying risk factors associated with adolescents' cyber aggression involvement based on their gender and their levels of peer attachment.

Acknowledgments: This work was supported by the project "Employment of Best Young Scientists for International Cooperation Empowerment" (CZ.1.07/2.3.00/30.0037) co-financed from European Social Fund and the state budget of the Czech Republic. This work was also partially supported by JSPS KAKENHI Grant-in-Aid for Young Scientists (B) Grant Number 26870535.

Author Contributions: Michelle F. Wright developed the study proposal, analyzed data, and wrote and edited the manuscript. Ikuko Aoyama coordinated data collection, collected data, and edited the manuscript. Shanmukh V. Kamble coordinated data collection, collected data, and edited the manuscript. Zheng Li coordinated data collection, collected data, and edited the manuscript. Shruti Soudi coordinated data collection, and collected data. Li Lei coordinated data collection. Chang Shu coordinated data collection.

Conflicts of Interest: The authors declare no conflict of interest.

References

1. Ybarra, M.L.; Diener-West, M.; Leaf, P. Examining the overlap in internet harassment and school bullying: Implications for school intervention. *J. Adolesc. Health* **2007**, *1*, S42–S50.
2. Wright, M.F.; Li, Y. The association between cyber victimization and subsequent cyber aggression: The moderating effect of peer rejection. *J. Youth Adolesc.* **2013**, *42*, 662–674.
3. Grigg, D.W. Cyber-aggression: Definition and concept of cyberbullying. *Aust. J. Guid. Counsell.* **2010**, *20*, 143–156.

4. Bauman, S. Cyberbullying in a rural intermediate school: An exploratory study. *J. Early Adolesc.* **2010**, *30*, 803–833.

5. Patchin, J.W.; Hinduja, S. Traditional and nontraditional bullying among youth: A test of general strain theory. *Youth Soc.* **2011**, *43*, 727–775.

6. Pornari, C.D.; Wood, J. Peer and cyber aggression in secondary school students: The role of moral disengagement, hostile attribution bias, and outcome expectancies. *Aggress. Behav.* **2010**, *36*, 81–94.

7. Sontag, L.M.; Clemans, K.H.; Graber, J.A.; Lyndon, S. Traditional and cyber aggressors and victims: A comparison of psychosocial characteristics. *J. Youth Adolesc.* **2011**, *40*, 392–404.

8. Topcu, C.; Erdur-Baker, O. Affective and cognitive empathy as mediators of gender differences in cyber and traditional bullying. *Sch. Psychol. Int.* **2012**, *33*, 550–561.

9. Ang, R.P.; Goh, D.H. Cyberbullying among adolescents: The role of affective and cognitive empathy, and gender. *Child Psychiatry Hum. Dev.* **2010**, *41*, 387–397.

10. Fanti, K.A.; Demetriou, A.G.; Hawa, V.V. A longitudinal study of cyberbullying: Examining risk and protective factors. *Eur. J. Dev. Psychol.* **2012**, *9*, 168–181.

11. Wright, M.F. Longitudinal investigation of the associations between adolescents' popularity and cyber social behaviors. *J. Sch. Violence* **2014**, *13*, 291–314.

12. Campbell, M.; Spears, B.; Slee, P.; Bulter, D.; Kift, S. Victims' perceptions of traditional and cyberbullying and the psychosocial correlates of their victimization. *Emot. Behav. Diffic.* **2012**, *17*, 389–401.

13. Kowalski, R.M.; Limber, S.P. Psychological, physical, and academic correlates of cyberbullying and traditional bullying. *J. Adolesc. Health* **2013**, *53*, S13–S20.

14. Schenk, A.M.; Fremouw, W.J.; Keelan, C.M. Characteristics of college cyberbullies. *Comput. Hum. Behav.* **2013**, *29*, 2320–2327.

15. Beran, T.; Li, Q. The relationship between cyberbullying and school bullying. *J. Stud. Wellbeing* **2007**, *1*, 15–33.

16. Huang, Y.; Chou, C. An analysis of multiple factors of cyberbullying among junior high school students in Taiwan. *Comput. Hum. Behav.* **2010**, *26*, 1581–1590.

17. Katzer, C.; Fetchenhauer, D.; Belschak, F. Cyberbullying in chatrooms: Who are the victims? *J. Media Psychol.* **2009**, *21*, 25–36.

18. Heirman, W.; Walrave, M. Predicting adolescent perpetration in cyberbullying: An application of the theory of planned behavior. *Psicothema* **2012**, *24*, 614–620.

19. Festl, R.; Schwarkow, M.; Quandt, T. Peer influence, internet use and cyberbullying: A comparison of different context effects among German adolescents. *J. Child. Media* **2013**, *7*, 446–462.

20. Corcoran, L.; Connolly, I.; O'Moore, M. Cyberbullying in Irish schools: An investigation of personality and self-concept. *Ir. J. Psychol.* **2012**, *33*, 153–165.

21. Brighi, A.; Guarini, A.; Melotti, G.; Galli, S.; Genta, M.L. Predictors of victimisation across direct bullying, indirect bullying and cyberbullying. *Emot. Behav. Diffic.* **2012**, *17*, 375–388.

22. Gamez-Guadix, M.; Orue, I.; Smith, P.K.; Calvete, E. Longitudinal and reciprocal relations of cyberbullying with depression, substance use, and problematic internet use among adolescents. *J. Adolesc. Health* **2013**, *53*, 446–452.

23. Beckman, L.; Hagquist, C.; Hellstrom, L. Does the association with psychosomatic health problems differ between cyberbullying and traditional bullying? *Emot. Behav. Diffic.* **2012**, *17*, 421–434.

24. Laftman, S.B.; Modin, B.; Ostberg, V. Cyberbullying and subjective health: A large-scale study of students in Stockholm, Sweden. *Child. Youth Serv. Rev.* **2013**, *35*, 112–119.

25. Erdur-Baker, O. Cyberbullying and its correlation to traditional bullying, gender and frequent and risky usage of internet-mediated communication tools. *New Media Soc.* **2010**, *12*, 109–125.

26. Zhou, Z.; Tang, H.; Tian, Y.; Wei, H.; Zhang, F.; Morrison, C.M. Cyberbullying and its risk factors among Chinese high school students. *Sch. Psychol. Int.* **2013**, *34*, 630–647.

27. Jang, H.; Song, J.; Kim, R. Does the offline bully-victimization influence cyberbullying behavior among youths? Application of general strain theory. *Comput. Hum. Behav.* **2014**, *31*, 85–93.

28. Kwan, G.C.E.; Skoric, M.M. Facebook bullying: An extension of battles at school. *Comput. Hum. Behav.* **2013**, *29*, 16–25.

29. Internet Live Stats. Available online: http://www.internetlivestats.com/ (accessed on 15 November 2014).

30. Livingstone, S.; Smith, P.K. Annual research review: Harms experienced by child users of online and mobile technologies: The nature, prevalence and management of sexual and aggressive risks in the digital age. *J. Child Psychol. Psychiatry* **2014**, *55*, 635–654.

31. Park, S.; Na, E.; Kim, E. The relationship between online activities, netiquette and cyberbullying. *Child. Youth Serv. Rev.* **2014**, *42*, 74–81.

32. Li, J.; Gao, X.; Shi, G. Characteristics of cyberbullying among adolescents. *Chin. Ment. Health J.* **2013**, *27*, 43–48.

33. Barlett, C.P.; Gentile, D.A.; Anderson, C.A.; Suzuki, K.; Sakamoto, A.; Yamaoka, A.; Katsura, R. Cross-cultural differences in cyberbullying behavior: A short-term longitudinal study. *J. Cross Cult. Psychol.* **2013**, *45*, 300–313.

34. Strohmeier, D.; Aoyama, I.; Gradinger, P.; Toda, Y. Cybervictimization and cyberaggression in Eastern and Western countries: Challenges of constructing a cross-cultural appropriate scale. In *Principles of Cyberbullying Research: Definitions, Measures, and Methodology*; Bauman, S., Cross, D., Walker, J.L., Eds.; Routledge: New York, NY, USA, 2013; pp. 202–221.

35. Halder, D.; Jaishankar, K. Cyber gender harassment and secondary victimization: A comparative analysis of the United States, the UK, and India. *Vict. Offenders* **2011**, *6*, 386–398.

36. Nickerson, A.; Nagle, R. Parent and peer attachment in late childhood and early adolescence. *J. Early Adolesc.* **2005**, *25*, 223–249.

37. Huang, H.; Hong, J.S.; Espelage, D.L. Understanding factors associated with bullying and peer victimization in Chinese schools within ecological contexts. *J. Child Fam. Stud.* **2013**, *22*, 881–892.

38. Menzer, M.M.; Torney-Purta, J. Individualism and socioeconomic diversity at school as related to perceptions of the frequency of peer aggression in fifteen countries. *J. Adolesc.* **2012**, *35*, 1285–1294.

39. Nesdale, D.; Naito, M. Individualism-collectivism and the attitudes to school bullying of Japanese and Australian Students. *J. Cross Cult. Psychol.* **2005**, *36*, 537–556.

40. Singelis, T.M. The measurement of independent and interdependent self-construals. *Personal. Soc. Psychol. Bull.* **1994**, *20*, 580–591.

41. Bauman, S.; Toomey, R.B.; Walker, J.L. Associations among bullying, cyberbullying, and suicide in high school students. *J. Adolesc.* **2013**, *36*, 341–350.

42. Gradinger, P.; Strohmeier, D.; Spiel, C. Traditional bullying and cyberbullying. *J. Psychol.* **2009**, *217*, 205–213.

43. Hinduja, S.; Patchin, J.W. Cyberbullying: An exploratory analysis of factors related to offending and victimization. *Deviant Behav.* **2008**, *29*, 129–156.

44. Hu, Y.; Fan, C.; Zhang, F.; Zhou, R. Behavioral characteristics of different roles in cyberbullying and relation to depression in junior students. *Chin. Ment. Health J.* **2013**, *27*, 913–917.

45. Juvonen, J.; Graham, S.; Schuster, M. Bullying among young adolescents: The strong, the weak, and the troubled. *Pediatrics* **2003**, *112*, 1231–1237.

46. DeMonchy, M.; Pijl, S.; Zandberg, T. Discrepancies in judging social inclusion and bullying of pupils with behaviour problems. *Eur. J. Spec. Needs Educ.* **2004**, *19*, 317–330.

47. Leary, M.; Twenge, J.; Quinlivan, E. Interpersonal rejection as a determinant of anger and aggression. *Personal. Soc. Psychol. Rev.* **2006**, *10*, 111–132.

48. Laible, D.; Carlo, G.; Raffaelli, M. The differential relations of parent and peer attachment to adolescent adjustment. *J. Youth Adolesc.* **2000**, *29*, 45–59.

49. Burton, K.A.; Florell, D.; Wygant, D.B. The role of peer attachment and normative beliefs about aggression on traditional bullying and cyberbullying. *Psychol. Sch.* **2013**, *50*, 103–114.

50. Gorrese, A.; Ruggieri, R. Peer attachment: A meta-analytic review of gender and age differences and associations with parent attachment. *J. Youth Adolesc.* **2012**, *41*, 650–672.

51. Matsumoto, D.; Juang, L. *Culture and Psychology*; Wadsworth: Belmont, CA, USA, 2004.

52. Pearson, J.C.; Child, J.T. A cross-cultural comparison of parental and peer attachment styles among adult children from the United States, Puerto Rico, and India. *J. Intercult. Commun. Res.* **2007**, *36*, 15–32.

53. Laghi, F.; Pallini, S.; Baiocco, R.; Dimitrova, R. Parent and peer attachment and psychosocial adjustment in Chinese immigrant adolescents in Italy. *Adv. Immigr. Fam. Res.* **2014**, *1*, 259–273.

54. Yang, H.; Cai, T.; He, Y. Parent attachment, peers attachment and high school students' behavior problems. *Chin. J. Clin. Psychol.* **2010**, *18*, 107–108.

55. Li, Y.; Wang, M.; Wang, C.; Shi, J. Individualism, collectivism, and Chinese adolescents' aggression: Intracultural variations. *Aggress. Behav.* **2010**, *36*, 187–194.

56. Triandis, H.C.; Gelfand, M.J. Converging measurement of horizontal and verticial individualism and collectivism. *J. Personal. Soc. Psychol.* **1998**, *74*, 118–128.

57. Wright, M.F.; Li, Y.; Shi, J. Chinese adolescents' social status goals: Associations with behaviors and attributions for relational aggression. *Youth Soc.* **2012**, *46*, 566–588.

58. Armsden, G.C.; Greenberg, M.T. The Inventory of Parent and Peer Attachment: Relationships to well-being in adolescence. *J. Youth Adolesc.* **1987**, *16*, 427–454.

59. Marini, Z.A.; Dane, A.V.; Bosacki, S.L.; YLC-CURA. Direct and indirect bully-victims: Differential psychosocial risk factors associated with adolescents involve in bullying and victimization. *Aggress. Behav.* **2006**, *32*, 551–569.

60. Vassallo, S.; Edwards, B.; Renda, J.; Olsson, C.A. Bullying in early adolescence and antisocial behavior and depression six years later: What are the protective factors. *J. Sch. Violence* **2014**, *13*, 100–124.

61. Walden, L.M.; Beran, T.N. Attachment quality and bullying behavior in school-aged youth. *Can. J. Sch. Psychol.* **2010**, *25*, 5–18.

Mobile Technologies and the Incidence of Cyberbullying in Seven European Countries: Findings from Net Children Go Mobile

Brian O'Neill and Thuy Dinh

Abstract: The harmful effects of bullying and harassment on children have long been of concern to parents, educators, and policy makers. The online world presents a new environment in which vulnerable children can be victimized and a space where perpetrators find new ways to perform acts of harassment. While online bullying is often considered to be an extension of persistent offline behavior, according to EU Kids Online (2011), the most common form of bullying is in person, face-to-face. With the rise in use of mobile Internet technologies, this balance is changing. Increased levels of use and more time spent online accessed through a variety of devices has increased children's exposure to a range of online risks, including cyberbullying. This article presents the findings of the Net Children Go Mobile project, a cross-national study of children aged 9–16 in seven European countries. The research builds on the work of EU Kids Online and supports the identification of new trends in children's online experiences of risk and safety. The study finds that while overall levels of bullying have remained relatively static, levels of online bullying have increased, particularly among younger teens. The relationship between cyberbullying and the use of mobile Internet technologies is examined and factors contributing to increased levels of cyberbullying are highlighted.

Reprinted from *Societies*. Cite as: O'Neill, B.; Dinh, T. Mobile Technologies and the Incidence of Cyberbullying in Seven European Countries: Findings from Net Children Go Mobile. *Societies* **2015**, *5*, 384–398.

1. Introduction

The rapidity with which the Internet has been embraced by young people and the speed at which it has impacted on the environment for young people's informational, educational, and entertainment needs is remarkable. Young people have been at the fore in embracing new Internet technologies [1], adapting them effortlessly to new modes of social interaction [2] and forging new and often unexpected opportunities for learning [3]. Yet, a dual discourse counterpointing the diverse opportunities that the Internet affords with attendant risks and concerns with how best to manage young people's engagement with a complex amalgam of technologically-mediated content and contact risks has preoccupied policy makers, almost since its inception [4].

The harmful effects of bullying and harassment on children have long been of concern to parents, educators, and policy makers, long before the Internet became such a feature of contemporary life. That the online world presents a new environment in which vulnerable children can be victimized and a space where perpetrators find new ways to perform acts of harassment has been acknowledged by educators and online safety aspects as one of the main challenges facing children's online participation. Yet, the extent to which use of the Internet by young people has contributed to experiences of being bullied remains a challenging research question. Multinational studies such as EU Kids Online and Net Children Go Mobile have sought to enhance knowledge of European children's online opportunities, risks, and safety through the development of a robust evidence base towards understanding the online landscape that increasingly frames children and young people's experience. Children's accounts of risks and harm experienced through their use of the Internet provide the basis for the current study with a particular focus on the use of mobile Internet technologies such as smartphones, tablets, and other mobile connected devices. The study draws on children's responses from seven participating European countries and provides a baseline on which to assess trends in the situations that children find problematic. Bullying and online harassment feature as one of the risks asked about and while not the most prevalent of "risky" experiences that children describe, it is the one that was found to have the most severe impact.

Researching Young People's Internet Use

In response to growing policy concerns regarding online safety for children as well as a lack of reliable evidence in Europe, researchers have sought to develop better knowledge of European children's experiences and practices regarding risky and safer use of the Internet and new online technologies, and thereby to inform the promotion of a safer online environment for children. EU Kids Online has been one of the most prominent contributors in this regard. Beginning in 2006, EU Kids Online, with the support of the European Commission's (EC) Safer Internet Program, has in three successive phases of work sought to enhance knowledge of children's experiences and practices regarding risks and safety on the Internet. It has been acknowledged as the primary source in Europe of high-quality, independent, and comprehensive evidence underpinning a better and safer Internet for children in Europe [5].

The aim of the Net Children Go Mobile project, which followed EU Kids Online, is to study children's and young people's use of mobile Internet technologies and to examine consequences they may have for children's online well-being. Employing both quantitative and qualitative methodologies, the research focuses specifically on how new mobile conditions of Internet access and use (smartphones, tablets, other portable devices and use of Wi-Fi) bring greater or lesser risks to children's online safety. Given the rapid adoption of convergent mobile media and the changes associated with mobile Internet access at home, in school, and when out and about, mobile media technologies provide children with potential new opportunities, while at the same time exposing them to new risks.

The proliferation of mobile connected devices has greatly expanded children's and young people's opportunities to go online and access the Internet outside the confines of the home. Research has shown that the social context of Internet access and use is a major factor in shaping children's online experiences [6]. With mobile, "always-on" connectivity, the locations, time spent, and ways of using the Internet are likely to intensify, creating new challenges for parents, educators, and policy makers [7].

2. Theoretical Framework

Previous research [6,8,9] indicates that the patterns and social contexts of general Internet use are key factors shaping children's online activities and online risks encountered. Online experience is defined as a pathway composed of the online activities engaged in by children and the online and offline factors (family, social ecological environment, *etc.*) that shape children's behaviors toward the technological world. This approach, based on Bronfenbrenner's work [10], offers a re-conceptualization of the child's ecology as a multi-layered set of nested and interconnecting environmental systems, all of which influence the developing child but with varying degrees of directness. The perspective has evolved since its early inception and today acknowledges the role of the child's own characteristics, hence the model is now referred to as the bio-ecological model [10]. The framework recognizes the complex interdependencies between the institutions and structures that support or constrain children's opportunities and their agency in making choices and decisions online while negotiating these possibilities and constraints [11].

Children's Internet use may be investigated on two levels [6]. The most common way is to consider the child as the unit of analysis, examining both individual (demographic, psychological) factors and factors relating to their social environment (parents, peers, and teachers). This allows the analysis of the process and consequences of online activities contextualized within the "meso" and "macro" system of children's lives [11]. Parents are the most influential part of the ecology, as are, for example, school and childcare arrangements. As these have the most direct contact with the child, they are represented in the circle or layer immediately surrounding the individual (the microsystem).

This analysis builds on our previous work [12] exploring a child-centered approach to children's experiences, perspectives, and action in relation of the use of the Internet, contextualizing them within concentric circles of structuring social influences—family, community, and culture [6]. By using the bio-ecological approach

118

in which media are no longer investigated in their individual textuality or as a cluster of isolated material practices, but rather as "an overall technical social, cultural and place-based system, in which components are not decomposable or separable" [13].

Another plausible framework is the usage paradigm, which connects Internet use with online opportunities and risk [14,15]. This approach, characterized by the underlying rule "the more opportunities, the more risks" [8,16] implies that the more children use the Internet, the more they learn to reap its benefits and deal in healthy and non-harmful ways with potential risk. However, risk does not always result in harm; and risk taking can be beneficial in terms of building resilience [6].

3. Incidence of Bullying in Seven European Countries

Bullying was one of four types of online risk asked about in the Net Children Go Mobile survey. Young people were asked if they had themselves experienced bullying either online or offline; what impact this had on them; and what actions they took in attempting to deal with the problem, for example, who they spoke to or what action they took to deal with the problem.

Despite being a recurrent theme in research and in public and policy debates, there is no standard definition of "cyberbullying." Bullying has been defined as a form of aggression that is (a) intentional; (b) repetitive; and (c) involves a power imbalance between a victim and a perpetrator [17]. Accordingly, cyberbullying is defined as intentional and repeated aggression using any form of technological device such as the Internet or mobile phone.

To avoid adopting contested, adult, or emotionally-charged terms, bullying was defined in the Net Children Go Mobile study as follows: Sometimes children or teenagers say or do hurtful or nasty things to someone and this can often be quite a few times on different days over a period of time, for example. This can include: teasing someone in a way this person does not like; hitting, kicking or pushing someone around; intentionally leaving someone out of things. When people are hurtful or nasty to someone in this way, it can happen: in person face to face (a person who is together with you in the same place at the same time); by mobile phone (texts, calls, video clips); on the Internet (email, instant messaging, social networking, chatrooms); on whatever device you use to go online.

3.1. Survey Sample and Procedure

The main data used in this article is taken from the Net Children Go Mobile (NCGM) survey. A total of 3500 children who use the Internet were interviewed during winter 2013 and spring 2014, across seven European countries (UK, Denmark, Italy, Romania, Ireland, Portugal, and Belgium) [18]. Many of the questions asked in this survey replicate precisely those asked in the EU Kids Online survey conducted in 25 European countries in 2010 [8].

The NCGM survey involved a random stratified sample of around 500 children aged 9–16, who are Internet users, per country. The sampling frame started with a known population base taken from national registers, that is, the general population in most countries and the population of children aged 9–16 years in some others. Using official registers of geographical units, country regions were stratified to ensure that smaller geographical and rural areas were included. From each stratum (that is, those identified in the stratification process), random sampling points were selected with a selection probability proportionate to the number of children aged 9–16 living in the area. Different address selection methods imply different degrees of sample representativeness. The interview was conducted in children's homes, as a face-to-face interview. It included a self-completion section for sensitive questions. Average interview time per child was 40 min [18]. To ensure children's comprehension, the wording of these questionnaires was refined on the basis of cognitive testing with children of different age groups (9–10, 11–12, 13–14, 15–16) and gender in each country. The Net Children Go Mobile survey continued to use EU Kids Online's conceptual framework, which is operationalized in a child-centered, critical, contextual, and comparative approach [8].

For the purpose of comparison, the trends and patterns of cyberbullying incidences, between two periods of time (2010 and 2014) were identified. On several occasions we compared the findings of the Net Children Go Mobile survey with the 2010 EU Kids Online survey. When such comparisons are made we calculated an average number from the EU Kids Online survey only for the countries included in the Net Children Go Mobile survey, thus attempting to provide as direct a comparison as possible.

When direct comparisons are made to the EU Kids Online survey, the data are presented as "EUKO 2010" whereas the Net Children Go Mobile data are presented as "NCGM 2014."

3.2. Incidence of Bullying, Offline and Online

Table 1 presents the findings in response to the question of whether the child had been bullied online or offline in the past 12 months and whether this was an experience that had upset them. Prior research has shown that, while cyberbullying is less common than offline bullying [8], it is a very distressing and harmful experience [8]. Online bullying is often understood as an extension of persistent offline behavior. The shift from offline to online spaces means that the boundaries of space and time are becoming non-existent: one cannot leave a place and know that the bullying will end; rather, the bullying is likely to take place not only at the school yard but also after school, on a variety of platforms. Research has also shown that compared to face-to-face forms of bullying, the boundaries between the roles of victim, perpetrator, and bystanders are less easily drawn in online bullying [19].

Table 1. Child has been bullied online or offline in the past 12 months (%).

	Has not been bullied	Victim of bullying but not upset	Victim and a little upset	Victim and very upset
Row percentages	77	6	12	5
Age				
9–10	76	3	14	7
11–12	81	5	10	4
13–14	74	7	15	4
15–16	78	9	8	5
Gender				
Male	81	6	10	3
Female	74	6	14	6
SES				
Low	80	5	10	5
Medium	73	8	14	5
High	79	5	12	4
Country				
Belgium	87	5	7	1
Denmark	61	11	20	8
Ireland	78	6	10	6
Italy	87	5	7	1
Portugal	90	4	4	2
Romania	59	8	22	11
UK	79	3	12	6

Base: All children aged between 9 and 16 who use the Internet, NCGM 2014.

According to Net Children Go Mobile, nearly one in four (23%) 9–16-year-olds say that they have experienced some form of bullying, online or offline, in the past 12 months. For 6% of children, this was not an upsetting experience. However, the majority of children who have experienced bullying find it upsetting. Seventeen percent of children overall said they were "very" (5%) or "a little upset" (12%) about what happened. It is, however, the youngest children who report higher rates of being upset by being bullied (21%).

Gender differences are marked. The incidence of bullying is higher among girls overall and for those in their mid-teens, aged 13–14 years (26%). Girls are more likely to experience bullying (26%) than boys (19%) and more likely to be upset (20%) compared to 13% of boys.

Only slight differences by socioeconomic status are noted with children from middle SES homes reporting more frequent levels of bullying.

It is at the country level where the greatest differences in incidence of bullying are to be found. The average of 23% of 9–16-year-old children experiencing some form of bullying incorporates therefore a wide variation from high levels of bullying experienced in Romania (41%) and Denmark (39%) to much lower levels in Portugal (10%), Belgium, and Italy (both 13%). The UK and Ireland (21% and 22%, respectively) are the only two countries that lie close to the average of the seven countries in the NCGM survey.

Figure 1 compares the 2010 and 2014 findings by age and gender for bullying overall and for cyberbullying.

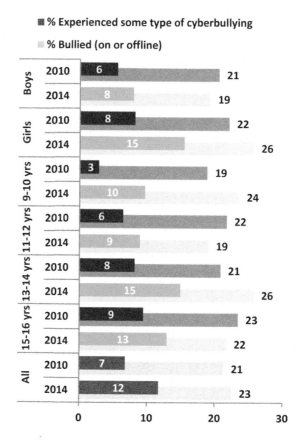

Figure 1. Being bullied off/online, by gender and age, comparing EUKO 2010 and 2014 NCGM 2014. Base: All children aged who use the Internet.

A comparison of the EUKO 2010 and NCGM 2014 findings reveals that offline bullying is no longer the dominant form of bullying experienced by young people. Overall levels of bullying have risen marginally from 21% to 23%. However, the number of children who report being bullied online or through any form on the Internet or mobile phones has nearly doubled from 7% to 12% in the period from 2011 to 2014. An increase in bullying among girls, and a slight decline among boys, is noteworthy. This is especially the case in relation to girls' reports of cyberbullying, where almost a doubling of online bullying from 8% to 15% is reported.

Age variations are also significant. There are increased reports of bullying among young children, 9–10 years of age, and among 13–14 year olds. Older teens aged 15–16 as well as 12–13report a slight decline in experiences of being bullied. However, reports of cyberbullying have increased among all groups. The most substantial increase is in fact among younger users, aged 9–10, where reports have trebled from 3% to 10% between 2011 and 2014, and doubled among 13–14-year-olds, from 8% to 15%.

3.3. What Form Does Cyberbullying Take?

Bullying can occur in many ways and in the survey children were asked if someone had treated them in a hurtful or nasty way and how this had happened. Children were also asked if they had behaved in this way to someone else. For purposes of comparison, forms of bullying included in the EU Kids Online survey were listed in addition to new forms of mobile media use. Table 2 presents the ways in which children have been bullied by age and gender.

Table 2. Ways in which children have been bullied/bullied others in the past 12 months, by age and gender (%).

	Ways in Which Children Have been Bullied					Ways in Which Children Have Bullied Others				
	9–12		13–16		All	9–12		13–16		All
	Girls	Boys	Girls	Boys		Girls	Boys	Girls	Boys	
In person/face-to-face	9	12	10	11	10	8	9	8	8	8
By mobile phone calls	1	1	1	2	2	2	2	3	1	2
By messages sent to me on my phone (SMS, text, or MMS)	2	2	6	2	3	2	2	4	2	3
On a social networking site	4	3	14	5	7	2	1	3	4	3
On a media sharing platform	0	0	2	1	1	0	1	1	1	1
By instant messaging	1	2	2	1	2	1	1	1	1	1
In a chatroom	1	1	1	0	1	0	1	1	1	1
By email					0					0
On a gaming website	3	2	1	1	2	2	1	1	2	2
Other	1	0	1	1	1	1	1	1	1	1
In any form on the Internet or through mobile phones	10	8	20	8	12	8	7	8	8	8

Base: All children who use the Internet, NCGM 2014.

While 10% of children have been bullied face-to-face, offline bullying, as noted above, is no longer the dominant mode of bullying behavior. In fact, 12% of children report being bullied through some technologically mediated form, online, or through mobile communication. The most common forms of cyberbullying reported is via a social networking site (SNS) at 7%. SMS messages and texts sent to the child's phone account for 3%, while phone calls, instant messaging, and gaming websites are each reported by 2% of children. Email, media sharing platforms, and chatrooms do not appear to be significant threats for online bullying.

Age differences are noteworthy. The youngest children are more likely to report being bullied face-to-face and on a gaming website. By contrast, teenagers are more likely to experience cyberbullying on social networking sites. Teenagers also report more experiences of cyberbullying via SMS and phone calls.

The gender differences in reports of being bullied are particularly significant. While bullying face-to-face is something of a constant across the age groups, more girls report being bullied at all, with gender being a factor in the different forms that cyberbullying takes. Overall, slightly more boys than girls reported being bullied face-to-face, especially in the younger age group. However, among teenagers, more than twice as many girls report being bullied online than boys (20% compared to 8%). Gender differences are marked in each of the dominant forms of cyberbullying: three times as many girls than boys report being bullied by SMS (6% *vs.* 2%), and girls report more than twice the amount of bullying on social networking sites (14% *vs.* 5%).

When it comes to children's accounts of bullying others, there are equal reports of bullying face-to-face as well as online bullying. Eight percent of young people report having bullied others either online or offline in the past 12 months. Younger boys are slightly more likely to have bullied others. Notably, while 13–14-year-old girls report the highest levels of being bullied on a social networking site (14%), just 3% say they have bullied others this way.

3.4. Prevalence of Cyberbullying on SNS and Mobile Platforms

The role of social networking sites is of particular interest. Social networking remains one of the most popular activities for young people online, with SNS being one of the most important venues for young people connecting, communicating, and socializing with peers, as well as identity building and self-expression [20]. EU Kids Online found in 2010 that over one-third of 9–12-year-olds and three-quarters of 13–16-year-olds who use the Internet in Europe have their own profile on a social networking site (SNS) [9]. Net Children Go Mobile reports a slight decline in this finding with 68% of children overall having at least one profile on a social networking site [21]. This is largely attributed to the decline in underage social networking use for 9–12-year-olds. Among teenagers 84% of 12–14-year-olds and 93% of 15–16-year-olds report having an SNS profile.

The role that social networking plays in experiences of cyberbullying, particularly for girls and younger children, is illustrated in Figure 2. The data shows that children, both boys and girls across all age groups, who have at least one SNS profile, are at least twice as likely to be cyberbullied as children who have no SNS profile. In particularly, 22% of 13–16-year-old girls who have at least one SNS profile are more likely to be cyberbullied, compared to 4% of girls from the same age group. Similarly, 9% of 13–16-year-old boys who have at least one SNS profile are more likely to be bullied compared to 1% of boys from the same age group. Again, gender and age differences are notable with girls and younger children (both with or without a SNS profile) are more likely to be cyberbullied.

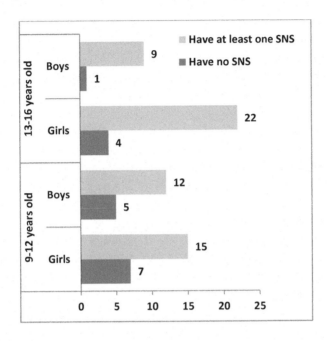

Figure 2. Children being cyberbullied, with or without SNS (%) by age and gender. *Base*: All children who use the Internet, NCGM 2014.

Yet, the pervasiveness of social networking among teenagers is just one factor in experiences of cyberbullying. The use of mobile technologies, one of the primary areas of interest for the Net Children Go Mobile study, also features strongly in young people's reports of cyberbullying. Table 3 shows that smartphone users (17%) and tablet users (15%) are more likely to have experienced any form of cyberbullying than children who do not use mobile devices at all (8%). Smartphone users are also more likely to have engaged in any form of cyberbullying. There are no differences among the different categories of Internet users in the likelihood of being bullied face-to-face and there is only a marginal difference in the likelihood of bullying others face-to-face.

Table 3. Ways in which children have been bullied in the past 12 months, comparing mobile and non-mobile Internet users (%).

	Among Smartphone Users	Among Tablet Users	Use Neither
Have experienced any form of cyberbullying	17	15	8
Been bullied in person, face-to-face	10	10	10
Have engaged in any form of cyberbullying	9	6	8
Have bullied others in person, face-to-face	8	9	8

Base: All children who use the Internet, NCGM 2014.

4. How Do Children Cope?

Building resilience and enabling young people to cope with online problems that may bother or upset them is an important objective of online safety education. Children try a range of coping strategies, when faced with upsetting experiences online. These include individual coping strategies such as trying to deal with the problem themselves; social coping strategies, which include seeking help from others; as well as technical solutions, such as blocking the sender or reporting the abuse using an online reporting tool.

According to EU Kids Online, the most common individual coping strategy for experiences of being bullied online was a proactive one whereby the child tried to solve the problem on his/her own (31%). This was followed by the more fatalistic strategy in that a quarter of children who had been bullied hoped the problem would go away by itself (24%) [8]. Net Children Go Mobile focused on social coping strategies and the forms of social support that children sought in the context of experiencing bullying. Findings from EU Kids Online have shown that most children who had been bullied (four in five or 77%) talked to somebody about it.

4.1. Seeking Social Support for Upsetting Experiences Online

In the Net Children Go Mobile project, children were asked: if they were to experience something on the Internet or when they were online that bothered them or made them upset, how likely or unlikely is it that they would talk to a parent, a sibling, friends, or others (Table 4).

Parents, both mothers and fathers, remain the primary source of social support in cases of experiencing something upsetting on the Internet. As shown in Table 4, younger children are more likely to talk to their parents than anyone else, with both girls and boys most likely to seek support from mothers (65% and 52%, respectively). However, parental support decreases with age. While teenagers are still most likely to seek support from a parent (and in this case mothers are the most likely source of social support), teenagers also turn in significant numbers to seek support from their peers.

126

Table 4. Who children are likely to talk about things that bothered them on the Internet, by age and gender.

Who Children Are Likely to Talk to When Something Bothers Them … (%)	9–12 Years		13–16 Years		All
% very likely …	Boys	Girls	Boys	Girls	
My father	43	39	29	23	33
My mother	52	65	32	44	48
My brother or sister	20	22	13	26	20
Other relatives	9	10	7	8	8
Friends	17	16	27	42	26
Teachers	10	8	4	7	7
Someone whose job is to help children	7	8	6	7	7
Another adult I trust	8	8	8	7	8

Base: All children who use the Internet, NCGM 2014.

Gender is a significant factor here. While older girls are more likely to talk with their friends (42%) and still more likely to turn to their mothers (44%), teenage boys continue to seek support from parents (29% for father and 32% for mother) more than friends (27%).

The importance of peer support in dealing with upsetting experiences of bullying is well established [22]. This survey finds that after parents, peers are the next most important form of social support. This is particularly noteworthy in the case of teenage girls, 42% of whom say they would turn to a friend about something that had upset them online. It is interesting to note also that siblings likewise offer an important form of social support: one in five of all children, a quarter of teenage girls, say that they would turn to a sibling if they were upset about something online.

Overall, children do not turn to teachers in any significant numbers. Given the importance of schools in reinforcing positive messages about online safety and in promoting effective strategies to deal with bullying, this low finding is perhaps surprising. Just 7% of children mention a teacher as a likely source of support, though younger children are somewhat more likely to talk to a teacher.

Table 5 shows that country variations are also pronounced here, with Portuguese and Belgian children more likely to look for social support (80% and 78%, respectively). By contrast, children in Denmark are the least likely to do so (56%). Mothers are the main source of support for children in all countries, especially in Portugal, Belgium, and the UK. In most countries, children are likely to talk to their mothers or fathers when something bothers them on the Internet, except Romania, where children choose their brother or sister or friends (25% and 24%, respectively) over their fathers (19%). In most countries, the percentages of children who talk to teachers when something bothers them are relatively low, varying from 4 to 7 percent, with the exception of Portuguese children (30%). However, overall, one in three children is still unlikely to ask for support from parents, peers, or teachers.

Table 5. Who children are likely to talk about things that bothered them on the Internet, by country (%).

Who Children Are Likely to Talk to When Something Bothers Them ... (%)	UK	RO	PT	IT	IE	DK	BE	All
%..very likely								
My father	35	19	53	23	31	24	45	33
My mother	50	36	68	40	45	33	62	48
My brother or sister	15	25	35	17	16	13	22	20
Other relatives	7	10	15	2	10	2	13	8
Friends	24	24	32	29	24	26	24	26
Teachers	6	6	20	3	7	4	5	7
Someone whose job is to help children	5	4	13	2	7	9	8	7
Another adult I trust	7	8	9	5	13	5	8	8
At least one of the above	64	63	80	63	65	56	78	67

Base: All children who use the Internet, NCGM 2014.

4.2. Past Experiences of Social Support

Most children (67%) say that they would talk to someone if something had bothered them online. But what about their previous experiences: have children in fact received support from parents, friends, or teachers in the past when something upset them on the Internet? Similarly, have parents, teachers, or friends spoken to them about what they would do if something ever bothered them online? Table 6 examines past experiences of having received social support from one of these sources.

Table 6 shows that parents are both the most important sources of mediation of online safety and the source of social support when something upsetting happened in the past. Fifty-seven percent of parents have spoken to their children about how to handle a problematic situation online and 41% have helped their children in the past with an upsetting experience. The role of parents in giving advice about how to cope is a constant with all age groups and somewhat higher for younger children. With the exception of older teens, parents are also the ones who have helped in specific situations that have occurred.

There is a gendered dimension to parental support. Both in terms of giving advice and actually intervening in situations where the child has been upset, parents are more likely to respond to girls than boys. There are also some interesting differences in SES in relation to parental support. While more parents from lower SES homes have spoken about how to handle an upsetting situation online, a higher proportion of parents from high SES homes have actually helped in a difficult situation that arose.

The role of peer support is one that rises steadily with age. Younger children, especially 9–10 years of age, seek social support primarily from parents. As children get older, peers become more important, equaling the role of parents for older teenagers. This is especially the case for girls, 37% of whom have been helped by friends when something upset them online.

Table 6. Social support provided by parents, friends, and teachers (%).

%	Have Helped Children in the Past When Something Bothered Them on the Internet			Have Talked to You about What You Would Do If Something on the Internet Ever Bothered You		
	Parents	Friends	Teachers	Parents	Friends	Teachers
All	41	32	23	57	33	40
Age						
9–10	42	17	22	58	19	37
11–12	43	28	21	60	28	39
13–14	42	38	21	55	39	39
15–16	36	41	27	56	42	45
Gender						
Male	36	26	21	51	28	36
Female	45	37	25	63	38	44
SES						
Low	36	32	24	65	30	30
Medium	39	32	24	60	34	34
High	51	32	24	50	35	35

Base: All children who use the Internet, NCGM 2014.

Despite the fact that just 7% of children say they would turn to a teacher if something bothered them online, one in five of all 9–16-year-olds have in fact been helped by teachers, rising to 27% of 15–16-year-olds. It is also notable that teachers actively engage with children of all ages, from 37% of 9–10-year-olds to 44% of 15–16-year-olds, on how to deal with upsetting experiences online. Again, somewhat more girls than boys report having been helped by teachers.

5. Conclusions

The findings presented by the Net Children Go Mobile project show a rise in cyberbullying compared to data revealed by EU Kids Online. EU Kids Online found that while cyberbullying was not the most prevalent risk that young people encounter online, it is the one that has the most severe impact [8]. Its findings showed that cyberbullying is a phenomenon that particularly affects teenagers, is closely associated with more intensive Internet use, and happens mostly on social networking sites [12]. With new data from seven of the original 25 countries, Net Children Go Mobile shows that while overall incidence of bullying has not increased since the EU Kids Online survey, cyberbullying is now more prevalent than face-to-face bullying and occurs most commonly on SNS.

This shift in experiences from bullying offline to online is most noticeable for girls and for early teenagers and is markedly a feature of increased use of mobile media technologies such as smartphones and tablets. More research is needed into the causes and contexts that give rise to bullying behavior. However, it is tempting to view the "always-on" connectivity afforded by portable and personal media as a contributory factor to increased reports of being bullied online. The question of whether this is a direct outcome of new media devices or rather, a result of changing ways in which children access and use the Internet requires further analysis. It is also the case that since the original EU Kids Online survey, extensive educational awareness campaigns have taken place, sensitizing young people to the phenomenon and raising awareness of bullying behavior, the role of bystanders and the blurred lines between being bullied and bullying. More generally, the Net Children Go Mobile project has tended to view the "more opportunities, more risks" hypothesis as a valid framework for understanding the changes associated with smartphones and tablets, changes that lead to more pervasive Internet access and use in children's everyday lives [21].

Acknowledgments: Funding support from the Department of Education and Skills, Central Policy Unit, and the National Digital Strategy Unit–Department of Communications Energy and Natural Resources-is gratefully acknowledged.

Author Contributions: Both authors made an equal contribution to this work.

Conflicts of Interest: The authors declare no conflict of interest.

References and Notes

1. Rice, R.; Haythornthwaite, C. *Handbook of New Media: Social Shaping and Social Consequences*; Lievrouw, L., Livingstone, S., Eds.; Sage: London, UK, 2006; pp. 92–113.
2. Boyd, D. *Taken Out of Context: American Teen Sociality in Networked Publics*; University of California: Berkeley, CA, USA, 2008.
3. Ito, M.; Horst, H.A.; Bittanti, M.; boyd, d.; Stephenson, B.H.; Lange, P.G.; Pascoe, C.J.; Robinson, L.; Baumer, S.; Cody, R.; *et al. Living and Learning with New Media: Summary of Findings from Digital Youth Project*; The MIT Press: Cambridge, MA, USA, 2009.
4. Attewell, P.; Suazo-Garcia, B.; Battle, J. Computers and Young Children: Social Benefit or Social Problem? *Social Forces* **2003**, *82*, 277–296.

5.	Kroes, N. *Towards a Better Internet for Children? Policy Pillars, Players and Paradoxes*; O'Neill, B., Staksrud, E., McLaughlin, S., Eds.; Nordicom/UNESCO Clearinghouse for Children and Media: Goteborg, Germany, 2013.

6.	*Children, Risk and Safety on the Internet: Research and Policy Challenges in Comparative Perspective*; Livingstone, S.; Haddon, L.; Görzig, A. (Eds.) Policy Press: Bristol, UK, 2012.

7.	Stald, G.; Green, L.; Barbovski, M.; Haddon, L.; Mascheroni, G.; Ságvári, B.; Scifo, B.; Tsaliki, L. *Online on the Mobile: Internet Use on Smartphones and Associated Risks among Youth in Europe*; EU Kids Online: London, UK, 2014.

8.	Livingstone, S.; Haddon, L.; Görzig, A.; Ólafsson, K. *Risks and Safety on the Internet: The Perspective of European Children. Full Findings*; EU Kids Online: London, UK, 2011.

9.	Livingstone, S.; Ólafsson, K.; Staksrud, E. *Social Networking, Age and Privacy*; EU Kids Online: London, UK, 2011.

10.	Bronfenbrenner, U.; Morris, P.A. The Bio-Ecological Model of Human Development. In *Handbook of Child Psychology*, 6th ed.; Damon, W., Lerner, R.M., Eds.; Theoretical Models of Human Development, John Wiley: New York, NY, USA, 2006; Volume 1, pp. 793–828.

11.	Livingstone, S.; Helsper, E. Children, Internet and risk in comparative perspective. *J. Child. Media* **2013**, *7*, 1–8.

12.	O'Neill, B.; Dinh, T. *Cyberbullying among 9–16 Year Olds in Ireland*; Digital Childhoods Working Paper Series, No.5; Dublin Institute of Technology, Centre for Social and Educational Research: Dublin, Ireland, 2013.

13.	Ito, M.; Baumer, S.; Bittanti, M.; boyd, d.; Cody, R.; Herr, B.; Horst, H.; Lange, P.; Mahendran, D.; Martinez, K.; *et al. Hanging Out, Messing Around, and Geeking Out: Kids Living and Learning with New Media*; MIT Press: Cambridge, MA, USA, 2009.

14.	Livingstone, S.; Haddon, L. *EU Kids Online: Final Report*; EU Kids Online: London, UK, 2009.

15.	De Haan, J. Maximising opportunities and minimizing risks for children online. In *Kids Online: Opportunities and Risks for Children*; Livingstone, S., Haddon, L., Eds.; The Policy Press: Bristol, UK, 2009.

16.	Livingstone, S.; Helsper, E. Balancing opportunities and risks in teenagers@ use of the Internet: the role of offline social-psychological factors in young people's vulnerability to online risks. *New Media Soc.* **2010**, *12*, 309–329.

17.	Jackson, C.L.; Cohen, R. Childhood victimization: Modeling the relation between classroom victimization, cyber victimization, and psychosocial functioning. *Psychol. Pop. Media Cult.* **2012**, *1*, 254–269.

18.	Mascheroni, G.; Ólafsson, K. *Net Children Go Mobile: Risks and Opportunities*, 2nd ed.; Educatt: Milano, Italy, 2014.

19.	Lampert, C.; Donoso, V. Bullying. In *Children, Risk and Safety on the Internet: Research and Policy Challenges in Comparative Perspective*; Livingstone, S., Haddon, L., Gorzig, A., Eds.; Policy Press: Bristol, UK, 2012; pp. 141–150.

20.	Van Dijck, J. Facebook as a Tool for Producing Sociality and Connectivity. *Telev. New Media* **2012**, *13*, 160–176.

21. Mascheroni, G.; Cuman, A. *Net Children Go Mobile. Final Report*; Educatt: Milano, Italy, 2014.

22. Burrell, N.A.; Zirbel, C.S.; Allen, M. Evaluating Peer Mediation Outcomes in Educational Settings: A Meta-Analytic Review. *Confl. Resolut. Q.* **2003**, *21*, 7–26.

Dutch Cyberbullying Victims' Experiences, Perceptions, Attitudes and Motivations Related to (Coping with) Cyberbullying: Focus Group Interviews

Niels C.L. Jacobs, Linda Goossens, Francine Dehue, Trijntje Völlink and Lilian Lechner

Abstract: Because of the negative effects of cyberbullying; and because of its unique characteristics; interventions to stop cyberbullying are needed. For this purpose, more insightful information is needed about cyberbullying victims' (*i.e.*, the target group) experiences, perceptions, attitudes and motivations related to (coping with) cyberbullying. Five schools with 66 low-educated Dutch adolescents between 12 and 15 (53% female) participated in 10 focus group interviews. Results show that victims do not perceive all behaviors as cyberbullying and traditional bullying is generally perceived as worse than cyberbullying. Cyberbullies are perceived as sad, cowards and embarrassing themselves. Victims are perceived as easy targets; they wear strange clothes, act in a provocative manner and have a bad appearance. These perceptions often depend on context, the level of anonymity, being in a fight or not, the person sending the message and his/her behavior. Further, victims reacted to cyberbullying by acting nonchalant, by not actually saying anything and seeking help from others (*i.e.*, parents are not often asked for help because they do not want to bother them; fear of restricted Internet privileges). It can be concluded that asking cyberbullying victims about their experiences in an open manner, and allowing them to discuss these experiences, likely results in new and insightful information compared to using self-reports. In this questioning the perception of adolescents is key to see what is perceived as cyberbullying.

Reprinted from *Societies*. Cite as: Jacobs, N.C.L.; Goossens, L.; Dehue, F.; Völlink, T.; Lechner, L. Dutch Cyberbullying Victims' Experiences, Perceptions, Attitudes and Motivations Related to (Coping with) Cyberbullying: Focus Group Interviews. *Societies* **2015**, *5*, 43–64.

1. Introduction

Worldwide, between 20% and 40% of adolescents are the victim of cyberbullying [1]. In the Netherlands, this percentage lies around 20% [2], which is similar to the worldwide prevalence. In addition, the Netherlands appears to have the highest percentage of Internet use among children between 9 and 16 years old [3]. Since heavy Internet use is related to cyberbullying and victimization [4,5], Dutch

133

children have an increased risk of being involved in cyberbullying. Cyberbullying is a repeated aggressive and intentional act, carried out by a group or an individual, using electronic forms of contact. This act is directed towards a victim who cannot easily defend him or herself [6]. Cyberbullying victimization appears to be related to a variety of negative consequences (e.g., anxiety [7], depression, emotional distress [8], suicidality [9,10], school violence and delinquency [11]). Because of the negative consequences, and because of the unique characteristics of cyberbullying (e.g., the bully can stay anonymous and reach a large audience in a relatively short amount of time [12]), some suggest that specific intervention programs are needed [13,14].

Nowadays, there are many anti-bullying websites and programs that are intended for adolescents, their parents and teachers. However, adolescents often do not (want to) talk to adults about their cyberbullying experiences [15–19]. Further, the interventions that currently exist do not specifically target cyberbullying [20], are often based on practical beliefs or commonsense approaches (*i.e.*, without a basis in theory or results of effectiveness [21]), are school-based anti-bullying interventions and/or aim at changing online risk and safety behaviors [22]. Research shows that participation in these interventions is not significantly related to change in Internet risk attitudes or behavior and, in case of the school-based anti-bullying interventions that were researched by Mishna *et al.* [22], do not affect the number of cyberbullying experiences had by students.

Until now (*i.e.*, to the authors knowledge), there are no specific anti-cyberbullying programs in the Netherlands (see the database of the Netherlands Youth Institute, www.nji.nl). A well-known program, the Finnish school-based anti-bullying program KiVa that is also implemented in the Netherlands, appears to be efficacious in addressing both traditional [23] and cyberbullying [24]. However, the unique effects of KiVa on traditional and cyberbullying are conditional on age (*i.e.*, once students were older than approximately 12.87 years, the effect of the treatment condition was no longer significant), and the effects on cyberbullying and cyber victimization were modest in size [23,24]. Williford *et al.* [24] therefore suggest that school-based anti-bullying interventions (e.g., KiVa) may need to incorporate additional components that aim specifically at reducing cyberbullying.

Hence, it is important to develop effective and evidence-based anti-cyberbullying interventions, preferably in a planned, systematic and theory-based manner [25]. These interventions should be based on thorough research and recommendations from the literature as well as directly from the target-group, and should: (1) not only increase victims' awareness of possible dangers but also give advice based on what victims need [21]; (2) increase victims' knowledge of effective coping strategies [26]; (3) reduce both traditional and cyberbullying because they often occur together [27]; and (4) use personalized information based on unique characteristics of a person [28,29]. Because most of the cyberbullying victims attend lower educational levels (*i.e.*, secondary vocational education as opposed to higher general secondary education and higher academic education) and are transferring to (junior) high school [30,31], an intervention should focus on this specific aged target-group. As mentioned before, KiVa appears to have no effects in this specific aged target-group. We therefore aim to develop a cyberbullying-specific intervention for Dutch adolescents (12–15 years) who start attending secondary vocational education [32].

To develop an intervention based on the above mentioned recommendations, insight is needed into cyberbullying victims' experiences, perceptions, attitudes and motivations related to (coping with) cyberbullying. It is important to consider these topics in adolescents' own language and words [33]. Focus group interviews could help in gaining more insightful information into what is already known, and to add this information to the current discussion about cyberbullying. A focus group interview is a guided discussion between people who share a number of characteristics. It is an adequate method for obtaining information about the ideas, feelings, attitudes and preferences of a target group. The interaction between participants often results in "in depth" information [34,35]. Focus group interviews are likely to enhance insight into the uniqueness of online experiences and needs of Dutch cyberbullying victims that will help them to combat cyberbullying.

The literature already provides general information about cyberbullying victims' experiences: they are called names, insulted, ignored, misled, hacked, and gossiped about via e-mail and messenger services [2,15,36–39]. They receive pornographic content (*i.e.*, pictures, videos), (their) pictures are forwarded [40] and manipulated, and humiliating websites are created [41]. The most common forms of cyberbullying victimization are name calling and insulting [19] or being contacted by strangers [41]. However, it is not always clear what these experiences constitute and how they take place. Researchers often use self-report questionnaires in which adolescents are not able to give detailed information about their experiences and perceptions concerning cyberbullying. In addition, these questionnaires are developed by researchers, leading to the possibility that some bullying behaviors are overseen, wrongly described, or that some online experiences are wrongly perceived as cyberbullying. It is also unknown whether cyberbullying experiences found in other countries or populations are without exceptions applicable to Dutch cyberbullying victims. Therefore, this study sets out to find more detailed information related to research question (RQ) 1:

(1) What kind of experiences do Dutch low-educated cyberbullying victims have with cyberbullying victimization and perpetration, and what do they look like?

The (qualitative) literature provides some information about adolescents' perceptions of cyberbullying. Adolescents, for example, perceive repeated, public and anonymous cyberbullying as worse than repeated, public and anonymous

135

traditional bullying [42]. Some adolescents perceive picture and video clip bullying as worse than traditional bullying; email, instant messaging, website and chat room bullying as comparable to traditional bullying; and phone call and text message bullying as less severe than traditional bullying [6,39]. Some negative online behaviors are not considered as cyberbullying but as "another way to bully just over the computer" [37] (p. 1224) or as teasing [2], cyber-teasing or cyber-arguing [41]. Vandebosch and van Cleemput [41] found that adolescents' perception of cyberbullying heavily depends on the context in which it takes place, and—in line with the definition of cyberbullying—on the power imbalance and intention to hurt. Although these studies provide important information about adolescents' perceptions, this information is not always conclusive. More information is needed (e.g., for intervention development) that is applicable to the target group, obtained without the use of self-developed and self-report questionnaires. RQ2 therefore is:

(2) How do Dutch low-educated cyberbullying victims perceive/consider experiences with cyberbullying and what is perceived as worse (traditional bullying, cyberbullying, different forms)?

Some studies suggest that a primary motivation for adolescents to cyberbully is anonymity [14,43–46], while for others it is not [19,47]. Apparently, the feeling of anonymity that many online activities entail may contribute to cyberbullying [48]. Other motivations to cyberbully that were found in individual interviews among high-school students (15–19 years) are for example jealousy, rejection, revenge, boredom, to make cyberbullies feel better about themselves, to try out new persona, and to seek approval [47]. Additionally, adolescents mentioned the lack of consequences and confrontation as reasons to cyberbully. Other studies suggest avoiding retaliation or punishment [49] and boy/girlfriend break ups [50] as motivations. Further, according to adolescents, people will become the victim of (traditional) bullying when they have a different appearance, and a bully when they have low self-esteem [51]. However, these sometimes inconclusive results—often found with self-developed self-report questionnaires—are yet to be found among Dutch victims of cyberbullying. RQ3 therefore is:

(3) Why do Dutch low-educated cyberbullying victims think people (cyber) bully (i.e., traditional and cyberbully) each other, who becomes/is a victim and who is a bully?

Research shows that having a positive attitude towards cyberbullying (e.g., cyberbullying is cool, fun, good) is associated with verbal, physical and cyberbullying and negative bystander behavior [14]. One study even found that the attitude towards cyberbullying was the strongest predictor (*i.e.*, compared to subjective norm and perceived behavioral control) of adolescents' intention to cyberbully [52].

Similarly, adolescents who have the tendency to think that aggression is appropriate are more likely to be a cyberbully [53]. Self-reported cyberbullies think that their actions are funny while cyberbully victims perceive their actions as hurtful [54], and those who are less concerned about the possible impact of cyberbullying are more likely to perpetrate in cyberbullying [31]. Although this information can (partly) be used in, for example, intervention development, more information—applicable to Dutch cyberbullying victims—is needed that is obtained without the use of self-developed and self-report questionnaires. RQ4 therefore is:

(4) Which attitudes do Dutch low-educated cyberbullying victims have towards cyberbullying?

Questionnaire-research provides information about adolescents' reactions to cyberbullying. In general, there are two types of ineffective reactions: victims either react passively (*i.e.*, one relinquishes the control of- and reactions to the stressful situation to others, or one lets other areas of life to be adversely affected by the stressful situation [55]) or aggressively (*i.e.*, one reacts to a stressful situation by physically/instrumentally, verbally or emotionally inflicting harm to oneself, another person or object). Examples of passive reactions are crying [15], doing nothing or feeling depressed/bad [56]. Examples of aggressive reactions are getting mad/angry or retaliating [2,57,58]. When victims do not react effectively, an incident can quickly and repeatedly reach a large audience [54,59]. There are, however, effective reactions that are considered to be helpful (e.g., confronting the bully [15], seeking social support [6,15,16,60,61] and blocking and deleting the bully [15,17,19]). Although many adolescents recommend asking parents for help [15,61], there are also adolescents who do not [4,16]. Asking teachers for help is generally not recommended [15,38]. Asking peers for help, [15,61] however, and acting in an assertive manner [62] are often recommended and commonly used. Again, it is unknown whether these findings—which are often collected with self-developed self-report questionnaires—are applicable to Dutch cyberbullying victims. RQ5 therefore is:

(5) How do Dutch low-educated cyberbullying victims cope with cyberbullying, and how do they perceive these coping strategies?

2. Materials and Methods

2.1. Recruitment and Participants

Twenty schools were contacted via e-mail, and were asked to contribute to the discontinuation of cyberbullying by participating in the focus group interviews. The schools were asked to seek for cyberbullying victims (*i.e.*, adolescents who (have) experience(d) cyberbullying), to provide a classroom and time to conduct the interviews. The students were subsequently told that we wanted to talk about their experiences with cyberbullying, and that their information could help us and other adolescents in combating cyberbullying. In total, five schools (response rate: 25%) located in the south of the Netherlands (provinces Limburg and Noord-Brabant) with 66 adolescents between 12 and 15 years old, participated in 10 focus group interviews; 53% was female. All participating students were attending the first class of secondary vocational education.

2.2. Procedure

Before the interviews took place, schools received informed consent forms (ICs). Students were instructed to sign the ICs, and to let their parents sign the ICs.

Each focus group consisted of six to eight (former) cyberbullying victims, with one group of four adolescents. In all interviews, two researchers were present: one as interviewer and discussion leader, the other taking notes and checking whether all questions/topics were discussed. The victims were asked permission to record the interview. We explained that no one else but the researchers had access to the recordings, and that they would be used only for research purposes. It was also stressed that all opinions and comments were welcome, and that there were no right or wrong answers. Furthermore, the rules of the focus group interviews were pointed out (e.g., respect each other's opinion, do not talk when someone else is talking). Four interviews were conducted as a pilot test for the intervention, two of them focusing solely on questions from the pilot test. These two interviews were not used in the analysis for this article.

The interviews lasted between 30 min and 1.5 h ($M = 59.1$ min, $SD = 23.35$ min), were semi-structured, but all included questions about experiences with-, perceptions of-, coping with- and attitudes about cyberbullying. Research indicates that a direct approach of asking about cyberbullying experiences (e.g., "Did you experience cyberbullying?") often results in low prevalence figures, because adolescents do not perceive all behaviors as cyberbullying [2,41], and because perception of cyberbullying appears to depend on context [54]. Because perceptions and contexts often differ between persons, we used an indirect approach (e.g., "Which of the following behaviors did you experience?"), in which we did not provide the adolescents with a definition of cyberbullying. This approach allowed us to ask follow-up questions about perceptions and contexts, and enables the adolescents to adjust their answers based on others' opinions.

The questions were printed out on paper prior to the interviews, to facilitate the interviewer and assistant in checking whether all topics were asked, and to allow for similarity in the main questions in each group. To ensure and stimulate discussion about cyberbullying, mostly open-ended questions were used. The main topics and example questions of the interviews are summarized in Table 1. When all questions were exhaustively answered the victims were thanked for their cooperation, and received some drinks and sweets.

Table 1. Interview schedule with predefined themes.

Theme	Example Questions
Experiencing cyberbullying	Which of the following cyberbullying events did you experience? What kind of cyberbullying event did you experience? What are the consequences of cyberbullying?
Performing cyberbullying	Which of the following cyberbullying events did you perform? Who cyberbullied someone else? What did you do? Why did you cyberbully someone else?
Perception of cyberbullying	How do you perceive cyberbullying? Did you perceive this behavior as cyberbullying? Why? What do you perceive as worse? Traditional or cyberbullying? Why?
Attitude about cyberbullying	What do you think about cyberbullying? What is worse? Traditional or cyberbullying? What is the worst thing about cyberbullying?
Motives for cyberbullying	Why do (you think) people cyberbully each other? Which characteristics does a victim of cyberbullying have? Which characteristics does a cyberbully have?
Coping with cyberbullying	How do you react to cyberbullying? How did your cyberbully react to your reaction? What are other possible reactions towards cyberbullying? Which reactions do you think are effective in stopping cyberbullying? Why? Do you talk about experiences with cyberbullying? With whom? Why (not)?

2.3. Data Analysis

All interviews were recorded and transcribed by the first and second author. In order to become familiar with the data, these two researchers read the transcripts repeatedly. Based on this process, and based on the questions asked in the interviews, a coding scheme was developed with main themes and subthemes (see first and second columns of Tables 3–8), using a data-driven thematic approach [63] in which we sought to find insightful information related to the research questions.

Victims talked about traditional bullying as well. Therefore, additional codes for traditional bullying were developed. Moreover, it was not always evident whether victims were talking about traditional or cyberbullying, in which case we refer to (cyber)bullying (*i.e.*, traditional and cyberbullying). The transcripts were subsequently analyzed independently by the first and second author using Qualicoder (www.qualicoder.com). Disagreement in coding was discussed. When no consensus could be reached, the third author was asked for her opinion until consensus was reached. During this process, the coding scheme was adjusted if necessary (*i.e.*, adding more elaborate definitions of categories and codes, adding additional codes). In Table 2, an overview of the (dis)agreements between coders can be found.

Table 2. Agreement and disagreement between coders.

Focus group	Coder 1		Coder 2		Agreement	Fragments without Consensus
	Number of fragments coded	Disagreement with coder 2	Number of fragments coded	Disagreement with coder 1		
Interview 1	197	74 (37,56%)	224	101 (45,09%)	123	19
Interview 2	88	20 (22,72%)	89	21 (23,60%)	68	0
Interview 3	220	31 (14,09%)	226	37 (16,37%)	189	0
Interview 4	128	19 (14,84%)	134	25 (18,66%)	109	0
Interview 5	24	6 (25%)	27	11 (40,74%)	18	0
Interview 6	41	5 (12,20%)	45	9 (20%)	36	0
Interview 7	4	0 (0%)	4	0 (0%)	4	0
Interview 8	18	1 (5,56%)	19	3 (15,79%)	17	0

2.4. Ethics Approval

The Ethical Commission of the psychology department of the Open University in the Netherlands judged the focus group interviews as non-medical research and concluded that the victims were not "subjected to procedures or required to follow certain rules of behavior" [64]. Therefore, ethical approval of the Regional Medical Ethics committee in the Netherlands was not necessary.

3. Results

First, experiences (*i.e.*, victimization and perpetration) with cyberbullying and traditional bullying will be discussed (3.1). Next, victims' perceptions of (cyber)bullying (*i.e.*, what is (not) seen as (cyber)bullying and characteristics of victims and bullies) is discussed (3.2), followed by motivations to cyberbully (3.3), attitudes (3.4), and coping strategies used in response to cyberbullying (3.5)). Although we did not set out to find information about consequences, victims talked about consequences (3.6). Each topic (1–5) has a table with (additional) examples (*i.e.*, Tables 3–9).

3.1. Experiences with Victimization and Perpetration in (Cyber)bullying

3.1.1. What Kind of Experiences do Dutch Low-Educated Cyberbullying Victims Have with Cyberbullying Victimization in Cyberbullying, and What do They Look Like?

Victims indicated having experienced 16 different forms (see Table 3 "subthemes") of cyberbullying victimization. The most common forms of cyberbullying victimization in several groups were being called names and being ridiculed. Being ignored by someone else and being threatened also occurred quite often, however, more among boys than girls. In four groups, victims experienced that someone—known (e.g., brother) or unknown to them—pretended to be someone else (*i.e.*, impersonation), which made it possible to bully anonymously. In three groups, victims experienced that others lied to them. In five groups, some victims received anonymous e-mails or phone-calls. Less common forms of cyberbullying victimization were, for example, one's picture being placed upon a voting website (two groups), receiving mail bombs (one group), being misled by someone else (one group), breaking into the computer (one group), receiving pornographic content (two groups), and being deleted by someone (one group).

Table 3. Main themes, subthemes and examples for experiences with traditional and cyberbullying.

Final Themes	Subthemes	Examples
	Being called names	Boy: "On the Internet I was playing around on Facebook, and this girl from my old school started calling me names ... "
	Being ignored	Girl: " ... I was in a fight with someone, I think, and then they ignored me."
	Being deleted	Girl: " ... she deleted me, now she isn't talking to me anymore, thank god!"
	Being gossiped about	No examples, only raised hands
	Being threatened	Boy: "Once, I received a text message which stated that someone would enter my room around midnight. However, it didn't happen."
	Being mislead	No examples, only raised hands
Experiences with cyberbullying	Being lied to	Girl: "Yeah, they just lied to me."
	Impersonation	Boy: "And from someone else, I don't know exactly who it was, but he sent me messages with four-letter words."
	Being placed upon a voting website	No examples, only raised hands
	Being threatened	Girl: " ... I got in a fight with a girl via Hyves* and she was calling me names and said: 'When I see you, I'll hit you in the face'."
	Uploading unwanted pictures	Girl: "They posted a picture of me on Hyves* while I was sleeping."
	Breaking in	Boy: "Nothing happened to my computer, but now and again someone took over the control over my mouse."
	Changing passwords	Girl: "On my MSN messenger, I don't know who it was. I wanted to log in but it didn't work anymore."

Table 3. *Cont.*

Final Themes	Subthemes	Examples
Experiences with traditional bullying	Receiving mail bombs	Boy: "Yesterday I checked my Inbox and then there were 493 unread messages about stuff you can buy."
	Receiving pornographic materials	Boy: "Once I went to Hyves* and someone added me and started sending me nasty pictures."
	Receiving anonymous e-mails/phone-calls	Boy: "The past few weeks someone was calling me and then my phone displays 'Blocked number'. The caller has a thing, a strange voice. And then I think I know who it is, but then he isn't."
	Being called names	Girl: "They call everybody hooker and bitch and so on."
	Being beaten up/ physical bullying	Boy: "Continuously calling me names, pushing me, stuff like that. They tried to throw me on the floor, stuff like that. Eight kids standing around me."
	Being threatened	Girl: "In this class, some girls came to my house."
	Being excluded	Girl: "They started making noises I didn't like and started gossiping about me and counting me out. I really didn't like that."

* Hyves was (until December 2013) a Dutch social networking site.

Inevitably, victims also talked about traditional bullying victimization. Victims from six groups indicated being bullied in a non-specified way. In the same six groups, victims were physically bullied (e.g., kicking, hitting, pushing), and in five groups they were called names. Other, less occurring traditional forms of bullying victimization were being threatened, being excluded and being gossiped about.

3.1.2. What Kind of Experiences do Dutch Low-Educated Cyberbullying Victims Have with Cyberbullying Perpetration, and What do They Look Like?

Victims mentioned performing nine specific forms of (cyber)bullying (*i.e.*, it was not always apparent whether they were talking about traditional or cyberbullying, some behaviors occur in both forms of bullying). For instance, in one group, all girls have ridiculed or called someone names. In another group, a girl said: "sometimes as a joke.". In a third group, a common form of perpetrating in traditional bullying was insulting someone. In the same group, some girls also gossiped about someone. Victims from three groups ignored someone once or twice. Almost all victims from one group also lied to someone. Other, less occurring perpetrations of cyberbullying were threatening someone, changing passwords and uploading unwanted pictures. Additionally, two boys impersonated themselves.

3.2. How do Dutch Low-Educated Cyberbullying Victims Perceive/Consider Experiences with Cyberbullying and What is Perceived as Worse?

In five groups, victims mostly talked about what was (not) seen as (cyber)bullying. There was no agreement on, for example, receiving a mail bomb and calling names, since a girl said: "Some people think the word 'loser' is calling names. However, when I call ——[1] a loser, she won't get angry. Right this morning I called her loser. I don't think that's bullying.". However, another girl said: "It depends, when you're in a fight you call each other names and offend each other as well, that doesn't mean that it's bullying. However, when they always do that, and with more people, then I think it is.". Similarly, there was no agreement on threatening. One girl said: "With threatening, people try to scare you and with bullying this isn't the case. Therefore I think it isn't bullying." and another girl said " ... when you say 'Watch out, tonight at eight o clock I will be standing in front of your house', then I think this is pretty bad.". Some even consider threatening as being worse than (cyber)bullying. In addition, on being offended no agreement was found. There was agreement on talking negative about family, which victims from different groups always considered as cyberbullying, and lying, which victims do not considered as cyberbullying, even when it is done repeatedly or by an unknown person.

Whether something was seen as (cyber)bullying depended on: (1) the context: for example, repetitiveness, anonymity and the person sending the message were mentioned; (2) the content of the message or photo; and (3) whether the person was willing to delete it (e.g., boys and girls: "It depends on what kind of picture it is and who posted the picture. It also depends on whether that person deletes the picture immediately when you ask for it.").

3.3. Why do Dutch Low-Educated Cyberbullying Victims Think People (Cyber)Bully Each Other, Who Becomes/Is a Victim and Who is a Bully?

Victims mentioned several possible reasons why others are (cyber)bullied; for example, clothing, having a bad appearance, and being an (easy) target (e.g., girl: "People sent out a certain message or ask for it."). In two groups, victims mentioned that others bully because they are in a bad mood, they want to be popular, they want to feel better about themselves, they are jealous or they act out on someone. Some said that bullies are insecure, while others said they are not. In one group, all victims agreed that everybody can be a bully.

---

[1] —— = anonymized name.

Table 4. Main themes, subthemes and examples for cyberbullying perpetration.

Final Themes	Subthemes	Examples
Performing cyberbullying	Calling names/ridiculing	Girl: "Calling names and ignoring, and ridiculing and stuff . . . "
	Changing passwords	Girl: "On my brother's phone, just as a joke."
	Gossiping	Girl: "For example gossiping, or directly to the person, just like —."
	Ignoring	No examples, only raised hands
	Insulting someone	Boy: "And, I don't know how I said it, but I think I said 'It doesn't smell so nice over here' while I was standing next to him. Well, like 'It smells over here'. It wasn't really nice."
	Lying to someone	No examples, only raised hands
	Misleading/impersonation	Boy: "A friend of mine received a text message, and then I send a message to the sender pretending to be my brother. I told him I was 17 and that I would get to him. He then stopped texting."
	Threatening	Boy: " . . . with a friend, we anonymously send a mail mentioning 'if you don't stop you'll die'."
	Uploading unwanted pictures	Girl: "Once I was in a bad fight with a girl, and then I Photo shopped her head on Lolo Ferrari and posted the picture on Hyves*, and stuff like that."

* Hyves was (until December 2013) a Dutch social networking site. —- Anonymized name.

Table 5. Main themes, subthemes and examples for perceptions of (cyber)bullying.

Final Themes	Subthemes	Examples
Perception of (cyber)bullying	Characteristics of a victim	Boy: " . . . they're insecure, but they also often walk alone. And that's an appearance like, I am just saying, I don't have any friends and thus I'm kind of bait."
	Characteristics of a bully	Girl: "Yes everybody can be a bully. Whether it's someone who's very small with glasses and whatever, or someone who's very tall and who looks like a bully . . . ")
	Seen as (cyber)bullying	Boy: "When you just had a fight, and when someone isn't talking back to you on Hyves*. I think this is cyberbullying because you try to make it up and that person perhaps doesn't even see your attempts, he just clicks your message away."
	Not seen as (cyber)bullying	Girl: "Sometimes I think calling names isn't bullying, sometimes you do that as friends..."

* Hyves was (until December 2013) a Dutch social networking site.

Table 6. Main themes, subthemes and examples for motivations for (cyber)bullying.

Final Themes	Subthemes	Examples
Motivations to bully/ being bullied	Cyberbullying victims	Girl: "So provoking others and being lonely, then you're being an easy target."
	Cyberbullying bullies	Girl: "A bully is insecure at the moment, I think."

3.4. Which Attitudes do Dutch Low-Educated Cyberbullying Victims have towards Cyberbullying?

When talking about being (cyber)bullied, a lot of negative attitudes were given (e.g., boy: "No, once I got bullied really bad, and now I know how it feels. It really isn't funny.") In several groups, victims considered both traditional and cyberbullying as cowardly. Other opinions about cyberbullies were given in response to someone talking about being cyberbullied (e.g., boy: "Then you're a really sad person."; and boy: " … I think they embarrass themselves."). In response to the question whether cyberbullying is worse than traditional bullying, a girl answered: "Yes, I think it is.". Others thought that traditional bullying was worse. Additionally, when talking about performing bullying, a girl mentioned: "I don't do that. When I don't like it myself, I'll not do it to others.".

Table 7. Main themes, subthemes and examples of attitudes about (cyber)bullying.

Final Themes	Subthemes	Examples
Attitudes	Cyberbullying	Girl: "I think it's cowardly when you don't have the balls to say something to me in real life, like 'you're a hooker'. When someone says that to me via the Internet, than he's a coward."
	Specific forms of (cyber)bullying	Girl: "When the four-letter words aren't that bad I don't mind that much."
	Cyberbullying compared to traditional bullying	Boy: "When they kick you or hit you offline, then I think it's worse than online."

3.5. How do Dutch Low-Educated Cyberbullying Victims Cope with Cyberbullying, and How do They Perceive These Coping Strategies?

3.5.1. Aggressive Coping

A wide variety of aggressive coping responses were given. In some groups, some of the victims got angry after being cyberbullied. However, the most often used and discussed aggressive coping strategy was retaliation, which was mentioned in four groups (e.g., girl: " . . . when someone does that (*i.e.*, offending or calling names) to me, yeah then I have the tendency to do the same."). The most used strategies in response to traditional bullying were fighting back (*i.e.*, getting physical), and retaliating (*i.e.*, calling names), which were mentioned in four groups. Many victims also got angry in response to traditional bullying. Only one girl mentioned that she once agreed to meet for a fight.

3.5.2. Passive Coping

In seven groups, the most often discussed passive coping strategy was doing nothing or ignoring the cyberbullying. Another way of doing nothing that was mentioned was sending the word "OK", as was described by a girl: "One reaction that works really well is sending an 'O' and a 'K'. 'OK' means okay, nobody likes that. Like you aren't responding.". Later on she told us: "Yes it's just on Twitter, when someone calls me a hooker, then I just say 'OK'.". Another passive coping strategy that was often mentioned in four groups was acting nonchalant or thinking "I don't care". A third, less often used passive coping strategy was thinking positive or putting things in perspective, which was mentioned in three groups.

3.5.3. Active Coping

Victims mentioned several strategies that can be considered as active coping. For example, in four groups, blocking and deleting was mentioned. Other frequently used strategies (*i.e.*, mentioned in five groups) were standing up for oneself, and sometimes the adolescents stood up for someone else. Additionally, victims also mentioned talking about the event. One girl mentioned that seeming self-assured is a good strategy to use, and a boy mentioned: "You could save it in your history, then it will be mentioned in history and then your parents and police will be able to read it.".

3.5.4. Seeking Support Coping

A lot of victims considered seeking social support as a good strategy to use. They mentioned support in general, but also specified their source of support (e.g., parents, teachers, siblings/family, friends). When talking about parents as a source of support, there was a lot of ambiguity. On the one hand, victims told us that they went to their parents and received effective help (e.g., boy: "Then my mother found out and went to my school. Since then they never bullied me again and I don't suffer from it anymore.") or did not receive help. On the other hand, some victims mentioned that they did not want to bother their parents (e.g., boy: "No, but I'll not tell my parents. It would only be bad for them, because they'll stress out and stuff. While that's not necessary at all, I think.") or that their help would be irritating (e.g., girl: "When you tell your parents they'll react like a parent. That's really annoying!").

Table 8. Main themes, subthemes and examples of coping with cyberbullying.

Final Themes	Subthemes	Examples
Aggressive coping	Getting angry online	Girl: "It doesn't make me sad, I just get really angry when people do stuff like that … "
	Retaliating/calling names online	Boy: "When someone does that to me, I do it back, to be honest."
	Agreeing to meet for a fight offline	Girl: "Very stupid, but then we waylaid for her. We did not really waylaid for her but agreed to waylay, this sounds really stupid, however different things happened."
	Fighting back/getting physical offline	Boy: "Only then he kept doing it. Okay, I wasn't supposed to do that, but I grabbed him in his neck, well not lifting him up, and I pushed him with his head against the door. And then I just reacted really angry. Anger attack. Because I warned him, but he kept doing it and kept provoking me."
	Getting angry offline	Girl: "Getting angry. Then I start yelling, hitting and I grab the nearest painful object and throw it at their heads."
	Retaliating/calling names offline	Boy: "When they call me names, then I do it back three times worse."

Table 8. *Cont.*

Final Themes	Subthemes	Examples
Active coping	Blocking and deleting	Boy: "Once I was on Hyves* and someone added me and started sending me nasty pictures. Then I told my mom. After that, I immediately deleted and blocked him."
	Seem self-assured	Girl: "Loosen up a little bit in class and try to not look insecure. People will respect you more and they'll stop bullying you eventually. That's how it went with me."
	Standing up for oneself	Boy: "Yeah I once said 'What you're saying to me, you wouldn't like it when I said that to you … "
	Standing up for someone else	Girl: "Then I completely freaked out on him and told him 'Go and cry to your mommy'. Because I don't stand it when they do something like that to my friends. I was really angry!"
	Talking about it	Girl: "After a time you just try to talk, because then you both will be more calm and will be able to talk about it. However, it depends on what the person said."
Passive coping	Doing nothing/ignoring (the message)	Boy: "Someone, I don't know who, called me names on Twitter and then I just let it happen, I didn't know him so I didn't reacted to it."
	Nonchalance/ I do not care	Girl: "When they call me for example a hooker via the Internet, then I just let that happen. I don't care. I just know that I am not."
	Quitting school	Girl: " … when it happened at my old school, I just thought 'I'll go to another school' … "
	Putting things in perspective/ positive thinking	Boy: "When they call me names, I always think ' Yeah, you can call me names, but the only thing you do is making yourself look smaller and you make a fool out of yourself."

Table 8. *Cont.*

Final Themes	Subthemes	Examples
Seeking support coping	Friends	Girl: "Most of my friends help me pretty good."
	Parents	Boy: "I just go to my mom, then I tell my mom and dad what's going on and they tell me what I should do."
	Teachers	Girl: "I went to talk to my mentor."
	Siblings/family	Girl: "Once my sister came to this school, they did not dare to bully me anymore. I wouldn't tell her, but when she hears I'm in trouble, she immediately comes and helps me."
	Not seeking support/loneliness	Girl: "Most of the time I don't talk about it to no one, really no one. And I keep it to myself."

* Hyves was (until December 2013) a Dutch social networking site.

When asked who turns to their friends for help, a boy mentioned: "Yes, I think that everybody does that.". Otherwise, mostly girls mentioned that they turned to their friends for help. Teachers were mentioned in six groups, however, talking to teachers was not always perceived as useful (e.g., boy: "Occasionally, I went to a teacher, however they hardly did something about it. They only said 'We'll keep an eye out' and even that they didn't do."). Other sources of support are siblings (*i.e.*, brothers and sisters) or family (*i.e.*, aunts, nephews). Some victims did not seek help. When asked whether they turn to someone for help a girl said: "No, I think it's my own problem, I can solve it myself.".

3.6. Consequences

Although we did not set out to find information concerning consequences, there were two types of consequences mentioned by the victims. The first type are the consequences of (cyber)bullying victimization. Several victims from different groups mentioned feeling depressed, bad and angry. Some said that the consequences of experiencing (cyber)bullying could last a lifetime (e.g., boy: "Most of the bullies forget the event, but victims experience the consequences for the rest of their lives.").

The second type were consequences of certain coping strategies in response to cyberbullying. Consequences of getting angry were, for example, fights or the bully going offline. For some, getting angry helped, for others it did not. Additionally, a boy mentioned that ignoring and positive thinking helped. Active coping and seeking support often resulted in the discontinuation of cyberbullying (e.g., girl: "I just say to them: 'If you want to call me names, come and find me and say it to my face.' Then they stop saying things to me." or boy: "On the Internet I was just playing around on Facebook and then there was a girl who attended my previous school, and she started calling me names and then I then blocked her and didn't accept her on my profile."). After that, the bullying stopped. However, in some cases acting active/effectively did not help (e.g., boy: "Yeah I once said 'What you're saying to me, you wouldn't like it when I said that to you', however it didn't help.").

Table 9. Main themes, subthemes and examples of consequences of (coping with) (cyber)bullying victimization.

Final Themes	Subthemes	Examples
Consequences	Victimization	Girl: "A really bad feeling..."
	Coping	Boy: "I became more angry and angry, so eventually there was a big fight, however since then they don't do anything anymore."

4. Discussion & Conclusions

In this study, we aimed to find relevant insightful information into Dutch cyberbullying victims' experiences, perceptions, attitudes and motivations related to (coping with) cyberbullying. We expected that focus group interviews would enable us to get this information. Indeed, this study found new and insightful information that, for example, can be used in intervention development. Before discussing the results, however, a notable finding was made: a lot of victims spontaneously talked about experiences with traditional bullying as well (*i.e.*, physical bullying, being called names, being threatened, and being excluded). This finding can be explained by the large overlap between involvement in traditional and cyberbullying [4,65]: about 40% of the adolescents who had experienced online harassment did also experienced traditional bullying [66]. Subsequently, cyberbullying is seen as another form of bullying [39,43]. This suggests that interventions should focus on both forms of bullying [27].

In answering RQ1 (*i.e.*, What kind of experiences do Dutch low-educated cyberbullying victims have with cyberbullying victimization and perpetration, and what do they look like?), all participants were victimized but many also perpetrated in cyberbullying (often in response to someone else bullying them). Indeed, the literature shows correlations between victimization and perpetration of cyberbullying [67]. Similar to Juvonen and Gross [19], this study found that being called names and being ridiculed (*i.e.*, insulted) were the most often mentioned victimization behaviors. Besides confirming earlier findings, this study also found new cyberbullying victimization (e.g., being posted upon a voting website, breaking into the computer) and perpetration behaviors (e.g., lying to someone else, changing passwords). It seems that when asking victims about their experiences in an open manner, and allowing them to discuss these experiences, more information is found compared to using self-report questionnaires. Additionally, victims automatically talked about possible consequences (e.g., feeling depressed, bad, angry) of being victimized online. Furthermore, although some research mentions that boys are more often the perpetrators of cyberbullying [2,68], a prominent finding of the present study is that mostly girls perpetrated in the above mentioned behaviors. A possible explanation could be that cyberbullying is in some respects like indirect bullying, in which girls are more often involved [6].

Several studies (e.g., [69,70]) recommend that one should explicitly ask participants about their involvement in specific negative behaviors. In relation to RQ2 (*i.e.*, How do Dutch low-educated cyberbullying victims perceive/consider experiences with cyberbullying and what is perceived as worse?), this study found that victims do not perceive all specific negative behaviors as cyberbullying (*i.e.*, being lied to online, calling names) and thus this approach could give a distorted picture. Apparently, calling names is considered as "normal" communication (*i.e.*, even friends call each other names). Victims do not agree with each other on perceiving certain behaviors as cyberbullying (e.g., calling names/being offended, receiving mail bombs, threatening). Victims did perceive—and agreed on—talking negatively about family as cyberbullying. Additionally, being deleted by someone was not completely perceived as negative (*i.e.*, adolescent experienced relief) as was found in [42]. Although some victims perceived cyberbullying as worse than traditional bullying (as was found in [42]), most agreed on traditional bullying being worse than cyberbullying: offline, a message cannot be deleted or ignored, and people can physically hurt you. Furthermore, considering something as cyberbullying in this study indeed depends on the context [4,41] and the level of anonymity [48]. A new finding is that it depends whether the persons involved are in a fight (or not) and on the behavior of the person sending the message (e.g., willing to delete it).

Regarding RQ3 (*i.e.*, Why do Dutch low-educated cyberbullying victims think people (cyber)bully each other, who becomes/is a victim and who is a bully?) this study found motivations to cyberbully reported in previous studies (e.g., jealousy, boredom, to redirect feelings, to feel better, to seek approval, confrontation). Although victims indicated being an occasional victim or bully of cyberbullying, they mostly mentioned motivations why others are being cyberbullied or why others cyberbully, not motivations why they got bullied or why they bully. When talking about motivations, the perspective changes from talking about personal experiences (RQ1) to talking about what others experienced (RQ3). Apparently, victims do not see themselves as cyberbullying victims, but rather as adolescents who once or twice experienced cyberbullying. Similarly, they do not see themselves as cyberbullies but rather as adolescents who occasionally tease someone else, and therefore cannot be called bullies. These findings suggest that the repeated nature, as mentioned in Smith's *et al.* [6] definition of cyberbullying, really is important in the perception of cyberbullying: single or occasional events are not often perceived as cyberbullying. Future studies should look into which frequency of cyberbullying determines when and if an adolescent perceives something as cyberbullying. In addition, as discussed before, some behaviors are not seen as cyberbullying (e.g., gossiping, calling each other names while being friends), and perception depends on the context and/or being in a fight. In case of these behaviors—contexts and being in a fight—apparently adolescents do not always see themselves as cyberbully or cyberbullying victim. Nevertheless, according to the majority of the participants of this study, everybody can be a cyberbully, and cyberbullies are often insecure. Further, victims mentioned that one's appearance (e.g., easy targets, wear strange clothes, provoke and have a bad appearance) determines becoming a (cyber)bullying victim, which was previously found in traditional bullying [51]. Unfortunately, it was not always clear whether the victims were talking about cyberbullying or only about traditional bullying.

In relation to RQ4 (*i.e.*, Which attitudes do Dutch low-educated cyberbullying victims have towards cyberbullying?), victims provided several negative attitudes (e.g., someone who perpetrates in cyberbullying is sad, a coward and embarrasses him/herself). However, some of these victims also perpetrated (once or twice) in (cyber)bullying, suggesting that having a negative attitude towards (cyber)bullying does not mean that one will not (cyber)bully themselves. A possible explanation—found in response to asking victims about motivations—could be that victims do not perceive themselves as (cyber)bully when they, for example, retaliate or bully occasionally (*i.e.*, once or twice). Further, and new to the literature, some victims disapproved of perpetrating cyberbullying behavior because of reciprocal reasons (e.g., "When I don't like it myself, I'll not do it to others.").

In exploring RQ5 (*i.e.*, How do Dutch low-educated cyberbullying victims cope with cyberbullying, and how do they perceive these strategies?), this study found aggressive, passive as well as active/effective strategies. The most often mentioned aggressive strategies that were also found in the literature were getting angry [58] —which often resulted in the bully going offline, the message being changed or deleted by the bully, or in a fight—and retaliating [2,71]. The most often mentioned passive strategy that was also found in the literature was doing nothing or ignoring the bully [2], which appeared to be a successful strategy. New to the literature were acting nonchalant and reacting by not actually saying anything (e.g., sending "OK" as a response), which was perceived as helpful.

The most often used active/effective strategies that were also previously found in the literature were blocking and deleting [15,17,19], confronting the bully or standing up for oneself [15], and seeking parents', teachers', siblings/family's and friends' support [6,15,16,60,61]. In general, these strategies are effective in discontinuing bullying, although some adolescents also experienced that the cyberbullying continued. Additionally, victims also stood up for someone else. Further, victims either mentioned talking to adults and receiving effective help (e.g., comfort, parents intervening) or mentioned not wanting to talk to adults because they (as found in the literature): (1) do not want to bother their parents [16]; (2) have the feeling that adults would not be able to help them [72]; (3) have the perception that their friends are more tech-savvy [15]; (4) have experienced that teachers would not react [16]; (5) have the feeling that parents were able to restrict or deny their access to the internet, which could isolate them from their friends and peers [4]; and (6) wanted to solve the problem themselves. Moreover, adolescents mentioned a preference of turning to their friends and other family members (e.g., siblings, nieces/nephews) for support [72].

This study has several strengths and limitations. This study seemed to result into more insightful information than when using a quantitative design. Subsequently, this led to some findings that are not previously reported in the literature. However, this study did not compare qualitative with quantitative designs but merely compared qualitative with quantitative results, suggesting that we cannot conclude that qualitative designs result in more information than quantitative designs. Furthermore, this study is one of the first qualitative studies that included adolescents that had just started to attend lower secondary vocational education. A limitation of this study, on the other hand, is the voluntary cooperation of participants. This may bias the results in that the opinions of victims who do not want/dare to talk about their experiences are overseen. Another limitation is the fact that there were no "pure cyberbullies" included in this study, which may have led to one-sided views. Future research should focus on the views of "pure cyberbullies", because this information might be helpful in reducing cyberbullying as well. Additionally, in this study we did not ask specifically who perceived themselves as a bully or as a victim, and when one perceived themselves as a bully or victim, which may have led to less interpretable results. Future research should also consider these self-perceptions.

In conclusion, the focus group method seems to be promising in finding unstudied concepts related to cyberbullying. It appears that victims perceive traditional and cyberbullying to be related, suggesting that interventions should focus on both forms of bullying. Furthermore, an indirect approach of asking about experiences (e.g., Which of the following behaviors did you experience?) could result in an overestimation of prevalence figures, because victims do not perceive all behaviors as cyberbullying. A direct approach (e.g., How many times were you cyberbullied?) could result in an underestimation of prevalence figure. Therefore, victims should be asked whether they perceive certain behaviors as (cyber)bullying, and they should be given a clear definition of cyberbullying, in addition to asking them indirectly about cyberbullying. Further, both boys and girls are victims and perpetrators of cyberbullying, suggesting that interventions should offer a wide variety of information to both boys and girls. Furthermore, an intervention should not communicate that it focuses on victims of cyberbullying, because a lot of adolescents do not perceive themselves as victims. It appears that the focus group method results in at least the same findings as questionnaire research; however, this study also found some new and unstudied concepts. These results can be used in the development of effective interventions with a primary focus on cyberbullying. However, since a lot of overlap exists between traditional and cyberbullying, as suggested by this study, these interventions can have a secondary focus and effect on traditional bullying as well. These results can also directly provide content for a program in a language that members of the target group speak and understand.

Author Contributions: N.J. and L.G. conceived of the study, recruited participants and drafted the manuscript. N.J. conducted the interviews, T.V. (twice) and L.G. (six times) assisted N.J. in conducting the interviews. N.J. and L.G. independently coded the transcripts, compared the coding and adjusted the coding scheme. F.D. and T.V. served as back-up coders in case of disagreement between N.J. and L.G., F.D. and T.V. helped recruiting participants, helped to draft the manuscript and helped in drafting the final manuscript. L.L. supervised the whole research and helped with drafting and writing the final manuscript. N.J. processed all feedback from the other authors and reviewers. All authors read and approved of the final manuscript.

Conflicts of Interest: The authors declare no conflict of interest.

References

1. Tokunaga, R.S. Following you home from school: A critical review and synthesis of research on cyberbullying victimization. *Comput. Human Behav.* **2010**, *26*, 277–287.
2. Dehue, F.; Bolman, C.; Völlink, T. Cyberbullying: Youngsters' experiences and parental perception. *Cyberpsychol. Behav.* **2008**, *11*, 217–223.
3. Livingstone, S.; Haddon, L.; Görzig, A.; Olafsson, K. *Risks and Safety on the Internet: The Perspective of European Children: Full Findings and Policy Implications from the EU Kids Online Survey of 9–16 Year Olds and Their Parents in 25 Countries 2011*; LSE: London, UK.
4. Kowalski, R.M.; Limber, S.P.; Agatston, P.W. *Cyber Bullying: Bullying in the Digital Age*; Blackwell Publishing: Malden, MA, USA, 2008.
5. Ybarra, M.L.; Mitchell, K.J. Youth engaging in online harassment: Associations with caregiver-child relationships, Internet use, and personal characteristics. *J. Adolesc.* **2004**, *27*, 319–336.

6. Smith, P.K.; Mahdavi, J.; Carvalho, M.; Fisher, S.; Russell, S.; Tippett, N. Cyberbullying: Its nature and impact in secondary school pupils. *J. Child Psychol. Psychiatry* **2008**, *49*, 376–385.

7. Campbell, M.A.; Spears, B.; Slee, P.; Butler, D.; Kift, S. Victims' perceptions of traditional and cyberbullying, and the psychosocial correlates of their victimisation. *Emot. Behav. Difficulties* **2012**, *17*, 389–401.

8. Perren, S.; Dooley, J.; Shaw, T.; Cross, D. Bullying in school and cyberspace: Associations with depressive symptoms in Swiss and Australian adolescents. *Child Adolesc. Psychiatry Ment. Health* **2010**, *4*, 1–10.

9. Hinduja, S.; Patchin, J.W. Bullying, Cyberbullying, and Suicide. *Arch. Suicide Res.* **2010**, *14*, 206–221.

10. Schneider, S.K.; O'Donnell, L.; Stueve, A.; Coulter, R.W.S. Cyberbullying, school bullying, and psychological distress: A regional census of high school students. *Am. J. Public Health* **2012**, *102*, 171–177.

11. Hinduja, S.; Patchin, J.W. Offline Consequences of Online Victimization. *J. Sch. Violence* **2007**, *6*, 89–112.

12. Smith, P.K.; del Barrio, C.; Tokunaga, R.S. Definitions of bullying and cyberbullying: How useful are the terms. In *Principles of Cyberbullying Research: Definitions, Measures Methodology*; Bauman, S., Cross, D., Walker, J., Eds.; Routledge: London, UK, 2013; pp. 26–45.

13. Kiriakidis, S.P.; Kavoura, A. A Review of the Literature on Harassment Through the Internet and Other Electronic Means. *Fam. Community Health* **2010**, *11*, 82–93.

14. Williams, K.R.; Guerra, N.G. Prevalence and Predictors of Internet Bullying. *J. Adolesc. Health* **2007**, *41*, S14–S21.

15. Aricak, T.; Siyahhan, S.; Uzunhasanoglu, A.; Saribeyoglu, S.; Ciplak, S.; Yilmaz, N.; Memmedov, C. Cyberbullying among Turkish adolescents. *Cyberpsychol. Behav.* **2008**, *11*, 253–261.

16. Hoff, D.L.; Mitchell, S.N. Cyberbullying: Causes, effects, and remedies. *J. Educ. Adm.* **2009**, *47*, 652–665.

17. Kowalski, R.M.; Limber, S.P. Electronic Bullying Among Middle School Students. *J. Adolesc. Heal.* **2007**, *41*, S22–S30.

18. Perren, S.; Corcoran, L.; Cowie, H.; Dehue, F.; Garcia, D.; Mc Guckin, C.; Ševčíková, A.; Tsatsou, P.; Völlink, T. Cyberbullying and traditional bullying in adolescence: Differential roles of moral disengagement, moral emotions, and moral values. *Eur. J. Dev. Psychol.* **2012**, *9*, 195–209.

19. Juvonen, J.; Gross, E.F. Extending the school grounds?—Bullying experiences in cyberspace. *J. Sch. Health.* **2008**, *78*, 496–505.

20. Slonje, R.; Smith, P.K.; Frisén, A. The nature of cyberbullying, and strategies for prevention. *Comput. Human Behav.* **2013**, *29*, 26–32.

21. Snakenborg, J.; van Acker, R.; Gable, R.A. Cyberbullying: Prevention and Intervention to Protect Our Children and Youth. *Prev. Sch. Fail* **2011**, *55*, 88–95.

22. Mishna, F.; Cook, C.; Saini, M.; Wu, M.; MacFadden, R. Interventions to Prevent and Reduce Cyber Abuse of Youth: A Systematic Review. *Res. Soc. Work Pract.* **2011**, *21*, 5–14.

23. Kärnä, A.; Voeten, M.; Little, T.D.; Poskiparta, E.; Kaljonen, A.; Salmivalli, C. A Large-Scale Evaluation of the KiVa Antibullying Program: Grades 4–6. *Child Dev.* **2011**, *82*, 311–330.

24. Williford, A.; Elledge, L.C.; Boulton, A.J.; dePaolis, K.J.; Little, T.D.; Salmivalli, C. Effects of the KiVa antibullying program on cyberbullying and cybervictimization frequency among Finnish youth. *J. Clin. Child Adolesc. Psychol.* **2013**, *42*, 820–833.

25. Bartholomew, L.K.; Parcel, G.S.; Kok, G.; Gottlieb, N.H. *Planning Health Promotion Programs: An Intervention Mapping Approach*; Jossey-Bass: San Francisco, CA, USA, 2006.

26. Tenenbaum, L.S.; Varjas, K.; Meyers, J.; Parris, L. Coping strategies and perceived effectiveness in fourth through eighth grade victims of bullying. *Sch. Psychol. Int.* **2011**, *32*, 263–287.

27. Olweus, D. Invited expert discussion paper Cyberbullying: An overrated phenomenon? *Eur. J. Dev. Psychol.* **2012**, *9*, 1–19.

28. Noar, S.M.; Benac, C.N.; Harris, M.S. Does tailoring matter? Meta-analytic review of tailored print health behavior change interventions. *Psychol. Bull.* **2007**, *133*, 673–693.

29. Krebs, P.; Prochaska, J.O.; Rossi, J.S. A meta-analysis of computer-tailored interventions for health behavior change. *Prev. Med. (Baltim.)* **2010**, *51*, 214–221.

30. Wade, A.; Beran, T. Cyberbullying: The new era of bullying. *Can. J. Sch. Psychol.* **2011**, *26*, 44–61.

31. Walrave, M.; Heirman, W. Cyberbullying: Predicting Victimisation and Perpetration. *Child Soc.* **2011**, *25*, 59–72.

32. Jacobs, N.C.; Völlink, T.; Dehue, F.; Lechner, L. Online Pestkoppenstoppen: Systematic and theory-based development of a web-based tailored intervention for adolescent cyberbully victims to combat and prevent cyberbullying. *BMC Public Health* **2014**, *14*, 396.

33. Parris, L.; Varjas, K.; Meyers, J.; Cutts, H. High School Students' Perceptions of Coping with Cyberbullying. *Youth Soc.* **2011**, *44*, 284–306.

34. Kreuger, R.A.; Casey, M.A. *Focus Groups. A Practical Guide for Applied Research*; Sage Publications: Thoasand Oaks, CA, USA, 2000.

35. Creswell, J.W. *Research Design: Qualitative, Quantitative and Mixed Method Approaches*; Sage Publications: Thoasand Oaks, CA, USA, 2003.

36. Beran, T.; Li, Q. Cyber-harassment: A study of a new method for an old behavior. *J. Educ. Comput. Res.* **2005**, *32*, 265–277.

37. Patchin, J.W.; Hinduja, S. Bullies Move Beyond the Schoolyard: A Preliminary Look at Cyberbullying. *Youth Violence Juv. Justice* **2006**, *4*, 148–169.

38. Price, M.; Dalgleish, J. Cyberbullying: Experiences, impacts and coping strategies as described by Australian young people. *Youth Stud. Aust.* **2010**, *29*, 51–59.

39. Slonje, R.; Smith, P.K. Cyberbullying: Another main type of bullying? *Scand. J. Psychol.* **2008**, *49*, 147–154.

40. Li, Q. New bottle but old wine: A research of cyberbullying in schools. *Comput. Human Behav.* **2007**, *23*, 1777–1791.

41. Vandebosch, H.; van Cleemput, K. Defining cyberbullying: A qualitative research into the perceptions of youngsters. *Cyberpsychol. Behav.* **2008**, *11*, 499–503.

42. Sticca, F.; Perren, S. Is cyberbullying worse than traditional bullying? Examining the differential roles of medium, publicity, and anonymity for the perceived severity of bullying. *J. Youth Adolesc.* **2013**, *42*, 739–750.

43. Mishna, F.; Saini, M.; Solomon, S. Ongoing and online: Children and youth's perceptions of cyber bullying. *Child Youth Serv. Rev.* **2009**, *31*, 1222–1228.

44. Dehue, F.; Bolman, C.; Völlink, T.; Pouwelse, M. Cyberbullying and traditional bullying in relation with adolescents' perception of parenting. *J. CyberTherapy Rehabil.* **2012**, *5*, 25–34.

45. Katzer, C.; Fetchenhauer, D.; Belschak, F. Cyberbullying: Who Are the Victims? *J. Media Psychol. Theor. Methods Appl.* **2009**, *21*, 25–36.

46. Smith, P.; Mahdavi, J.; Carvalho, M.; Tippett, N. An investigation into cyberbullying, its forms, awareness and impact, and the relationship between age and gender in cyberbullying. Available online: http://webarchive.nationalarchives.gov.uk/20130401151715/http://www.education.gov.uk/publications/eOrderingDownload/RBX03-06.pdf (accessed on 5 December 2013).

47. Varjas, K.; Talley, J.; Meyers, J.; Parris, L.; Cutts, H. High school students' perceptions of motivations for cyberbullying: An exploratory study. *West J. Emerg. Med.* **2010**, *11*, 269–273.

48. Chen, H.-G.; Chen, C.C.; Lo, L.; Yang, S.C. Online privacy control via anonymity and pseudonym: Cross-cultural implications. *Behav. Inf. Technol.* **2008**, *27*, 229–242.

49. Compton, L.; Campbell, M.A.; Mergler, A. Teacher, parent and student perceptions of the motives of cyberbullies. *Soc. Psychol. Educ.* **2014**.

50. Strom, P.; Strom, R.; Walker, J.; Sindel-Arrington, T.; Beckert, T. Adolescent Bullies on Cyber Island. *NASSP Bull.* **2011**, *95*, 195–211.

51. Frisen, A.; Jonsson, A.; Persson, C. Adolescents' perception of bullying: Who is the victim? Who is the bully? What can be done to stop bullying? *Adolescence* **2007**, *42*, 749–761.

52. Heirman, W.; Walrave, M. Predicting adolescent perpetration in cyberbullying: An application of the theory of planned behavior. *Psicothema* **2012**, *24*, 614–620.

53. Calvete, E.; Orue, I.; Estévez, A.; Villardón, L.; Padilla, P. Cyberbullying in adolescents: Modalities and aggressors' profile. *Comput. Human Behav.* **2010**, *26*, 1128–1135.

54. Vandebosch, H.; van Cleemput, K. Cyberbullying among youngsters: Profiles of bullies and victims. *New Media Soc.* **2009**, *11*, 1349–1371.

55. Field, T.; McCabe, P.M.; Schneiderman, N. *Stress and Coping*; Erlbaum: Hillsdale, NJ, USA, 1985.

56. Völlink, T.; Bolman, C.A.W.; Dehue, F.; Jacobs, N.C.L. Coping with Cyberbullying: Differences Between Victims, Bully-victims and Children not Involved in Bullying. *J. Community Appl. Soc. Psychol.* **2013**, *23*, 7–24.

57. Monks, C.P.; Robinson, S.; Worlidge, P. The emergence of cyberbullying: A survey of primary school pupils' perceptions and experiences. *Sch. Psychol. Int.* **2012**, *33*, 477–491.

58. Ortega, R.; Elipe, P.; Mora-Merchán, J.A.; Genta, M.L.; Brighi, A.; Guarini, A.; Smith, P.K.; Thompson, F.; Tippett, N. The emotional impact of bullying and cyberbullying on victims: A European cross-national study. *Aggress Behav.* **2012**, *38*, 342–356.

59. Patchin, J.W.; Hinduja, S. Traditional and Nontraditional Bullying Among Youth: A Test of General Strain Theory. *Youth Soc.* **2011**, *43*, 727–751.

60. Stacey, E. Research into cyberbullying: Student perspectives on cybersafe learning environments. *Informatics Educ.* **2009**, *8*, 115–130.

61. Topçu, C.; Erdur-Baker, O.; Capa-Aydin, Y. Examination of cyberbullying experiences among Turkish students from different school types. *Cyberpsychol. Behav.* **2008**, *11*, 643–648.

62. Machmutow, K.; Perren, S.; Sticca, F.; Alsaker, F.D. Peer victimisation and depressive symptoms: Can specific coping strategies buffer the negative impact of cybervictimisation? *Emot. Behav. Difficulties* **2012**, *17*, 403–420.

63. Braun, V.; Clarke, V. Using thematic analysis in psychology. *Qual. Res. Psychol.* **2006**, *3*, 77–101.

64. Centrale Commissie Mensgebonden onderzoek CCMO (Central Committee on Human Research). Available online: http://www.ccmo.nl/en/help-mij-op-weg (accessed on 9 January 2015).

65. Ybarra, M.L.; Diener-West, M.; Leaf, P.J. Examining the Overlap in Internet Harassment and School Bullying: Implications for School Intervention. *J. Adolesc. Health* **2007**, *41*, S42–S50.

66. Varjas, K.; Henrich, C.C.; Meyers, J. Urban Middle School Students' Perceptions of Bullying, Cyberbullying, and School Safety. *J. Sch. Violence* **2009**, *8*, 159–176.

67. Li, Q. Cyberbullying in Schools: A Research of Gender Differences. *Sch. Psychol. Int.* **2006**, *27*, 157–170.

68. Hopkins, L.; Taylor, L.; Bowen, E.; Wood, C. A qualitative study investigating adolescents' understanding of aggression, bullying and violence. *Child Youth Serv. Rev.* **2013**, *35*, 685–693.

69. Vaillancourt, T.; McDougall, P.; Hymel, S.; Krygsman, A.; Miller, J.; Stiver, K.; Davis, C. Bullying: Are researchers and children/youth talking about the same thing? *Int. J. Behav. Dev.* **2008**, *32*, 486–495.

70. Riebel, J.; Jäger, R.S.; Fischer, U.C. Cyberbullying in Germany—An exploration of prevalence, overlapping with real life bullying and coping strategies. *Psychol. Sci. Q.* **2009**, *51*, 298–314.

71. Perren, S.; Corcoran, L.; Cowie, H.; Dehue, F.; Garcia, D.; Mc Guckin, C.; Sevcikova, A.; Tsatsou, P.; Völlink, T. Tackling cyberbullying: Review of empirical evidence regarding successful responses by students, parents, and schools. *Int. J. Conf. Violence* **2012**, *6*, 283–292.

72. Hunter, S.C.; Boyle, J.M.E.; Warden, D. Help seeking amongst child and adolescent victims of peer-aggression and bullying: The influence of school-stage, gender, victimisation, appraisal, and emotion. *Br. J. Educ. Psychol.* **2004**, *74*, 375–390.

The Development of a Self-Report Questionnaire on Coping with Cyberbullying: The Cyberbullying Coping Questionnaire

Niels C.L. Jacobs, Trijntje Völlink, Francine Dehue and Lilian Lechner

Abstract: The negative effects and the continuation of cyberbullying seem to depend on the coping strategies the victims use. To assess their coping strategies, self-report questionnaires (SRQs) are used. However, these SRQs are often subject to several shortcomings: the (single and topological) categorizations used in SRQs do not always adequately differentiate among various coping responses, in addition the strategies of general SRQs fail to accurately measure coping with cyberbullying. This study is therefore aimed to develop a SRQ that specifically measures coping with cyberbullying (*i.e.*, Cyberbullying Coping Questionnaire; CCQ) and to discover whether other, not single and topological, categorizations of coping strategies can be found. Based on previous SRQs used in the (cyber)bullying (*i.e.*, traditional and cyberbullying) literature (*i.e.*, 49 studies were found with three different SRQs measuring coping with traditional bullying, cyberbullying or (cyber)bullying) items and categorizations were selected, compared and merged into a new questionnaire. In compliance with recommendations from the classical test-theory, a principal component analysis and a confirmatory factor analysis were done, and a final model was constructed. Seventeen items loaded onto four different coping categorizations: mental-, passive-, social-, and confrontational-coping. The CCQ appeared to have good internal consistency, acceptable test-retest reliability, good discriminant validity and the development of the CCQ fulfilled many of the recommendations from classical test-theory. The CCQ omits working in single and topological categorizations and measures cognitive, behavioral, approach and avoidance strategies.

Reprinted from *Societies*. Cite as: Jacobs, N.C.L.; Völlink, T.; Dehue, F.; Lechner, L. The Development of a Self-Report Questionnaire on Coping with Cyberbullying: The Cyberbullying Coping Questionnaire. *Societies* **2015**, *5*, 460–491.

1. Introduction

Coping has two widely recognized major functions both of which are often represented in stressful encounters: emotion regulation and problem solving. By employing cognitive and behavioral strategies, an individual either reduces, masters or tolerates the internal and external demands that are the consequence of stressful events. According to the transactional model of stress and coping, the choice of these strategies is influenced by appraisals. These are evaluations of how important a situation is to one's well-being and how able one is to cope with, or change the situation [1,2]. Several categories of coping have been suggested, such as problem-focused-, emotion-focused-, passive-, aggressive-, distancing-, or avoidance-coping [3]. In the case of cyberbullying, it appears that the negative consequences are influenced by the use of ineffective coping strategies [4], and the use of ineffective coping appears to keep the online and offline bullying going [5–12]. Worldwide, a lot of adolescents are the victims of cyberbullying [13], and as a result they suffer from a range of negative consequences such as anxiety [14], depression, emotional distress [15,16], suicidality [17,18], school violence and delinquency [19]. For the most part they are also related to traditional bullying [20,21], and, especially, the combination of traditional and cyberbullying (*i.e.*, (cyber)bullying) seems to result in the most mental health and social problems compared to being bullied "only" in one way [22,23]. Hence, insight into (adequate) coping seems highly relevant in the field of cyberbullying.

To assess coping strategies of cyberbullying (and traditional) victims, researchers often use self-report questionnaires (SRQs) in which they ask victims to describe, aggregate or report their coping responses to a general stressor. In general, the use of SRQs has many advantages: it is a low-cost way of conducting research on a large scale, it is the most direct way to assess the construct of coping, it has high(er) apparent validity, and is less time-consuming than conducting interviews [24,25]. However, the current existing SRQs are also subject to several disadvantages. Firstly, in general, researchers agree that coping strategies (*i.e.*, items) cluster into primary coping categories, and that these categories contain either cognitive- *versus* behavioral-, avoid- *versus* approach- or problem-focused *versus* emotion-focused strategies [3,26]. Unfortunately, these single (*i.e.*, problem- *versus* emotion-focused) and topological (e.g., active *versus* passive, cognitive *versus* behavioral, avoid *versus* approach) categorizations are not optimal categories because coping is likely to serve many functions and is multidimensional [3,27]. For example, avoidance strategies can be both problem-focused and emotion-focused [26], and the coping strategy "justification" is neither an approach nor avoidant style of coping [28]. Hence, there still appears to be a gap between the acknowledged need of researchers to be able to identify categorizations of coping behavior and the development of measures that can distinguish these categorizations. In addition, the lack of consensus about core categories hinder comparing and cumulating results from different studies [3]. For example, some researchers suggest that coping categories should be changed into a more fine-grained distinction of hierarchical arranged coping strategies with the higher order categories proximity seeking, mastery and accommodation (e.g., [3,29,30]), while other researchers keep using single or topological categorizations (e.g., problem-focused *versus* emotion-focused coping [4,31]).

Secondly, the vast majority of SRQs are not designed to specifically assess coping with cyberbullying, but are designed to assess coping with stressful events in general. This general coping approach lacks the specificity of coping in bullying situations, because appraisals influence choice of coping strategies [1]. For example, appraising an online situation as harmful can be quite different compared to an offline situation as harmful. The appraisal harmfulness in online name calling (*i.e.*, cyberbullying) appears to depend on knowing the cyberbully in the offline world, on the cyberbully being a member of existing social groups, and on the transfer of cyberbullying to bullying in the offline world [22]. The appraisal of harmfulness in offline bullying may depend on the appearance of, for example the one calling names (e.g., tall *versus* small) and non-verbal communication. This difference in appraisal can lead to a different choice of coping strategies online (e.g., deleting a message) compared to offline (e.g., fighting back). Similarly, context also seems to play an important role in cyberbullying [32–34], leading an adolescent choosing a different coping strategy online compared to offline.

Other research based on appraisals (e.g., "Is there a threat such as cyberbullying?" and "Do I have the resources to address the cyberbullying?"), has shown that theories such as the transactional model of stress and coping [1] have to be adjusted to include coping strategies specifically for cyberbullying [26]. Online, it seems adolescents choose between reactive coping strategies (*i.e.*, acceptance, avoidance, justification or seeking social support) *versus* preventive ones (*i.e.*, increase security and awareness, talk in person), instead of between problem-focused *versus* emotion-focused ones. The appraisal "nothing can be done" leads to the use of other coping strategies (e.g., adopting the belief that there is no way to prevent cyberbullying) compared to the appraisal "something can be done" [26] (e.g., increasing security and awareness) when cyberbullied. Offline, these appraisals could lead to, for example, running away or asking the bully to stop in a confident manner, respectively. Furthermore, many SRQs do not assess concrete "online" coping strategies (e.g., saving evidence by taking a screenshot [35]), and online it might be easier to be passive (*i.e.*, online you can easily delete a message or close a window, offline you cannot). When these "online" coping strategies are not included in a SRQ, possible important strategies are not assessed. Consequently, when currently existing coping SRQs are used to enable, for example tailoring [36], in interventions, these interventions fail to provide participants with specific advice on how to cope more effectively with cyberbullying.

It, thus, seems that coping SRQs used in the cyberbullying literature are subject to two major shortcomings: (1) the (single and topological) categorizations used in existing SRQs do not adequately differentiate among various coping responses;

and (2) the strategies of general SRQs do not completely and adequately measure concrete coping with cyberbullying, which make adequate intervention more difficult. Online, it is likely that specific coping strategies—that are part of coping categorizations—exist, such as saving evidence [35], blocking and deleting [33,37,38], contacting service providers [39], and reacting by not actually saying anything [40]. This study therefore aims to develop a new SRQ that specifically measures cyberbullying victims' coping strategies and to discover whether other, not single and topological, categorizations of coping strategies can be found. Underlying this line of reasoning is the transactional model of stress and coping [1] that states that appraisals influence choice of coping strategies. Based on his review, Garcia [41] suggested that a new coping questionnaires should be an adapted and modified version of coping measures that already exists. Therefore, we conducted a preliminary study in which we made an overview of all coping SRQs used in the traditional and cyberbullying literature. Based on the items and categorizations found in this overview, and based on multiple recommendations from classical test-theory (see Sveinbjornsdottir and Thorsteinsson [34] for an overview), in the main study the Cyberbullying Coping Questionnaire (CCQ) was developed, with the purpose to find better fitting categorizations of coping strategies for cyberbullying. In the main study, we further tested the CCQ for suitability, reliability and (discriminant) validity.

2. Preliminary Study: Coping SRQs' Literature Review

An overview of all coping SRQs used in the traditional and cyberbullying literature is made with categorizations and study information.

2.1. Materials and Methods

Google Scholar, PsychINFO and PubMed were used to search for published and peer-reviewed studies, no later than the end of November 2014. The studies were selected on their usage of SRQs to investigate the coping strategies of adolescents in response to (cyber) bullying. The search items included "cyberbullying", "online bullying", "bullying", "traditional bullying", "peer victimization", "coping", "cope", and "scale". Only studies that used an SRQ to measure coping with (cyber)bullying were included. These studies were scanned for scales that measured more than one coping category (e.g., Naylor and Cowie [42] only measured peer support systems and thus was not included). Furthermore, the articles found were scanned for additional references that may not have surfaced in the initial search.

2.2. Results

An overview of all SRQs and their characteristics can be found in Table 1. To conclude, forty-nine studies were found that used 35 different SRQs to assess coping with (cyber)bullying: 12 studies used seven SRQs to measure coping with cyberbullying (however, we could not access the following study, [43]); 38 studies used 28 different SRQs to measure coping with traditional bullying (however, we could not access studies [44] and [45]); and three studies used three SRQs to measure coping with both traditional and cyberbullying. In eight studies, a questionnaire was developed or an existing questionnaire was adapted in order to measure coping with cyberbullying specifically. The most often used SRQs to assess coping with cyberbullying were the Adolescent Coping Scale (ACS; [46]) and an adapted version of the Utrechtse Coping List—Adolescents (UCL-A; [47]). The most often used SRQs to assess coping with traditional bullying were the Self-Report Coping Measure (SRCM; [48]) and the Survey for Coping with Rejection Experiences (SCORE; [49]).

3. Main Study: Developing and Testing the CCQ

Based on the overview of coping SRQs from the preliminary study, the Cyberbullying Coping Questionnaire (CCQ) was developed with the purpose of formulating better fitting categorizations of coping strategies for cyberbullying.

3.1. Materials and Methods

The following will be described: the procedure of selecting items, constructing the questionnaire, and analyzing the CCQ for suitability, reliability and (discriminant) validity. During this process, the following recommendations that are based on classical test-theory for the development of a psychological test were leading (see [34]): (1) test items must be clear, short, contain one statement, and are easy to understand; (2) a criterion of four items per factor should be used, and twice as many items as will be included in the final version are needed; (3) a minimum of 10 participants per item and a minimum of 500 participants should be used; (4) factor structure should be determined with factor analysis (FA) using oblique rotation; (5) the scree-test should be used in combination with parallel analysis (PA) to determine the amount of extracting factors. The factor loadings should be at least 0.30 when $N \leq 500$, 0.25 when $N \leq 1000$, and inter-item correlation should lie between 0.20 and 0.40; (6) when the sample is at least 100, test-retest correlation ≤ 0.70 for a four-week interval, ≤ 0.60 for a four- to ten-week interval, and ≤ 0.50 for an interval longer than ten weeks; (7) concurrent validity ≤ 0.70 unless scales are of poor quality, and replication through either Exploratory Factor Analysis (EFA) cross-validation or Confirmatory Factor Analysis (CFA) is proven when 90% of items and factor structures hold (given $N \leq 500$); (8) second-order Factor Analysis (FA) is safely conducted if earlier FA used oblique rotation and scree-tests; and (9) tests should consist of 20–50 items.

Table 1. Characteristics of self-report coping questionnaires used in (cyber)bullying research among adolescents.

Scale	Used in, Total Items, N, Ages	TB/CB	Categorizations	α	Notes
Self-Report Coping Measure (SRCM; [48])	a. [5] (34 items, $N = 408$, age 9–12)	TB	1. Social support seeking		Participants had to judge the items on a 5-point LS.
	b. [6] (34 items, $N = 329$, age 9–13)		2. Problem-solving		1. α's ranged from 0.64–0.86. No adjustments were made
	c. [29] (22 items, $N = 456$, age 9–10)		3. Distancing		2. α's were (1) 0.71, (2) 0.77, (3) 0.61, (4) 0.64 and (5) 0.67
	d. [9] (20 items, $N = 305$, age 12–16)		4. Internalizing		3. The stem of the SRQ was changed into "When I have a problem with another kid at school, I . . . ". Some items were removed because they loaded on multiple factors; α's were (1) 0.75, (2) 0.72, (3) 0.70, (4) 0.57 and (5) 0.60
	e. [12] (18 items, $N = 452$, age 12–14)		5. Externalizing		4. A modified version of the SRCM with 20 items (four per factor) was used. Participants were asked to apply the questionnaire to bullying situations
	f. [50] (25 items, $N = 463$, age 12–15)				5. The SRQ included a definition of traditional bullying. In addition to the usual factors, seeking support was split up into adults and peers, and the factors submission, nonchalance and escape were added
	g. [51] (34 items, $N = 311$, age 10–13)				6. The hypothetical situation was changed into "When in my classroom someone repeatedly bullies another classmate, I usually . . . ". Externalizing was not included. α's were (1) 0.80, (2) 0.84, (3) 0.78, and (4) 0.68
	h. [52] (34 items, $N = 255$, age 11–14)				7. In addition to items from the SRCM, items from the HICUPS [55] were used. Some items from the internalizing, externalizing and support seeking scale (SRCM) and avoidant scale (HICUPS) were used, preceded by "When bullied . . . "
	i. [53] (23 items, $N = 317$, age $M = 10.6$; $SD = 0.99$)				i Items were judged on a 4-point LS. A modified 23 item version [56] was used
	j. [54] (43 items, $N = 220$)				j A modified version of the SRCM in addition to scales from [57] (i.e., (6) conflict resolution, (7) revenge) were used. α's were (1) 0.89, (2) 0.88/0.85, (3) 0.67/0.71, (4) 0.74/0.80, (5) 0.72/0.77, (6) 0.75/0.74, and (7) 0.82/0.88

Table 1. *Cont.*

Scale	Used in, Total Items, N, Ages	TB/CB	Categorizations	α	Notes
Adolescent Coping Scale (ACS) [46]	a. [58] (79 items, $N = 50$, age 13–14) b. [59] (18 items, $N = 652$, age 11–17) c. [60] (26 items, $N = 1223$, age 12–16)	CB TB	1. Problem-solving (focus on problem solving, work hard & achieve, focus on positive, seek diversions, physical recreation, seek to belong, invest in friends) 2. Reference to others (seek social support, spirituality, professional help, social action) 3. Non-productive coping (worry, ignore problem, wishful thinking, tension reduction, self-blame, not coping, keep to self)		Items are judged on a 5-point LS. α's are based on means of subscales. a. CB, no adjustments were made b. an adapted version of the ACS: the Coping Scale for Children—Short form (CSC-SF; [61]) was used to measure coping with TB and CB. The CSC-SF measured two factors: approach (α = 0.69) and avoidant (α = 0.70) coping. The questionnaire asked participants to judge items on a 3-point LS c. The authors developed the Coping with Bullying questionnaire based on 20 items of the ACS and 6 additional items. The questionnaire consisted of the productive other-focused, productive self-focused, and nonproductive avoidance scale (α's were not mentioned)
Survey for Coping with Rejection Experiences (SCORE; [49])	a. [49] (28 items, $N = 225$, age 9–12) b. [62] (27 items, $N = 126$, age 9–11) c. [63] (28 items, $N = 79$, age 7–12)	TB	1. Active 2. Aggression 3. Denial 4. Rumination/avoidance		a. The questionnaire measures strategies used to cope with relational aggression. Two specific peer experiences (being teased by schoolmates, being excluded from a group activity) are described. Participants judge items on a 4-point LS. α's ranged from 0.69–0.84 for the teasing situation, and from 0.70–0.87 for the exclusion situation b. The questionnaire was modified to assess how children perceive relational aggression in the context of their close friendships c. Ruminative, positive reappraisal and aggressive coping scales were used. α's ranged from 0.61–0.77 for the teasing situation, and from 0.63–0.84 for the exclusion situation

Table 1. Cont.

Scale	Used in, Total Items, N, Ages	TB/CB	Categorizations	α	Notes
Utrechtse Coping List—Adolescents (UCL-A; [47])	a. [4] (24 items, N = 325, age 11–12) b. [31] (26 items, N = 325, age 11–12)	CB	a.1 Problem focused (confronting, social support) a.2 Emotion focused (palliative, avoidance, optimistic, express emotions) b.1 Depressive/emotional expression b.2 Avoidance/palliative b.3 Social support seeking	0.59 0.85 0.91 0.57 0.76	The questionnaire that measures coping with cyberbullying is an adapted version of the UCL-A, items were rewritten for coping with cyberbullying, and are judged on a 4-point LS
The Coping Strategy Indicator (CSI; [64])	[65] (33 items, N = 375, age M = 15.98, SD = 1.41)	CB	1. Problem solving 2. Seeking social support 3. Avoidance	0.85 0.87 0.69	The questionnaire is based on previous measures (e.g., [1] and suggestions from students and colleagues. Items are judged on a 3-point LS
Cognitive Emotion Regulation Questionnaire—Kids version(CERQ-k; [66])	[67] (36 items, N = 131, age 9–11)	TB	1. Refocus on planning 2. Rumination 3. Putting into perspective 4. Catastrophizing 5. Positive refocusing 6. Positive reappraisal 7. Acceptance 8. Self-blame 9. Other-blame	0.75 0.73 0.68 0.67 0.79 0.67 0.62 0.79 0.79	The study initially focused on anxious children. However, 61% of these experienced bullying. The CERQ-k is an adapted (i.e., simplified and shortened) version of the CERQ [68]. Participants had to judge items on a 5-point LS
Children's Coping Strategies Checklist (CCSC; [69])	[70] (45 items, N = 230, age 8–13)	TB	1. Active 2. Avoidant 3. Distraction 4. Support seeking	0.84 0.75 0.63 0.89	Participants had to judge items on a 4-point LS. The four broad coping categories consist of: (1) cognitive decision-making, direct problem solving, positive cognitive restructuring, seeking understanding; (2) cognitive avoidance, avoidant actions; (3) distracting actions, physical release of emotions; and (4) problem-focused support, emotion focused support
German Coping Questionnaire for Children and Adolescents [71]	[72] (36 items, N = 409, age 10–16)	TB	1. Emotion-focused 2. Problem-focused 3. Maladaptive	0.69 0.85 0.87	Participants had to judge items on a 5-point LS. The three main scales consisted of nine subscales: (1) minimization, distraction/recreation; (2) situation control, positive self-instructions, social support; and (3) passive avoidance, rumination, resignation, aggression

Table 1. *Cont.*

Scale	Used in, Total Items, N, Ages	TB/CB	Categorizations	α	Notes
Coping Styles Questionnaire (CSQ; [73])	[74] (48 items, N = 99, age 18–21)	TB	1. Rational 2. Detached 3. Emotional 4. Avoidance	0.77 0.71 0.85 0.75	The CSQ normally consists of 60 items. In this study, a 48-item version was used in which male participants had to judge items on a 4-point LS. This study focused on bullying in prisons
Ways of Coping Checklist (WCCL; [75])	[8] (35 items, N = 459, age 9–14)	TB	1. Problem-focused 2. Seek social support 3. Wishful thinking 4. Avoidance	0.82 0.77 0.73 0.28	Participants had to judge item on a 4-point LS
Life Events and Coping Inventory (LECI; [76])	[77] (52 items, N = 510, age 10–12)	TB	1. Aggression 2. Distraction 3. Self-destruction 4. Stress-recognition 5. Endurance	0.81 0.80 0.77 0.75 0.62	Participants had to judge items on a 4-point LS, specifically for which behaviors they used at school
Coping Scale for Children—Short Form (CSC-SF; [61])	c. [78] (16 items, N = 379, age 10–13)	TB	1. Approach 2. Avoidant	0.69 0.70	Items had to be rated on a 3-point LS
The Problem-solving Style Inventory [79]	[80] (28 items, N = 236, age 12–15)	TB	1. Helplessness 2. Control 3. Creativity 4. Confidence 5. Approach style 6. Avoidance style 7. Support-seeking	0.80 0.71 0.75 0.78 0.73 0.71 0.73	Higher scores mean more positive problem-solving style
Coping Orientation to Problem Experienced (COPE; [81])	[82] (60 items, N = 1339, age 17–29)	TB	1. Problem-focused 2. Emotion-focused 3. Avoidant	0.92	Participants judge items on a 4-point LS. Only the α for the complete questionnaire was mentioned
How I Cope Under Pressure Scale (HICUPS; [55])	[51] (45 items, N = 311, age 10–13)	TB	1. Active 2. Distraction 3. Avoidance 4. Support Seeking	0.88 - 0.65 0.86	Six items based on the avoidant actions subscale were used. Participants judged these items on a 5-point LS. Information about the scales, α's and ages were found in [55]

Table 1. Cont.

Scale	Used in, Total Items, N, Ages	TB/CB	Categorizations	α	Notes
Revised Ways of Coping (RWC; [83])	[84] (66 items, N = 98, grade 6–12)	TB	1. Problem-focused 2. Wishful thinking 3. Detachment 4. Seeking social support 5. Focusing on the positive 6. Self-blame 7. Tension reduction 8. Keep to self		The questionnaire measures styles used in relation to a distinguishable event. In this study, all participants were girls. They were asked to judge the items on a 4-point LS for relational aggression. α's ranged from 0.59–0.88
**	[85] (29 items, N = 573, age 12–13)	TB	1. Counter aggression 2. Helplessness 3. Nonchalance	0.87 0.75 0.77	Participants were asked to indicate on a 3-point LS how victims (including themselves) fit the situations. Two situations were dropped from the scale
Children's Emotional Dysregulation Questionnaire (CEDQ)*	[52] (9 items, N = 255, age 11–14)	TB	1. Anger 2. Sadness 3. Fear	0.71 0.72 0.76	Participants judge items on a 5-point LS. Higher scores reflect greater emotional dysregulation
**	[86] (9 items, N = 394, age M = 16.4, SD = 1.09)	TB	1. Avoidance 2. Health behavior 3. Increased eating	0.73 0.80 0.80	This study focused on weight-based victimization. Participants were asked to judge 28 items on a 5-point LS. A subset of nine items was used
**	[87] (10 items, N = 509, age 11–14)	TB	1. Problem focused 2. Seeking social support 3. Attending positive life events	0.92	Participants were asked to indicate how often each strategy (i.e., item) helped when being picked upon (based on [88]). α was only provided for the whole scale
**	[89] (14 items, N = 765, age M = 13.18, SD = 0.63)	CB	1. Distant advice 2. Assertiveness 3. Helplessness 4. Close support 5. Retaliation	0.67 0.49 0.36 0.65 -	Items were based on the results of a qualitative pilot study [90]. Students were asked what a hypothetical victim would do in a situation (situations varied between students) and had to rate the 14 items on a 4-point LS
Items from LAPSuS project [91]	[92] (11 items, N = 1987, age 6–19)	CBTB	1. Aggressive 2. Helpless 3. Cognitive 4. Technical	-	Items were not specific for cyberbullying, participants were asked to rate the items on a 4-point LS with in mind being cyberbullied, physically or verbally bullied. The model had to be rejected (bad fits on RMSEA and Chi square test)

Table 1. Cont.

Scale	Used in, Total Items, N, Ages	TB/CB	Categorizations	α	Notes
**	[93] (26 items, N = 2092, age 12–18)	CB	1. Technological coping 2. Reframing 3. Ignoring 4. Dissociation 5. Cognitive avoidance 6. Behavioral avoidance 7. Seeking support 8. Confrontation 9. Retaliation	-	List of coping strategies was developed based on extensive literature review on coping strategies in general and coping strategies in cyberbullying. Classification was based on [94]. Participants indicated *yes*, *no*, or *not applicable* for each item
**	[95] (16 items, N = 830, age 8–14)	TB	-	-	Participants had to judge a list of 16 items on a 4-point LS (except for items related to making new friends). Items were based on coping responses validated in previous research
Questionnaire of Cyberbullying (QoCB)*	[38] (21 items, N = 269, age 12–19)	CB	-	-	A number of questions multiple-choice questions measured blocking the message or person, telling person to stop harassing, changing usernames, telling friends, telling parents, telling teachers, ignoring and not telling anyone
**	[96] (11 items, N = 571, all ages)	CB	-	-	Participants had to indicate *yes* or *no* for each behavior
**	[97] (4 items, N = 548, age < 25)	CB TB	-	-	The questionnaire included items on offline and online coping strategies. Participants were asked to indicate which strategy/strategies they had used, and how helpful these strategies were on a 3-point LS
**	[98] (10 items, N = 219, age 18–40)	TB	-	-	Participants were asked to indicate which of 10 coping strategies they have used (e.g., I talked to the bullies, I tried to ignore it) in response to TB
**	[7] (12 items, N = 1852, age 4–19)	TB	-	-	Participants had to indicate which of the 12 given strategies they have used in responding to TB
**	[99] (3 items, N = 207, age 13–14)	TB	-	-	For each type of bullying (physical, verbal, social), participants first had to give an open answer about—And then had to choose a coping strategy from a list of eight to ten strategies and indicate how useful this strategy was
**	[100] (1 items, N = 2308, age 10–14)	TB	-	-	Participants were asked "What did you usually do when you were bullied at school?"

Table 1. *Cont.*

Scale	Used in, Total Items, N, Ages	TB/CB	Categorizations	α	Notes
**	[101] (N = 348, age 9–11)	TB	-	-	The questionnaire was based on previous studies. Participants were asked to indicate on a checklist which coping behaviors they displayed
**	[102] (N = 1835, age 11–14)	TB	-	-	Participants were asked to name all coping strategies they have used in response to TB. Later, these answers were coded independently by two authors
Internet Experiences Questionnaire (IEQ)*	[103] (N = 856, age 16–24)	CB	-	-	Participants could select as many options as applicable to adequately describe their behavioral reactions
**	[104] (7 items, N = 323)	TB	-	-	Participants were asked to indicate on a 3-point LS what they would do in response to being hit, teased, or left out of activities. Four items were adapted from [105], the other items came from the literature

Note: * Developed for this study; ** Developed for this study without a name; CB: Cyberbullying; TB: Traditional Bullying; LS: Likert scale.

3.1.1. Item Selection

Based on Table 1, the shortcomings mentioned in the introduction, and the recommendations of Sveinbjornsdottir and Thorsteinsson [34], four adolescent coping SRQs were selected as item pools for the CCQ. The UCL-A (1) and a SRQ which assesses coping with cyberbullying (2) were selected because: (a) the UCL-A was used in cyberbullying research [4,31], (b) the SRQ that assesses coping with cyberbullying was based on the UCL-A, and (c) both instruments assess cognitive and behavioral problem-focused coping, cognitive and behavioral emotion-focused coping and depressive/emotional coping with a low number of items (*i.e.*, 24/26 items). The CERQ (3) was selected because: (a) its diversity in different coping categories (*i.e.*, nine different scales) in combination with the low number of items (*i.e.*, 36); and (b) in contrast to other SRQs, it assesses one's cognitions after experiencing a negative event and it assesses how these cognitions are used in emotion-regulation [106]. The ACS (4) was selected because: (a) it was the most often used SRQ in the cyberbullying literature; (b) it was also used in traditional bullying literature; (c) it includes a non-productive scale and a reference to other scales; and (d) it also has a short form (*i.e.*, CSC-SF). Drawbacks of this latter scale, however, are the lack of important information on the development, and some poor psychometric properties (e.g., poor choices of item selection, FA model and rotation, not meeting accepted criteria, and missing of important reliability and validity analysis [34]).

The first two authors of this paper compared all items from the above-mentioned four adolescent coping SRQs with each other and merged and/or deleted items that appeared to measure the same. Next, these items were transformed to cyber specific situations (e.g., "I ask for help" was changed into "I ask for help on an Internet forum").

3.1.2. Initial Scale Construction (Preliminary PCA to Reduce Number of Items)

Construction of the CCQ followed. Selected items were compared with the items and coping categories from the COPE, SRCM, LECI, GCQCA, WCCL and SRCS for completeness. Items that appeared to measure the same strategy were merged into one item. This resulted in 65 items that had to be rated on a 5-point Likert scale (1 = *never*; 2 = *sometimes*; 3 = *regularly*; 4 = *often*; 5 = *almost always*). As an introduction to the questionnaire, participants were told: *In this questionnaire, cyberbullying is bullying via the Internet and via mobile phones. Do you react to cyberbullying? For each sentence, indicate whether you "never", "sometimes", "regularly", "often", or "almost always" did this.* In several focus group interviews (*i.e.*, partly described and published in [40], partly described in an internal report [107]), adolescents from the target population indicated that they do not like to read a lot and prefer short questionnaires. In addition, the CCQ was going to be used to tailor the online tailored advice sessions of *Online Pestkoppenstoppen* (the intervention aims to teach cyberbullying victims how to cope more effectively with cyberbullying [108]) to the aggressive or passive coping strategies used by cyberbullying victims. Several preliminary (not published) PCAs were conducted based on data from 278 adolescents (age 15–22, $M = 17.54$, $SD = 1.38$; 89.9% female) in order to try and find a three-factor structure (*i.e.*, aggressive-, passive-, and active coping), and in order to reduce the number of items as much as possible. After a first preliminary PCA, four items were deleted due to low correlations with other items, 16 items were deleted due to factor loadings on multiple factors or no or insufficient loadings, and two items were deleted due to high skewness values. Based on discussions between the first three authors of this article, three items were added in order to better measure active coping, and three items were merged into one item (that all measured retaliating). Consequently, 44 items were used in a second preliminary PCA. Eight items were deleted due to factor loadings on multiple factors or no or insufficient loadings, and four groups of items were merged into one factor, leading to the deletion of five items. After reviewing the found factor structure, four items were added, again, based on discussions between the authors (*i.e.*, improve the active coping factor). Finally, 35 items remained (see Table 2) that were used for the second principal component analysis (PCA) that is described below.

Table 2. Overview of questions of Cyberbullying Coping Questionnaire (CCQ).

Item No.	Item Content
Item 1	I wait for the cyberbullying to stop
Item 2	I ask for help on a forum
Item 3	I focus on solving the cyberbullying problem immediately
Item 4	I vent my emotions to myself
Item 5	I think that other people are experiencing things that are much worse
Item 6	I tell the cyberbullies when their behavior is bothering me
Item 7	I think the cyberbullying event will make me a "stronger" person
Item 8	I retaliate by cyberbullying
Item 9	I try not to think about the cyberbullying
Item 10	I think that the cyberbullying is not hurting me personally
Item 11	I try to find a new way to stop the cyberbullying
Item 12	I express my feelings
Item 13	I think that I cannot change anything about the cyberbullying event
Item 14	I laugh about the cyberbully/event
Item 15	I delete the message from my profile or e-mail
Item 16	I constantly think how terrible the cyberbullying is
Item 17	I let the cyberbullying happen without reacting
Item 18	I try to find the cause of the cyberbullying
Item 19	I act as if the cyberbullying did not happen
Item 20	I throw or break stuff
Item 21	I contact the people behind the website
Item 22	I think that there are worse things in life
Item 23	I think that the cyberbullying will stop
Item 24	I talk about the cyberbullying event with friends, family or someone I trust
Item 35	I show my irritation to the cyberbully

Table 2. *Cont.*

Item No.	Item Content
Item 25	I weep with grief
Item 26	I save print screens, messages and text messages as evidence
Item 27	I think about fun things that are not related to cyberbullying
Item 28	I ignore the cyberbullies
Item 29	I ask someone (parent, teacher, friend, peer) for help
Item 30	I cannot think about anything else than being cyberbullied
Item 31	I tell the cyberbullies to stop
Item 32	I joke about the cyberbullying event
Item 33	I think that it is just a game with the computer or telephone
Item 34	I think about which steps I need to take to stop the cyberbullying
Item 35	I show my irritation to the cyberbully

3.1.3. Participants

The baseline data obtained for the intervention study on *Online Pestkoppenstoppen* [108] was used for the PCA and confirmatory factor analysis (CFA), consisting of 211 participants (62.6% female) with mean age 12.56 (SD = 0.65). Of all participants, 31.28% was a victim, while 67.30% was a bully/victim (3 missing values). Furthermore, 92.9% indicated attending lower level educational school (vocational, theoretical, mixed or special needs). In order to be able to calculate test-retest reliability, the second wave of measurements (after a month) was used, in which 68 participants (80.9% female) with mean age 12.40 (SD = 1.69) remained.

3.1.4. Analysis

Although some researchers suggest that a coping questionnaire should be developed through using FA rather than PCA [34,109], Field [110] states that the procedure and solutions of PCA and FA differ little from each other. Furthermore, PCA is a psychometrically sound procedure, and it is conceptually less complex then FA. The aim of the PCA in this study was to identify groups or clusters of items that measure new, not single or topological, categorizations among the items of the CCQ. Additionally, CFA was used to test the models found in the PCA. SPSS 20 was used for the PCA, to calculate bivariate correlations (of participants' scores on each found categorization of the CCQ) between the first and second wave of measurement (*i.e.*, test-rest reliability) and bivariate correlations between participants' scores on the found categorizations and scores on the Rosenberg Self-Esteem Scale (*i.e.*, RSE, [111]) (*i.e.*, discriminant validity). R was used to conduct the CFAs and to compute Cronbach's alpha, omega and the greatest lower bound.

3.2. Results

3.2.1. Principal Components Analysis

Prior to performing the Principal Component Analysis (PCA), the suitability of the data for factor analysis was checked. Seven items (*i.e.*, item 8, 14, 20, 21, 30, 32 and 33; Table 2) were removed due to high skewness values (≥ 2) as well as low variance across response options [112,113]. Furthermore, seven items were deleted due to low correlation ($r = < 0.3$) with other items (*i.e.*, item 4, 7, 10, 12, 13, 15 and 25). Because of the ordinal measurement level, a nonlinear principal component analysis (NPCA) was conducted with optimal scaling (*i.e.*, categories of ordered or unordered (discrete) variables are assigned with numeric values [114]). However, many of the variables showed a (roughly) linear transformation (*i.e.*, making numeric treatment possible). The remaining 21 items were therefore analyzed with a PCA. The Kaiser-Meyer-Olkin (KMO) measure verified the sampling adequacy for the analysis, KMO = 0.82, and all KMO values for individuals were >0.71 [110]. Bartlett's test of sphericity, χ^2 (210) = 1367.11, $p < 0.001$, indicated that correlations between items were sufficiently large for PCA.

The PCA revealed five components with eigenvalues exceeding Kaiser's criterion of one. These components explained 56.54% of the variance. Based on the relatively small sample size, parallel analysis and the scree plot's inflexions (*i.e.*, a graph of each eigenvalue (Y-axis) plotted against the factor with which it is associated (X-axis)), it was decided to retain four components. The four-component solution explained 51.47% of the variance. To aid in interpretation an oblique (direct oblimin) rotation was performed [115] and the pattern (*i.e.*, factor loadings/regression coefficients for each variable on each factor) and structure (*i.e.*, correlation coefficients between each variable and factor) matrixes were checked [110]. Item 22 and item 34 were removed based on similar loadings on two factors in the structure and pattern matrix, and item 16 was removed based on too low loadings on the patterns matrix and similar loadings on the structure matrix. Consequently, item 2 had to be removed due to too low correlations to other items.

A third PCA was conducted with 17 items. The Kaiser-Meyer-Olkin measure verified the sampling adequacy for the analysis, KMO = 0.81, and all KMO values for individuals were >0.69 [110]. Bartlett's test of sphericity, χ^2 (136) = 1058.72, $p < 0.001$, indicated that correlations between items were sufficiently large for PCA. Five components had eigenvalues over Kaiser's criterion of one. They explained 62.53% of the variance. Given Kaiser's criterion, parallel analysis and the scree plot's inflexion, five components were retained. However, the oblique rotation failed to converge in 25 iterations, therefore four components were retained in the final analysis that explained 56.47% of the variance.

Table 3. Summary of exploratory factor analysis with direct oblimin rotation for the Cyberbullying Coping Questionnaire (CCQ) thoughts questionnaire (N = 211).

Item	Pattern Coefficients				Structure Coefficients				Communalities
	Mental Coping	Passive Coping	Social Coping	Confrontational Coping	Mental Coping	Passive Coping	Social Coping	Confrontational Coping	
9	**0.729**	0.248	-0.057	-0.148	**0.711**	0.343	0.138	0.043	0.589
3	**0.695**	-0.025	0.160	0.051	**0.748**	0.102	0.355	0.270	0.588
11	**0.660**	0.034	0.083	0.263	**0.712**	0.132	0.157	**0.422**	0.572
18	**0.619**	-.091	0.337	-0.064	**0.679**	0.044	**0.476**	0.172	0.566
5	**0.583**	0.026	0.019	0.299	**0.672**	0.128	0.246	**0.460**	0.537
19	0.193	**0.742**	-0.068	-0.124	0.256	**0.758**	0.055	-0.058	0.616
17	-0.159	**0.738**	0.188	-0.234	-0.060	**0.731**	0.191	-0.206	0.633
28	-0.195	**0.722**	-0.004	0.343	0.003	**0.706**	0.116	0.318	0.618
23	0.143	**0.599**	-0.034	0.149	0.263	**0.621**	0.116	0.202	0.435
1	0.153	**0.544**	0.093	-0.136	0.223	**0.574**	0.176	-0.054	0.371
27	0.052	**0.437**	0.057	0.394	0.238	**0.468**	0.216	**0.438**	0.402
26	-0.169	0.142	**0.783**	0.004	0.063	0.220	**0.757**	0.138	0.614
29	0.150	0.022	**0.748**	0.016	0.358	0.144	**0.795**	0.223	0.655
24	0.210	-0.002	**0.699**	0.061	**0.414**	0.124	**0.769**	0.272	0.641
6	0.198	-0.034	-0.070	**0.740**	0.371	0.015	0.142	**0.776**	0.637
31	-0.004	0.049	0.277	**0.719**	0.269	0.113	**0.442**	**0.781**	0.689
35	0.110	-0.209	0.365	**0.412**	0.286	-0.129	**0.458**	**0.514**	0.438
Eigen values	4.69	2.34	1.39				1.18		
% of variance	27.59	13.77	8.15				6.97		
α	0.77	0.73	0.73				0.68		
Ω	0.77	0.73	0.75				0.7		
GLB	0.77	0.79	0.76				0.73		

Note: Factor loadings over 0.40 appear in bold; GLB = Greatest Lower Bound.

To aid in the interpretation of these four components, an oblique (direct oblimin) rotation was performed. The rotation revealed that the four components showed a number of strong loadings. Table 3 shows the components loadings after rotation, communalities and reliabilities. The items that cluster on the same components suggest that component 1 represents mental coping (*i.e.*, items 3, 5, 9, 11, 18), component 2 represents passive coping (*i.e.*, items 1, 17, 19, 23, 27, 28), component 3 represents social coping (*i.e.*, items 24, 26, 29) and component 4 represents confrontational coping (*i.e.*, items 6, 31, 35). There were moderate correlations (component 1 and 2: $r = 0.15$; component 2 and 3: $r = 0.13$; component 3 and 4: $r = 0.22$; component 1 and 3: $r = 0.27$; component 1 and 4: $r = 0.27$; component 2 and 4: $r = 0.04$) between components.

3.2.2. Confirmatory Factor Analysis

To test whether PCA's structure of coping strategies (*i.e.*, the model) really fits the data, a CFA was conducted by using the statistical program R. Model fit was assessed using the Maximum Likelihood (ML) estimator with the following fit indices [116,117]: (1) chi square (x^2) with non-significant values reflecting good fit [118]; (2) the relative chi-square (x^2/df) lower than 2 [119]; (3) the Comparative Fit Index (CFI) and the Tucker Lewis Index (TLI) with values larger than 0.90 [112,120]; (4) the Root Mean Square Error of Approximation (RMSEA) with values smaller than 0.06 (values between 0.08 and 0.1 are mediocre and values above 0.1 are poor [117]); and (5) the Standardized Root Mean Square Residual (SRMR) with values lower than 0.08 indicate an acceptable fit [117].

The evaluation of the model fit was not satisfactory for most fit indices (see Table 4 first row) suggesting a rejection of the model. However, modification indices (MIs; indicating how to improve the model) clearly indicate that item 17 ("I let the cyberbullying happen without reacting") and item 7 ("I think about fun things that are not related to cyberbullying") should also load on the mental coping factor, which is plausible since both items can be strategies with a positive effect as well as mental strategies. In addition, MIs indicate that item 9 ("I try not to think about the cyberbullying") should also load on the passive coping factor, which is plausible since this item also expresses a degree of being passive.

Finally, MIs indicate that item 9 ("I try not to think about the cyberbullying") and 19 ("I act as if the cyberbullying did not happen") should correlate with each other, which is also plausible since both items in a way measure ignoring the cyberbullying. After modifying the model, the fit indices are all acceptable (however, RMSEA is not significant anymore) (see Table 3 second row). Furthermore, this model is significantly better fitting than a 1-factor model ($\Delta x^2(9) = 294.1$, $p < 0.001$; see Table 4). The final model is displayed in Figure 1, and its reliabilities in Table 5.

Table 4. Fit indices for first and second solution of Confirmatory Factor Analysis (CFA).

Model	χ^2	df	χ^2/df	$\Delta\chi^2$	Δdf	CFI	TLI	RMSEA	SRMR
1st solution	240.16 ***	113	2.13	-	-	0.868	0.841	0.073 ** (CI 90%: 0.060–0.086)	0.079
2nd solution	189.87 ***	109	1.74	294.1***	9	0.916	0.895	0.059 (CI 90%: 0.045–0.073)	0.058

Note: *** $p < 0.001$; ** $p < 0.01$; $N = 223$; CI = Confidence Interval.

Table 5. (Test-retest) reliabilities of the CFA model.

Coping categories	α	Ω	GLB	Test-retest r
Mental coping	0.7	0.72	0.74	0.65 *
Passive coping	0.73	0.73	0.8	0.47 *
Social coping	0.73	0.75	0.76	0.74 *
Confrontational coping	0.68	0.7	0.73	0.60 *

Note: * $p < 0.01$.

3.2.3. Test-Retest Reliability

A test-retest reliability of at least 0.60 was expected for a four to ten week interval [34]. See Table 5 for test-retest reliabilities for an interval of a month.

3.2.4. Discriminant Validity

Evidence for discriminant validity was assessed for the four factors of the CCQ based on correlations with the RSE. Low correlations were expected and found: all factors of the CCQ correlated between $r = -0.10$ and $r = 0.09$, which lie within the expected range.

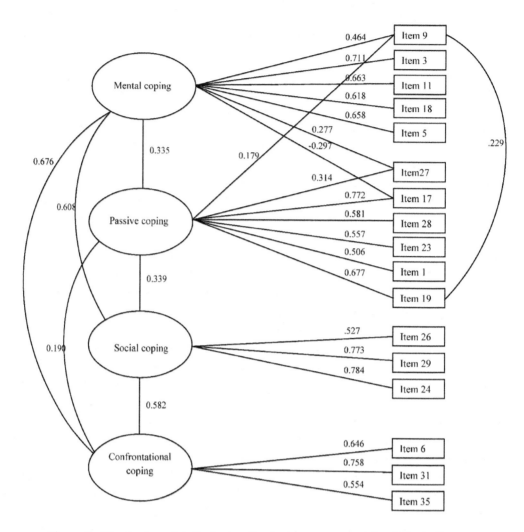

Figure 1. The final model displaying the factor structure of the Cyberbullying Coping Questionnaire including factor loadings.

4. Discussion

Researchers have attempted to measure coping with (cyber)bullying, using different self-report questionnaires (SRQs) that assess coping. Many of these SRQs are subject to different shortcomings: there is a lack of consensus about coping categories, SRQs fail to distinguish between categorizations, and often they do not specifically assess coping with cyberbullying [34,41] due to the deviating contexts and appraisals online [1,22,32]. Despite the importance of context and appraisals [22,32,33], SRQs measure coping in general or are preceded with a definition of cyberbullying.

In addition, they fail to see that online situations, contexts and appraisals, deviate from offline situations, which will lead to the selection of different coping strategies (e.g., online it is easier to be passive; you can close a window or shut down your computer). This study is therefore aimed to develop a SRQ, based on currently existing coping SRQs that are used in the (cyber)bullying literature, that specifically measures cyberbullying victims' coping strategies used in response to cyberbullying, and to formulate better fitting categorizations of coping strategies for cyberbullying. Consequently, the Cyberbullying Coping Questionnaire (CCQ) could be used in, for example, interventions that offer tailored advice to cyberbullying victims [108].

Although the initial model had to be adjusted based on modification indices, the evaluation of the final version (i.e., Figure 1) of the CCQ resulted in a four-factor model that fits the data well. The model has good internal consistency, acceptable test-retest reliability and good discriminant validity [34]. The development of the CCQ also fulfilled many of the recommendations from classical test-theory (see [34]): (1) the factor structure was determined with an oblique rotation; (2) the amount of extracting factors was determined with scree-tests in combination with parallel analysis; (3) factor loadings were at least 0.30; (4) the items of the CCQ seem to be clear and contain one statement, however, further research is needed to (further) determine the clarity and easiness of understanding; (5) with the final version of the CCQ consisting of 17 items, the recommendation of 10 participants per item was fulfilled; (6) factor structure was determined with a principal component analysis using oblique rotation, (7) the scree-test and parallel analysis determined the amount of extracting factors; and (8) factor loadings were at least 0.30. We failed to include at least 500 participants, and although initially twice as many items as in the final version were included, the recommendation of four items per factor was not fulfilled: two factors consist of three items.

The four factors of the CCQ all included both cognitive and behavioral items, avoidance and approach items [26], and active and passive items. The CCQ thus appears to omit working in single (*i.e.*, problem- *versus* emotion-focused) and topological (*i.e.*, cognitive *versus* behavioral, avoid *versus* approach, active *versus* passive) categorizations [3,27], but includes these types of categorization in each factor. The first factor that was found, the mental coping categorization, appears to capture one's mental attempts to deal with, or solve, the cyberbullying. Three items in this categorization represent a focus on problem-solving (e.g., "I focus on solving the cyberbullying problem immediately"), which is associated with reductions in cyberbullying frequency and less health complaints and depression [4]. The other four items represent victims' awareness about the stressful situation and the mental attempt to control the stress by mentally disconnecting from, or changing the way, they perceive the situation (e.g., "I think that other people are experiencing things that are much worse"). Hence, with this categorization of coping strategies, the victim does not necessarily solve the cyberbullying, but tries to find ways to stop the bullying while trying not to get too upset about the cyberbullying event (*i.e.*, it minimizes the painful impact of the stressful situation).

The second factor, the passive coping categorization, captures the way individuals manage cyberbullying events without actually solving the problem or trying to change the situation (e.g., "I ignore the bullies"). These items are possibly the only strategies one can use when situations appear to be uncontrollable. They are not necessarily negative; they appear to de-escalate and resolve the bullying [10]. Victims often recommend these strategies [37], but they are not always helpful [93]. Indeed, the victim fails at confronting the bully, and thus the use of the strategies in this categorization places the victim at risk for future victimization [5–12]. Furthermore, the use of such passive coping strategies is associated with more health complaints and depression than problem-solving coping [4], and the use of ineffective coping strategies appears to maintain online and offline bullying [5–12]. This is, however, an unavoidable categorization of coping; Parris *et al.*, [26] suggested that any model that attempts to measure coping should also include inaction.

The confirmatory factor analysis (CFA) indicates that there are three items that load on both the mental and passive coping categorizations (e.g., "I try not to think about the cyberbullying", "I let the cyberbullying happen without reacting", "I think about fun things that are not related to cyberbullying"). These strategies appear to indicate an active and mental attempt not to think about the cyberbullying, but also indicate a tendency to be inactive and thus being passive. Similarly to the strategies of the passive coping categorization, these strategies do not solve the problem but probably will relieve stress, because the victim tries to reinterpret the situation. In addition, two items (*i.e.*, "I try not to think about the cyberbullying" and "I act as if the cyberbullying did not happen") appear to be correlated: they both measure passive coping, however in a mental or behavioral way, respectively.

The third factor, the social coping categorization, constitutes actual behavior that one displays after being cyberbullied (e.g., "I ask someone (parent, teacher, friend, peer) for help"). These strategies are proactive because the victim actually tries to solve or cope with the problem in a constructive way, and these strategies are social because the victim uses his peer group. This strategy seems to strengthen the individual as well as solve the problem [34]. It is possible that a victim saves evidence in order (to be able) to show the actual behavior which is upsetting them when talking to someone else or asking for help.

The fourth and final factor, the confrontational coping categorization, appears to measure adolescents' strategies towards the cyberbully (e.g., "I tell the cyberbullies to stop"). Because the victim confronts the cyberbully with his or her behavior, for example by showing their irritation [10], these strategies can be interpreted as somewhat aggressive or as active but sometimes insufficient coping [92].

This strategy does not diminish the stress, however, it can help in solving the cyberbullying problem. Cyberbullies are often not aware of the consequences of their behavior because they consider the cyberbullying as an imaginary act of bullying (*i.e.,* dissociative imagination [33]) or they are not confronted with the emotional reaction of the victim (*i.e.,* the cockpit effect [121]). Hence, this coping categorization can lead to the discontinuation of cyberbullying by confronting the cyberbully with—and thus making him/her aware of—(the consequences of) his/her behavior.

This study is subjected to some strengths and limitations. A strength of this study is that the resulting SRQ omits single and topological categorizations [3,27]. These kinds of categorizations can result in too much heterogeneity among strategies [48] in which too many strategies (e.g., "I tell the cyberbullies to stop" and "I ask someone for help") are categorized into one coping factor (e.g., problem-solving coping), while they can be categorized in two factors (e.g., confrontational and social coping respectively). Therefore, it is highly likely that this SRQ will measure one's preferred coping strategies instead of measuring the extent in which contrasting coping strategies are used. In addition, this study found a four-factor (*i.e.,* mental, passive, social and confrontational coping) structure with categorizations that are internally valid, theoretically meaningful, and that measures both cognitive *versus* behavioral and approach *versus* avoidance natured strategies. Furthermore, the CCQ is an adapted and modified version of coping measures that already exist [41]. Finally, many of the recommendations from classical test-theory (e.g., [34]) are fulfilled during the development.

This study also has some limitations. To begin with, the number of participants was low (*i.e.,* 211), while classical test-theory suggests a minimum of 500 participants. Therefore, it is hard to assess construct validity and generalizability. Secondly, concurrent validity was not calculated as suggested [34]. Due to the length of the questionnaire, and the characteristics of the participant group (e.g., low educated, practical students who do not like to read) it was decided to keep the complete questionnaire as short as possible. Therefore, no additional SRQ that measures coping was used. Future studies should do this in order to establish concurrent validity. Thirdly, while performing factor analysis, several decisions (e.g., the number of factors to extract, the suitability of items for factor analysis) had to be made. This process has a certain subjectivity. Although not likely, it is possible that other researchers would have made different decision leading to a slightly different factor structure. Fourthly, the data used was part of an intervention study that aims to improve effective coping. Because the sample was relatively small, the second measurement of the experimental condition (*i.e.,* at the second measurement 31 out of 68 participants had received the first out of three advice sessions in which they learned how to change irrational thoughts into rational thoughts [108]) was not excluded for the test-retest analysis. Without the experimental condition, the

181

test-retest reliability only increased for the social coping factor (*i.e.*, α's were 0.89 for social, 0.62 for mental, 0.41 for passive, and 0.59 for confrontational coping), however N was 37. Moreover, coping with cyberbullying was changed by the intervention only in the second and third session, and the second measurement came before the second session. Nevertheless, just to be sure, future studies should validate the test-retest part of this study (*i.e.*, Figure 1) with data not obscured by an experimental design, and should take into account adolescents' opinions on meaningful and clear coping strategies, cultural backgrounds and developmental stages [41]. Finally, an assumption of this study was that online appraisals differ from offline appraisals, consequently leading to cyberbullying victims selecting different coping strategies compared to traditional bullying victims. However, this study did not explicitly measure appraisals. Future studies should also look into the appraisals of online victims of cyberbullying, and compare them with appraisals of offline victims.

In conclusion, this study seems to be a promising start in constructing a SRQ that measures coping with cyberbullying specifically. Many of the recommendations that come from classical test-theory were met, leading to a reliable and valid measure of coping. According to the results of this study, cyberbullying victims cope in a mental, passive, social or confrontational manner when faced with stress (*i.e.*, cyberbullying). Among these categorizations are both cognitive and behavioral and approach and avoidance strategies instead of cognitive *versus* behavioral and approach *versus* avoidance strategies. This SRQ thus seems to treat coping as a multidimensional process in which strategies serve multiple functions, instead of the many existing SRQs that consider coping to consist of single or topological categorizations.

Author Contributions: N.J. conceived of the study, conducted the preliminary study, recruited participants, conducted the analysis, and drafted the manuscript. N.J. and T.V. compared all items from the four selected adolescent coping SRQs with each other and merged and/or deleted items. F.D. controlled this process. F.D. and T.V. helped recruiting participants, helped to draft the manuscript and helped in drafting the final manuscript. L.L. supervised the whole research and helped with drafting and writing the final manuscript. N.J. processed all feedback from the other authors and reviewers. All authors read and approved of the final manuscript.

Conflicts of Interest: The authors declare no conflict of interest.

References

1. Lazarus, R.S.; Folkman, S. *Stress, Appraisal, and Coping*; Springer: New York, NY, USA, 1984.
2. Folkman, S.; Lazarus, R.S. An analysis of coping in a middle-aged community sample. *J. Health Soc. Behav.* **1980**, *21*, 219–239.
3. Skinner, E.A.; Edge, K.; Altman, J.; Sherwood, H. Searching for the structure of coping: A review and critique of category systems for classifying ways of coping. *Psychol. Bull.* **2003**, *129*, 216–269.

4. Völlink, T.; Bolman, C.A.W.; Eppingbroek, A.; Dehue, F. Emotion-Focused Coping Worsens Depressive Feelings and Health Complaints in Cyberbullied Children. *J. Criminol.* **2013**, *2013*, 1–10.

5. Andreou, E. Bully/Victim Problems and their Association with Coping Behaviour in Conflictual Peer Interactions Among School-age Children. *Educ. Psychol.* **2001**, *21*, 59–66.

6. Bijttebier, P.; Vertommen, H. Coping with peer arguments in school-age children with bully/victim problems. *Br. J. Educ. Psychol.* **1998**, *68*, 387–394.

7. Craig, W.; Pepler, D.; Blais, J. Responding to Bullying: What Works? *Sch. Psychol. Int.* **2007**, *28*, 465–477.

8. Hunter, S.C.; Boyle, J.M.E. Appraisal and coping strategy use in victims of school bullying. *Br. J. Educ. Psychol.* **2004**, *74*, 83–107.

9. Kristensen, S.M.; Smith, P.K. The use of coping strategies by Danish children classed as bullies, victims, bully/victims, and not involved, in response to different (hypothetical) types of bullying. *Scand. J. Psychol.* **2003**, *44*, 479–88.

10. Mahady Wilton, M.M.; Craig, W.M.; Pepler, D.J. Emotional Regulation and Display in Classroom Victims of Bullying: Characteristic Expressions of Affect, Coping Styles and Relevant Contextual Factors. *Soc. Dev.* **2000**, *9*, 227–245.

11. Perry, D.G.; Hodges, E.V.E.; Egan, S.K.; Juvonen, J.; Graham, S. Determinants of chronic victimization by peers: A review and new model of family influence. In *Peer Harass. Sch. Plight Vulnerable Vict*; Guilford Press: New York, NY, USA, 2001; pp. 73–104.

12. Skrzypiec, G.; Slee, P.; Murray-Harvey, R.; Pereira, B. School bullying by one or more ways: Does it matter and how do students cope? *Sch. Psychol. Int.* **2011**, *32*, 288–311.

13. Kowalski, R.M.; Giumetti, G.W.; Schroeder, A.N.; Lattanner, M.R. Bullying in the digital age: A critical review and meta-analysis of cyberbullying research among youth. *Psychol. Bull.* **2014**, *140*, 1073–1137.

14. Campbell, M.A.; Spears, B.; Slee, P.; Butler, D.; Kift, S. Victims' perceptions of traditional and cyberbullying, and the psychosocial correlates of their victimisation. *Emot. Behav. Difficulties* **2012**, *17*, 389–401.

15. Perren, S.; Dooley, J.; Shaw, T.; Cross, D. Bullying in school and cyberspace: Associations with depressive symptoms in Swiss and Australian adolescents. *Child Adolesc. Psychiatry Ment. Health* **2010**, *4*, 1–10.

16. Ybarra, M.L.; Mitchell, K.J. Youth engaging in online harassment: associations with caregiver-child relationships, Internet use, and personal characteristics. *J. Adolesc.* **2004**, *27*, 319–336.

17. Hinduja, S.; Patchin, J.W. Bullying, cyberbullying, and suicide. *Arch. Suicide Res.* **2010**, *14*, 206–221.

18. Schneider, S.K.; O'Donnell, L.; Stueve, A.; Coulter, R.W.S. Cyberbullying, school bullying, and psychological distress: A regional census of high school students. *Am. J. Public Health* **2012**, *102*, 171–177.

19. Hinduja, S.; Patchin, J.W. Offline Consequences of Online Victimization. *J. Sch. Violence* **2007**, *6*, 89–112.

20. Ortega, R.; Elipe, P.; Mora-Merchán, J.A.; Genta, M.L.; Brighi, A.; Guarini, A.; Smith, P.K.; Thompson, F.; Tippett, N. The emotional impact of bullying and cyberbullying on victims: A European cross-national study. *Aggress. Behav.* **2012**, *38*, 342–356.

21. Gradinger, P.; Strohmeier, D.; Spiel, C. Traditional bullying and cyberbullying: Identification of risk groups for adjustment problems. *Z. Psychol. Psychol.* **2009**, *217*, 205–213.

22. Ševčíková, A.; Šmahel, D.; Otavová, M. The perception of cyberbullying in adolescent victims. *Emot. Behav. Difficulties* **2012**, *17*, 319–328.

23. Van den Eijnden, R.; Vermulst, A.; van Rooij, T.; Meerkerk, G.J. *Monitor Internet en Jongeren: Pesten op Internet en het Psychosociale Welbevinden van Jongeren*; IVO: Rotterdam, The Netherlands, 2006. (In Dutch)

24. Black, C.; Wilson, G.T. Assessment of eating disorders: Interview *versus* questionnaire. *Int. J. Eat. Disord.* **1996**, *20*, 43–50.

25. Gravetter, F.J.; Forzano, L.B. *Research Methods for the Behavioral Sciences*; Wadsworth/Thomson Learning: Belmont, CA, USA, 2006.

26. Parris, L.; Varjas, K.; Meyers, J.; Cutts, H. High School Students' Perceptions of Coping With Cyberbullying. *Youth Soc.* **2011**, *44*, 284–306.

27. Compas, B.E.; Connor-Smith, J.K.; Saltzman, H.; Thomsen, A.H.; Wadsworth, M.E. Coping with stress during childhood and adolescence: Problems, progress, and potential in theory and research. *Psychol. Bull.* **2001**, *127*, 87–127.

28. Roth, S.; Cohen, L.J. Approach, avoidance, and coping with stress. *Am. Psychol.* **1986**, *41*, 813–819.

29. Kochenderfer-Ladd, B.; Skinner, K. Children's coping strategies: Moderators of the effects of peer victimization? *Dev. Psychol.* **2002**, *38*, 267–278.

30. Šleglova, V.; Cerna, A. Cyberbullying in Adolescent Victims: Perception and Coping. *Cyberpsychol. J. Psychosoc. Res. Cybersp.* **2011**, *5*. Article 4. Available online: www.cyberpsychology.eu/view.php?cisloclanku=2011121901&article=4.

31. Völlink, T.; Bolman, C.A.W.; Dehue, F.; Jacobs, N.C.L. Coping with Cyberbullying: Differences Between Victims, Bully-victims and Children not Involved in Bullying. *J. Community Appl. Soc. Psychol.* **2013**, *23*, 7–24.

32. Vandebosch, H.; Van Cleemput, K. Cyberbullying among youngsters: Profiles of bullies and victims. *New Media Soc.* **2009**, *11*, 1349–1371.

33. Kowalski, R.M.; Limber, S.P. Electronic Bullying Among Middle School Students. *J. Adolesc. Health* **2007**, *41*, S22–S30.

34. Sveinbjornsdottir, S.; Thorsteinsson, E.B. Adolescent coping scales: A critical psychometric review. *Scand. J. Psychol.* **2008**, *49*, 533–548.

35. Van Ouytsel, J.; Walrave, M.; Vandebosch, H. Correlates of Cyberbullying and How School Nurses Can Respond. *NASN Sch. Nurse* **2014**.

36. Noar, S.M.; Benac, C.N.; Harris, M.S. Does tailoring matter? Meta-analytic review of tailored print health behavior change interventions. *Psychol. Bull.* **2007**, *133*, 673–693.

37. Dehue, F.; Bolman, C.; Völlink, T. Cyberbullying: Youngsters" experiences and parental perception. *Cyberpsychol. Behav.* **2008**, *11*, 217–223.

38. Aricak, T.; Siyahhan, S.; Uzunhasanoglu, A.; Saribeyoglu, S.; Ciplak, S.; Yilmaz, N.; Memmedov, C. Cyberbullying among Turkish adolescents. *Cyberpsychol. Behav.* **2008**, *11*, 253–261.

39. Smith, P.; Mahdavi, J.; Carvalho, M.; Tippett, N. An investigation into cyberbullying, its forms, awareness and impact, and the relationship between age and gender in cyberbullying. Available online: http://webarchive.nationalarchives.gov.uk/20130401151715/http://www.education.gov.uk/publications/eOrderingDownload/RBX03-06.pdf (accessed on 5 December 2013).

40. Jacobs, N.C.L.; Goossens, L.; Dehue, F.; Völlink, T.; Lechner, L. Dutch Cyberbullying Victims' Experiences, Perceptions, Attitudes and Motivations Related to (Coping with) Cyberbullying: Focus Group Interviews. *Societies* **2015**, *5*, 43–64.

41. Garcia, C. Conceptualization and measurement of coping during adolescence: A review of the literature. *J. Nurs. Scholarsh* **2010**, *42*, 166–185.

42. Naylor, P.; Cowie, H. The effectiveness of peer support systems in challenging school bullying: The perspectives and experiences of teachers and pupils. *J. Adolesc.* **1999**, *22*, 467–479.

43. Kokkinos, C.M.; Antoniadou, N.; Dalara, E.; Koufogazou, A.; Papatziki, A. Cyber-Bullying, Personality and Coping among Pre-Adolescents. *Int. J. Cyber Behav. Psychol. Learn.* **2013**, *3*, 55–69.

44. Sharp, S. How much does bullying hurt? The effects of bullying on the personal wellbeing and educational progress of secondary aged students. *Educ. Child Psychol.* **1995**, *12*, 81–88.

45. Martin, J.; Gillies, R.M. How Adolescents Cope With Bullying. *Aust. J. Guid. Couns.* **2004**, *14*, 195–210.

46. Frydenberg, E.; Lewis, R. *The Adolescent Coping Scale: Administrator's Manual*; Australian Council for Educational Research: Melbourne, Australia, 1993.

47. Bijstra, J.O.; Jackson, S.; Bosma, H.A. De Utrechtse Coping Lijst voor Adolescenten. *Kind En Adolesc.* **1994**, *15*, 67–74.

48. Causey, D.L.; Dubow, E.F. Development of a self-report coping measure for elementary school children. *J. Clin. Child Psychol.* **1992**, *21*, 47–59.

49. Sandstrom, M.J. Pitfalls of the peer world: How children cope with common rejection experiences. *J. Abnorm. Child Psychol.* **2004**, *32*, 67–81.

50. Pozzoli, T.; Gini, G. Active Defending and Passive Bystanding Behavior in Bullying: The Role of Personal Characteristics and Perceived Peer Pressure. *J. Abnorm. Child Psychol.* **2010**, *38*, 815–827.

51. Terranova, A.; Harris, J.; Kavetski, M.; Oates, R. Responding to Peer Victimization: A Sense of Control Matters. *Child Youth Care Forum* **2011**, *40*, 1–16.

52. Spence, S.; De Young, A.; Toon, C.; Bond, S. Longitudinal examination of the associations between emotional dysregulation, coping responses to peer provocation, and victimisation in children. *Aust. J. Psychol.* **2009**, *61*, 145–155.

53. Visconti, K.J.; Sechler, C.M.; Kochenderfer-Ladd, B. Coping with peer victimization: The role of children's attributions. *Sch. Psychol. Q.* **2013**, *28*, 122–140.

54. Shelley, D.; Craig, W.M. Attributions and Coping Styles in Reducing Victimization. *Can. J. Sch. Psychol.* **2009**, *25*, 84–100.

55. Ayers, T.S.; Sandler, I.N. Manual for the Children's Coping Strategies Checklist and the How I Coped Under Pressure Scales. Available online: http://prc.asu.edu/docs/CCSC-HICUPS%20%20Manual2.pdf (accessed on 1 August 2014).

56. Kochenderfer-Ladd, B.; Pelletier, M.E. Teachers' views and beliefs about bullying: Influences on classroom management strategies and students' coping with peer victimization. *J. Sch. Psychol.* **2008**, *46*, 431–453.

57. Kochenderfer-Ladd, B. Peer Victimization: The Role of Emotions in Adaptive and Maladaptive Coping. *Soc. Dev.* **2004**, *13*, 329–349.

58. Lam, C.W.C.; Frydenberg, E. Coping in the Cyberworld: Program Implementation and Evaluation—A Pilot Project. *Aust. J. Guid. Couns.* **2009**, *19*, 196–215.

59. Lodge, J.; Frydenberg, E. Cyber-Bullying in Australian Schools: Profiles of Adolescent Coping and Insights for School Practitioners. *Aust. Educ. Dev. Psychol.* **2007**, *24*, 45–58.

60. Murray-harvey, R.; Skrzypiec, G.; Slee, P.T. Effective and Ineffective Coping With Bullying Strategies as Assessed by Informed Professionals and Their Use by Victimised Students. *Aust. J. Guid. Couns.* **2012**, *22*, 122–138.

61. Lodge, J. Exploring the measurement and structure of children's coping through the development of a short form of coping. *Aust. Educ. Dev. Psychol.* **2006**, *23*, 35–45.

62. Waasdorp, T.E.; Bagdi, A.; Bradshaw, C.P. Peer Victimization Among Urban, Predominantly African American Youth: Coping With Relational Aggression Between Friends. *J. Sch. Violence* **2009**, *9*, 98–116.

63. Southam-gerow, K.L.; Goodman, M.A. The regulating role of negative emotions in children's coping with peer rejection. *Child Psychiatry Hum. Dev.* **2010**, *41*, 515–534.

64. Amirkhan, J.H. A factor analytically derived measure of coping: The Coping Strategy Indicator. *J. Pers. Soc. Psychol.* **1990**, *59*, 1066–1074.

65. Palladino, B.E.; Nocentini, A.; Menesini, E. Online and offline peer led models against bullying and cyberbullying. *Psicothema* **2012**, *24*, 634–639.

66. Garnefski, N.; Rieffe, C.; Jellesma, F.; Terwogt, M.M.; Kraaij, V. Cognitive emotion regulation strategies and emotional problems in 9–11-year-old children: The development of an instrument. *Eur. Child Adolesc. Psychiatry* **2007**, *16*, 1–9.

67. Jellesma, F.C.; Verhulst, A.F.; Utens, E.M.W.J. Cognitive coping and childhood anxiety disorders. *Eur. Child Adolesc. Psychiatry* **2010**, *19*, 143–150.

68. Garnefski, N.; Kraaij, V.; Spinhoven, P. Negative life events, cognitive emotion regulation and emotional problems. *Pers. Individ. Dif.* **2001**, *30*, 1311–1327.

69. Ayers, T.S.; Sandier, I.N.; West, S.G.; Roosa, M.W. A Dispositional and Situational Assessment of Children's Coping: Testing Alternative Models of Coping. *J. Pers.* **1996**, *64*, 923–958.

70. Zimmer-Gembeck, M.J.; Lees, D.; Skinner, E.A. Children's emotions and coping with interpersonal stress as correlates of social competence. *Aust. J. Psychol.* **2011**, *63*, 131–141.

71. Hampel, P.; Dickow, B.; Petermann, F. Reliability and validity of the German Coping Questionnaire for Children and Adolescents (Ger-man). *Z. Diff. Diagn. Psychol.* **2002**, *23*, 273–289.

72. Hampel, P.; Manhal, S.; Hayer, T. Direct and relational bullying among children and adolescents: Coping and psychological adjustment. *Sch. Psychol. Int.* **2009**, *30*, 474–490.

73. Roger, D.; Jarvis, G.; Najarian, B. Detachment and coping: The construction and validation of a new scale for measuring coping strategies. *Pers. Individ. Dif.* **1993**, *15*, 619–626.

74. Grennan, S.; Woodhams, J. The impact of bullying and coping strategies on the psychological distress of young offenders. *Psychol. Crime Law* **2007**, *13*, 487–504.

75. Halstead, M.; Johnson, S.B.; Cunningham, W. Measuring Coping in Adolescents: An Application of the Ways of Coping Checklist. *J. Clin. Child. Psychol.* **1993**, *22*, 337–344.

76. Dise-Lewis, J.E. The Life Events and Coping Inventory: An assessment of stress in children. *Psychosom. Med.* **1988**, *50*, 484–499.

77. Olafsen, R.N.; Viemerö, V. Bully/victim problems and coping with stress in school among 10- to 12-year-old pupils in Åland, Finland. *Aggress. Behav.* **2000**, *26*, 57–65.

78. Lodge, J.; Feldman, S.S. Avoidant coping as a mediator between appearance-related victimization and self-esteem in youn Asutralian adolescents. *Br. J. Dev. Psychol.* **2007**, *25*, 633–642.

79. Cassidy, T.; Long, C. Problem-solving style, stress and psychological illness: Development of a multifactorial measure. *Br. J. Clin. Psychol.* **1996**, *35*, 265–277.

80. Cassidy, T.; Taylor, L. Coping and psychological distress as a function of the bully victim dichotomy in older children. *Soc. Psychol. Educ.* **2005**, *8*, 249–262.

81. Carver, C.S.; Scheier, M.F.; Weintraub, J.K. Assessing coping strategies: A theoretically based approach. *J. Pers. Soc. Psychol.* **1989**, *56*, 267–283.

82. Newman, M.L.; Holden, G.W.; Delville, Y. Coping With the Stress of Being Bullied: Consequences of Coping Strategies Among College Students. *Soc. Psychol. Personal. Sci.* **2010**.

83. Folkman, S.; Lazarus, R.S. If it changes it must be a process: Study of emotion and coping during three stages of a college examination. *J. Pers. Soc. Psychol.* **1985**, *48*, 150–170.

84. Remillard, A.M.; Lamb, S. Adolescent Girls' Coping With Relational Aggression. *Sex Roles* **2005**, *53*, 221–229.

85. Salmivalli, C.; Karhunen, J.; Lagerspetz, K.M.J. How do the victims respond to bullying? *Aggress. Behav.* **1996**, *22*, 99–109.

86. Puhl, R.M.; Luedicke, J. Weight-based victimization among adolescents in the school setting: Emotional reactions and coping behaviors. *J. Youth Adolesc.* **2012**, *41*, 27–40.

87. Harper, C.R.; Parris, L.N.; Henrich, C.C.; Varjas, K.; Meyers, J. Peer Victimization and School Safety: The Role of Coping Effectiveness. *J. Sch. Violence* **2012**, *11*, 267–287.

88. Tenenbaum, L.S.; Varjas, K.; Meyers, J.; Parris, L. Coping strategies and perceived effectiveness in fourth through eighth grade victims of bullying. *Sch. Psychol. Int.* **2011**, *32*, 263–287.

89. Machmutow, K.; Perren, S.; Sticca, F.; Alsaker, F.D. Peer victimisation and depressive symptoms: Can specific coping strategies buffer the negative impact of cybervictimisation? *Emot. Behav. Difficulties* **2012**, *17*, 403–420.

90. Machmutow, K.; Perren, S. Coping with cyberbullying: Successful and unsuccessful coping strategies. In Poster presented at the 3rd COST workshop on cyberbullying, Turku, Finland, 13 May 2011.

91. Jäger, T.; Jäger, R.S. *LAPSuS: Landauer Anti-Gewalt-Programm für Schülerinnen und Schüler*; Zentrum für Empirische Pädagogische Forschung: Landau, Germany, 1996. (In German)

92. Riebel, J.; Jäger, R.S.; Fischer, U.C. Cyberbullying in Germany—An exploration of prevalence, overlapping with real life bullying and coping strategies. *Psychol. Sci. Q.* **2009**, *51*, 298–314.

93. Machackova, H.; Cerna, A.; Sevcikova, A.; Dedkova, L.; Daneback, K. Effectiveness of coping strategies for victims of cyberbullying. *Cyberpsychol. J. Psychosoc. Res. Cybersp.* **2013**, *7*. Article 5. Available online: http://www.cyberpsychology.eu/view.php?cisloclanku=2014012101&article=5 (accessed on 30 July 2014).

94. Perren, S.; Corcoran, L.; Cowie, H.; Dehue, F.; Garcia, D.; Mc Guckin, C. Cyberbullying and traditional bullying in adolescence: Differential roles of moral disengagement, moral emotions, and moral values. *Eur. J. Dev. Psychol.* **2012**, *9*, 195–209.

95. Hunter, S.C.; Boyle, J.M.E.; Warden, D. Help seeking amongst child and adolescent victims of peer-aggression and bullying: The influence of school-stage, gender, victimisation, appraisal, and emotion. *Br. J. Educ. Psychol.* **2004**, *74*, 375–390.

96. Patchin, J.W.; Hinduja, S. Bullies Move Beyond the Schoolyard: A Preliminary Look at Cyberbullying. *Youth Violence Juv. Justice* **2006**, *4*, 148–169.

97. Price, M.; Dalgleish, J. Cyberbullying: Experiences, impacts and coping strategies as described by Australian young people. *Youth Stud. Aust.* **2010**, *29*, 51–59.

98. Hunter, S.C.; Mora-Merchan, J.; Ortega, R. The Long-Term Effects of Coping Strategy Use in Victims of Bullying. *Span. J. Psychol.* **2004**, *7*, 3–12.

99. Kanetsuna, T.; Smith, P.K. Pupil Insights into Bullying, and Coping with Bullying—A Bi-National Study in Japan and England. *J. Sch. Violence* **2002**, *1*, 5–29.

100. Smith, P.K.; Shu, S. What Good Schools can Do About Bullying: Findings from a Survey in English Schools After a Decade of Research and Action. *Childhood* **2000**, *7*, 193–212.

101. Hunter, S.C.; Boyle, J.M.E. Perceptions of control in the victims of school bullying: The importance of early intervention. *Educ. Res.* **2002**, *44*, 323–336.

102. Naylor, P.; Cowie, H.; Rey, R. Coping strategies of secondary school children in response to being bullied. *Child Adolesc. Ment. Health* **2001**, *6*, 114–120.

103. Schenk, A.M.; Fremouw, W.J. Prevalence, Psychological Impact, and Coping of Cyberbully Victims Among College Students. *J. Sch. Violence* **2012**, *11*, 21–37.

104. Elledge, L.C.; Cavell, T.A.; Ogle, N.T.; Newgent, R.A.; Faith, M.A. History of peer victimization and children's response to school bullying. *Sch. Psychol. Q.* **2010**, *25*, 129–141.

105. Kochenderfer, B.J.; Ladd, G.W. Victimized children's responses to peers' aggression: Behaviors associated with reduced *versus* continued victimization. *Dev. Psychopathol.* **1997**, *9*, 59–73.

106. Garnefski, V.; Kraaij, N.; Spinhoven, P. *Manual for the Use of the Cognitive Emotion Regulation Questionnaire*; DATEC: Leidorp, The Netherlands, 2002.

107. Jacobs, N.C.L.; Völlink, T.; Dehue, F.; Lechner, L. *Procesevaluatie van Online Pestkoppenstoppen*; Open University: Heerlen, The Netherlands, 2014. (In Dutch)

108. Jacobs, N.C.L.; Völlink, T.; Dehue, F.; Lechner, L. Online Pestkoppenstoppen: Systematic and theory-based development of a web-based tailored intervention for adolescent cyberbully victims to combat and prevent cyberbullying. *BMC Public Health* **2014**, *14*, 396.

109. Conway, J.M.; Huffcutt, A.I. A review and evaluation of exploratory factor analysis practices in organizational research. *Organ Res. Methods* **2003**, *6*, 147–168.

110. Field, A. *Discovering Statistics Using SPSS*, 3rd ed.; SAGE Publications Limited: Los Angeles, CA, USA; London, UK; New Delhi, India; Singapore, Singapore; Washington, DC, USA, 2009.

111. Rosenberg, M. *Conceiving the Self*; Basic Books: New York, NY, USA, 1979.

112. Tabachnick, B.G.; Fidell, L.S. *Using Multivariate Statistics*, 5th ed.; Allyn & Bacon: Boston, MA, USA, 2007.

113. Linting, M.; van der Kooij, A. Nonlinear principal components analysis with CATPCA: A tutorial. *J. Pers. Assess.* **2012**, *94*, 12–25.

114. Linting, M.; Meulman, J.J.; Groenen, P.J.F.; van der Kooij, A.J. Nonlinear principal components analysis: Introduction and application. *Psychol. Methods* **2007**, *12*, 336–358.

115. Kline, P. *An Easy Guide to Factor Analysis*; Routledge: London, UK, 1994.

116. Jackson, D.L.; Gillaspy, J.A.; Purc-Stephenson, R. Reporting practices in confirmatory factor analysis: An overview and some recommendations. *Psychol. Methods* **2009**, *14*, 6–23.

117. Kenny, D.A. Measuring Model Fit 2012. Available online: http://davidakenny.net/cm/fit.htm (accessed on 2 July 2014).

118. Bollen, K.A. *Structural Equations with Latent Variables*; John Wiley & Sons: New York, NY, USA, 1989.

119. Arbuckle, J.L. *Amos 20 User's Guide*; IBM: Chicago, IL, USA, 2001.

120. Tabachnick, B.G.; Fidell, L.S. *Using Multivariate Statistics*, 4th ed.; Allyn & Bacon: Boston, MA, USA, 2001.

121. Heirman, W.; Walrave, M. Assessing Concerns and Issues about the Mediation of Technology in Cyberbullying. *Cyberpsychol. J. Psychosoc. Res. Cybersp.* **2008**, *2*, 1–12.

189

The Coping with Cyberbullying Questionnaire: Development of a New Measure

Fabio Sticca, Katja Machmutow, Ariane Stauber, Sonja Perren,
Benedetta Emanuela Palladino, Annalaura Nocentini, Ersilia Menesini,
Lucie Corcoran and Conor Mc Guckin

Abstract: Victims of cyberbullying report a number of undesirable outcomes regarding their well-being, especially those who are not able to successfully cope with cyber victimization. Research on coping with cyberbullying has identified a number of different coping strategies that seem to be differentially adaptive in cases of cyber victimization. However, knowledge regarding the effectiveness of these strategies is scarce. This scarcity is partially due to the lack of valid and reliable instruments for the assessment of coping strategies in the context of cyber victimization. The present study outlines the development of the Coping with Cyberbullying Questionnaire (CWCBQ) and tests of its reliability and construct validity over a total of five questionnaire development stages. The CWCBQ was developed in the context of a longitudinal study carried out in Switzerland and was also used with Italian and Irish samples of adolescents. The results of these different studies and stages resulted in a questionnaire that is composed of seven subscales (*i.e.,* distal advice, assertiveness, helplessness/self-blame, active ignoring, retaliation, close support and technical coping) with a total of 36 items. The CWCBQ is still being developed, but the results obtained so far suggested that the questionnaire was reliable and valid among the countries where it was used at different stages of its development. The CWCBQ is a promising tool for the understanding of potential coping with experiences of cyber victimization and for the development of prevention and intervention programs.

Reprinted from *Societies*. Cite as: Sticca, F.; Machmutow, K.; Stauber, A.; Perren, S.; Palladino, B.E.; Nocentini, A.; Menesini, E.; Corcoran, L.; Guckin, C.M. The Coping with Cyberbullying Questionnaire: Development of a New Measure. *Societies* **2015**, *5*, 515–536.

1. Introduction

Cyberbullying can be defined as an intentional aggressive behaviour that is performed by a person or group of persons using electronic forms of communication repeatedly and over time against a victim who cannot easily defend himself or herself [1]. Over the last few decades, the phenomenon of cyberbullying has become a

190

major issue in many countries. Modecki, Minchin, Harbaugh, Guerra and Runions [2] reviewed and conducted a meta-analysis of a total of 80 studies on traditional bullying and cyberbullying, finding that the prevalence of cyber victimization (*i.e.*, suffering cyberbullying) is as high as 15%.

Given the often severe nature of cyberbullying, it is not surprising that experiencing it as a victim might lead to a number of undesirable outcomes. Indeed, research on cyber victimization has shown that cyber victims report increased depressive and psychosomatic symptoms [3–5], anxiety [6], lower levels of self-esteem [3,7,8], emotional distress, anger and sadness [5,9,10], social difficulties [11], academic problems and school absenteeism [8,12], suspensions from school and weapon carrying at school [13], deterioration of home life [9], substance use [14] and suicidal ideation [15]. In short, cyber victimization can potentially have negative effects on the victim's well-being, in particular if combined with other sources of stress, such as traditional victimization [16].

The list of potential negative outcomes of cyber victimization shows how distressing these experiences can be. However, not all cyber victims report undesirable outcomes that result from their cyber victimization experience [17–19]. Besides the variability in the nature, frequency and seriousness of the bullying experience [20–22], the use and the effectiveness of coping strategies might be one reason for these inter-individual differences in the effects of cyberbullying on well-being [18,19]. Coping can be defined as the effort to manage stress and related emotions and is crucial for the sustainment of emotional and psychological well-being in the case of adversity [23]. Two kinds of strategies with different main functions of coping are differentiated: problem-focused coping strategies, which are directed at managing the problem causing the distress, and emotion-focused coping strategies, which are directed at regulating the emotional response to the problem [24]. Problem-focused and emotion-focused coping should not be seen as two isolated types of coping, because in most cases of stress situations, they complement each other [23]. Individuals tend to use problem-focused coping when it is possible to exert control over the stressful situation and with enough resources. In contrast, they use emotion-focused coping when they think that they have limited resources and that they can do little to change the situation [24].

Perren *et al.* [25] reviewed a total of 36 studies on cyberbullying prevention strategies. The authors proposed three domains of responses to cyberbullying: reducing risks, combating cyberbullying and buffering the negative impact. Strategies for reducing risks included traditional anti-bullying programs and their various components that were found to be effective. Moreover, this included specific Internet safety strategies (e.g., not giving away passwords or using different ones) and parental mediation of children's and youth's online activities (e.g., accompanying them online, talking to them about their Internet experience).

Combating cyberbullying encompasses coping strategies that can be used when experiencing cyberbullying. These can be divided into technical solutions (e.g., blocking), confronting the cyberbully (e.g., constructive discussion or revenge), active ignoring (e.g., pretend that nothing happened, forgetting about it) and instrumental support (e.g., asking peers, parent or teachers for help). Lastly, buffering the negative impact includes emotional support from peers, parents and teachers and emotional coping, such as self-blame (maladaptive) and perpetrator blame (adaptive) [25].

Although Livingstone, Haddon, Görzig and Olaffson [26] concluded that children's coping strategies can be expected to be effective, Perren *et al.* [25] conclude their overview by stating that there is very little empirical evidence on the effectiveness of coping strategies in the context of cyberbullying and that research in this field is at its very beginning. The effectiveness of coping strategies is important, because the use of particular forms of coping seems to be strongly related to the emotional well-being of an individual [23]. Although it is important not to value a specific form of coping without reference to the context in which it is disposed, findings of empirical studies lead to the assumption that a problem-focused coping is often more adaptive than an emotion-focused coping [27]. Whereas problem-focused coping strategies are associated with positive affect and increased emotional regulation, emotional-focused coping strategies seem to be related with emotions of distress [28,29].

Consistent with this pattern, research on traditional victimization found that experiences of victimization were associated with less use of problem-focused coping strategies and with more psychological distress [30]. Therefore, victims are probably more likely to evaluate bullying as less changeable than non-victims. Furthermore, in the context of cyberbullying, victims seem to use emotion-focused coping strategies, like emotional expression, depressive coping and avoidance in daily life, more than other adolescents [31]. In the investigation of Völlink, Bolman, Eppingbroek and Dehue [32], only emotion-focused cyber-specific coping was associated with increased depressive feelings and other health complaints among cyber victims. This leads us to question if there are other, more effective coping strategies that may even buffer the negative short- and long-term consequences of cyber victimization on adolescents' mental health. The first longitudinal study of Machmutow *et al.* [18] showed that in contrast to helpless reactions and assertive coping, both of which were positively associated with depressive symptoms, seeking support from peers and family showed a significant buffering effect: cyber victims who were recommended to seek close support as a coping strategy showed lower levels of depressive symptoms over time. However, in the study by Völlink *et al.* [32], the buffering effect of problem-focused coping, measured with items about confronting coping and social support coping, was not confirmed. In sum, our knowledge about effective coping with cyberbullying is very limited [25].

As the issue of cyberbullying has emerged during the last two decades, research on coping with cyberbullying is as young as research on cyberbullying and as the phenomenon of cyberbullying itself. Examining how adolescents cope with experiences of cyber victimization and exploring which coping strategies are positively related to well-being (or negatively to undesirable outcomes) would yield important knowledge on how coping strategies mediate or moderate the association between experiences of cyber victimization and well-being and, lastly, on how to reduce the negative impact of cyber victimization. This knowledge would help teachers, parents, practitioners and cyber victims to cope with the negative experiences and to reduce the negative impact of bullying. One necessary condition for following this aim is the availability of a valid and reliable instrument for the assessment of coping strategies in relation to adolescents' experiences of cyber-victimization. To the best of our knowledge, no such instrument exists to date. For that reason, the aim of the present study was to develop a new instrument: the Coping with Cyberbullying Questionnaire (CWCBQ). The CWCBQ was developed in the context of a Swiss longitudinal study of cyberbullying in adolescence (netTEEN: "Wie nett sind Teens im Internet"; [18,21,22,33,34]). The entire process of the development of the CWCBQ is described in this paper, including qualitative pilot studies and assessments of its validity and reliability using data that were collected in Switzerland, Italy and Ireland.

2. Development of the Coping with Cyberbullying Questionnaire

The CWCBQ was developed to examine how adolescents would cope with hypothetical experiences of cyberbullying. The questionnaire underwent a total of five development stages. These stages are described hereunder.

Stage 1: In the context of an online pilot study that was carried out in late 2010, 127 German-speaking students were given a definition of cyberbullying and were asked a number of open-ended questions about their personal experience with cyber victimization. The questions were divided into four blocks: (1) "Have you ever suffered cyberbullying or did you ever witness how one of your friends suffered cyberbullying? How did you or your friend react to that?" (2) "In case you never experienced or witnessed cyberbullying, how would you react if someone bullied you through the Internet, emails or mobile phones?" (3) "What kind of behaviour do you think would help when experiencing cyberbullying?" (4) "What kind of reaction would worsen the situation?" Based on theoretical considerations [35–37], content analyses of the students' answers were conducted by one research assistant and yielded five coping dimensions: reactions toward the bully, ignoring, support, emotion-focussed reactions and technical solutions. These results marked the starting point for the development process of the quantitative questionnaire that is described in the following.

Stage 2: Based on these results from the qualitative pilot study, the first version of a quantitative coping questionnaire was developed. The coping questionnaire encompassed four subscales with a total of 14 items developed. The wording of the 14 items was based on the open-ended responses of the students that were gained in the pilot study and were simplified and modified to fit the format of the coping questionnaire (*i.e.*, "I would ... "). Further, a total of 32 different hypothetical cyberbullying scenarios were developed. These scenarios were systematically manipulated with respect to the severity and the publicity of the cyberbullying experience, as well as with respect to the gender of the hypothetical victim and acceptance in his or her peer group. This manipulation was used because it was assumed that both the use and the perceived success of a specific coping strategy depend on several characteristics of the cyberbullying experience at hand. These scenarios were then used during the second wave of data assessment in the longitudinal netTEEN-study carried out in Switzerland in May 2011. The coping questionnaire was distributed to students that managed to complete the other scales that were included in the netTEEN study [18,21,22,33,34] within time at their disposal (*i.e.*, 45 or 60 minutes depending on the school) and still had enough time left over to complete the coping questionnaire. A total of 765 students completed one of these coping questionnaires with a randomly-assigned scenario. Students were asked to imagine that they experienced something similar to what was described in the respective scenario and to rate how likely they were to use each of the 14 coping strategies on a scale ranging from one (definitely not) to four (definitely). The results of an exploratory factor analysis suggested that five subscales were present within the 14 items. These five subscales were in line with our expectations and were interpreted as: (1) distal advice; (2) close support; (3) assertiveness; (4) helplessness; and (5) retaliation [18]. All subscales were composed of three items, except retaliation, which was composed of a single item. One item had to be eliminated from the questionnaire, as the factor analysis indicated that the students had understood it ambiguously (*i.e.*, strong cross-loadings). However, the reliabilities of the five dimensions of the coping questionnaire that resulted from Stage 2 were not considered satisfactory, and the number of items was considered to be too low for the retaliation subscale. Therefore, a further stage of the questionnaire development process was initiated.

Stage 3: Results from Stage 2 were used as a starting point for a revision of the questionnaire. The questionnaire was revised based on theoretical considerations [36,38] and on students' open-ended answers obtained in Stage 1. The result of this revision was a questionnaire with a total of six subscales of three items each: (1) distal advice; (2) close support; (3) retaliation; (4) assertiveness; (5) active ignoring; and (6) helplessness/self-blame. Further, just one (Switzerland and Italy) or two (Ireland) cyberbullying scenarios were chosen (as opposed to the 32 scenarios that were used in

Stage 2). The scenario that was used in both Switzerland and Italy was the following: "Sometimes, the Internet or mobiles are used to bully others. Imagine that for a few weeks, you have been receiving nasty and threatening text messages. Aside from that, you found out that embarrassing pictures of you are being spread around". In Ireland, two different hypothetical scenarios of varying severity were developed. The wording of the scenarios was "Imagine that for the last few days, you frequently received text messages telling you that everyone in school thinks that you are a total loser" and "Imagine that yesterday, a friend told you that he or she saw a YouTube video of you from the last school trip. In this video, you are seen in an embarrassing state of undress for several minutes while changing your clothes". The purpose of this approach was to allow for the examination of coping preferences in different contexts. Although there is cyber-based victimization in both scenarios, the second scenario is exposing the individual to more public victimization and is also thought to be a more severe form of victimization, as it involves a video of the targeted person in a state of undress. In order to maximise the comparability between scenarios, we decided to use only data based on the first scenario for the analyses carried out at this step. As in previous versions of the questionnaire, students were asked to rate how likely they were to use each of the 18 coping strategies on a scale ranging from one (definitely not) to four (definitely). This version of the questionnaire was named the Coping with Cyberbullying Questionnaire (CWCBQ) and was used during the third assessment of the netTEEN study (November 2011). As the netTEEN study was carried out both in the German-speaking and the Italian-speaking part of Switzerland, the questionnaire was translated from its original German version to an Italian version. Further, the questionnaire was also translated from the German version to an English version to be used in Ireland. The translations were made by a total of six independent bilingual translators. Three of them worked on the Italian translation, and three worked on the English translation. The Italian version of the CWCBQ was also used in a study carried out in Italy [39], while the English version was used in a study carried out in Ireland [40]. In sum, the CWCBQ was used in Switzerland ($N = 803$), Italy ($N = 755$) and Ireland ($N = 2412$). While in Stage 2, the questionnaire was only distributed to those students that managed to complete the other scales, in Stage 3, the CWCBQ was distributed to all students. Note that the 803 students that participated in Stage 3 in Switzerland mostly also participated in Stage 2, as all assessments that were carried out in Switzerland were part of the longitudinal netTEEN study [18,21,22,33,34]. Given this unique opportunity resulting from a rich database, we examined the construct validity on the CWCBQ and tested it towards measurement invariance among the three countries.

Testing measurement invariance: Measurement invariance is a prerequisite for comparisons between different groups, such as different nations; only if measurement invariance is given can we be sure that, "under different conditions of observing and studying phenomena, measurement operations yield measures of the same attribute" [41]. Jöreskog [42] described multi-group confirmatory factor analysis (MGCFA) as a method to simultaneously perform factor analyses with different samples, and Steenkamp and Baumgartner [43] proposed a unified and sequential way to test for metric invariance among them. The authors outlined a testing strategy with increasingly restrictive levels of invariance. The less restrictive level is called configural invariance, followed by metric invariance and, finally, scalar invariance. Configural invariance means that the constructs are represented by the indicators among countries and is given when three conditions are met: (1) the same configuration of loadings and latent factors must be present (including cross-loadings); (2) all factor loadings must be both substantial and significant; and (3) the correlations among the latent factors must be lower than one (discriminant validity). Metric invariance means that the representation of the constructs is invariant across countries and is given when the factor loadings between indicators and latent constructs are invariant among countries. Finally, scalar invariance means that differences in the means of the indicators among countries are due to differences in the means of the latent constructs and is given when the intercepts of the indicators are invariant across countries.

Configural invariance: In the first step, we tested data from the three countries towards configural invariance. Thus, we modelled an MGCFA with three groups (Switzerland, Ireland, Italy). Following our theoretical model, for each group, we modelled an *a priori* CFA with six latent factors (*i.e.*, distal advice, close support, retaliation, assertiveness, active ignoring and helplessness/self-blame) represented by three indicators each. This model was not found to fit the data well (χ^2 = 2488.675; degrees of freedom (df) = 360; Comparative Fit Index (CFI) = 0.867; Root Mean Square Error of Approximation (RMSEA) = 0.067; Standardized Root Mean Square Residual (SRMR) = 0.072). Modification indices showed that the item "I would encourage my peers (e.g., my group of friends) to exclude the bully" from the retaliation subscale showed strong cross-loadings on a number of other latent factors, with particularly strong cross-loadings on assertiveness and close support in the Swiss sample. Given that the pattern of these cross-loadings was not in line with theoretical assumptions and that the cross-loadings were mainly found in the Swiss subsample, we decided to delete this item and to run the MGCFA without it. This adapted model was not found to fit the data well (χ^2 = 2128.580; df = 312; CFI = 0.878; RMSEA = 0.066; SRMR = 0.066). Modification indices showed that the item "I would take technical precautions (e.g., make my password more secure, change my mobile phone number and/or email address, *etc.*)" from the assertiveness subscale exhibited very strong cross-loadings on a number of other latent factors, with particularly strong cross-loadings on distal advice and close support in the Irish sample. Again, given that the pattern of these cross-loadings was not in line with theoretical assumptions and that the cross-loadings were mainly found in the Irish subsample, we decided to delete this item and to run the MGCFA without it. The resulting model was not found to fit the data well (χ^2 = 1645.204; df = 269; CFI = 0.903; RMSEA = 0.062; SRMR = 0.054). Modification indices showed that the item "I would avoid any further contact with the bully" from the active ignoring subscale exhibited very strong cross-loadings on a number of other latent factors, with particularly strong cross-loadings on retaliation, distal advice and close support in the Italian sample. Again, given that the pattern of these cross-loadings was not in line with theoretical assumptions and that the cross-loadings were mainly found in the Italian subsample, we decided to delete this item and to run the MGCFA without it. The resulting model showed a satisfactory fit to the data (see Table 1). All loadings were found to be significant and higher than 0.40, with most of them being higher than 0.60. Correlations between latent factors were found to be between −0.40 and 0.68. Thus, discriminant validity was also found among the subscales. Accordingly, all criteria for configural invariance among the three countries were met.

Table 1. Model fit indices for the three levels of measurement invariance (N = 3970).

Model	χ^2	df	CFI	RMSEA	SRMR
Configural	1181.946	225	0.926	0.048	0.048
Metric [1]	1220.372	243	0.925	0.055	0.051
Partial scalar [2]	1307.943	255	0.919	0.056	0.051

Notes: [1] Factor loadings equal among countries; [2] item intercepts partially equal among countries.

Metric invariance: In the second step, data from the three countries was tested towards metric invariance. All factor loadings were constrained to be equal among countries. The resulting model showed a satisfactory fit to the data (see Table 1). Given the large sample size of the present study, it was to be expected that the scaled chi-square test would indicate a significant deterioration in model fit as a consequence of the metric invariance constraints. However, simulation studies showed that with large sample sizes, the change in CFI might be a better indicator for model fit deterioration than the change in chi-square, as chi-square tests are notoriously affected by sample size [44]. The difference in CFI was found to be −0.001, which is ten-times smaller than the recommended threshold of −0.01 for accepting the null hypothesis of invariance [44]. Thus, it seemed eligible to conclude that metric invariance was given.

Scalar invariance: In the third and last step, data from the three countries was tested towards scalar invariance. All item intercepts were constrained to be equal among countries. The resulting model was not found to fit the data well (χ^2 = 1959.248; df = 261; CFI = 0.869; RMSEA = 0.070; SRMR = 0.072), which means that scalar invariance is not given for all latent constructs and countries. Modification indices were used to examine which item intercepts would have to be released to achieve a satisfactory model fit. Results indicated that the item "I would go to the police" from the distal advice subscale, the item "I would accept the situation as it is because there is nothing you can do to stop bullying" from the helplessness/self-blame subscale and the item "I would ignore all messages/pictures so that the bully would lose interest" from the active ignoring subscale were not found to have an invariant item intercept. These three item intercepts were then progressively released to reach partial scalar invariance. The resulting model showed a satisfactory fit to the data, and the reduction in CFI was found to be as small as -0.006. Table 2 lists the standardized factor loadings and the unstandardized item intercepts for each item and for each country. Descriptive statistics and reliabilities of the latent constructs can be found in Table 3. Correlations between the latent factors are listed in Table 4. Thus, although no full scalar invariance was found, partial scalar invariance was found.

Stage 4: Results from Stage 3 were satisfactory in that configural, metric and partial scalar invariance were found for 15 out of the 18 items, which, for instance, permits mean comparisons across the three countries for all six subscales [45]. However, three of the six subscales were left with only two items, which means that the respective latent factors would be under-identified in further analyses. Ideally, a latent factor should be just identified, which is the case when there are three indicators for each latent factor [46,47]. With this goal in mind and given the results from Stage 3, the CWCBQ was revised again, based on theoretical considerations and open-ended answers from Step 1. Those items that were excluded from the analyses in Stage 3 were nonetheless carried forward into this next stage of questionnaire development to make a replication of the results from Stage 3 potentially possible. The result of this revision was that all six subscales were composed of five items. Additionally, a seventh subscale of four items tapping into technical coping strategies was developed. Therefore, the revised version of the CWCBQ encompassed seven subscales with a total of 34 items. At this stage, the format of the CWCBQ was the same one as in Stage 3 (*i.e.*, only one scenario). Again, an Italian version of the CWCBQ was developed based on the German original version following the same translation procedure as described in Stage 3. This revised version of the CWCBQ was used in a follow-up study carried out among the Italian sample in mid-2012 [39]. In total, 358 students completed this version of the CWCBQ. Results of a CFA showed that the *a priori* model with the seven subscales did not fit the data well ($\chi^2 = 995.178$; df = 506; CFI = 0.835; RMSEA = 0.052; SRMR = 0.087). Modification indices indicated that a total of 10 items showed a pattern of cross-loadings that was not in line with theoretical expectations (one item each from the distal advice, assertiveness, retaliation, close support and technical coping subscales, two items from the helplessness/self-blame subscale and three items from the active ignoring subscale) and/or had loadings that were below 0.50. Therefore, these items were deleted, and the CFA was performed again without these items. Results of the CFA with seven subscales and 24 items showed that the model fit the data very well (χ^2 = 345.055; df = 231; CFI = 0.948; RMSEA = 0.037; SRMR = 0.051). Thus, the construct validity and the divergent validity of the questionnaire were found for the version of the CWCBQ presented in Table 5. Table 5 lists the standardized factor loadings and the unstandardized item intercepts for each item. Descriptive statistics and reliabilities of the latent constructs can be found in Table 3. Correlations between the latent factors are listed in Table 4.

Stage 5: Results from stage 4 were satisfactory in that the structure of the questionnaire was validated among the Italian sample. However, 10 items had to be deleted, which indicated that there is a core of items that seemed to have good psychometric properties (both in stage 3 and stage 4), while others were problematic. As a result, the number of items was relatively low in the different subscales. Therefore, the questionnaire was revised again based on results from stage 4, theoretical considerations and open-ended answers from step 1. In particular, the wordings of the items were streamlined (e.g., all references to "that person" were substituted by "the bully") and some items were reformulated with the aim to make them more coherent. Further, the aim was to have at least five items in every subscale. This revision resulted in all seven subscales having five items, except for technical coping, which was composed of six items. Therefore, the revised version of the CWCBQ encompassed seven subscales with a total of 36 items. The format of the CWCBQ was the same one as in stage 3 and 4 (*i.e.*, only one scenario, see Appendixes. A German, Italian, and an English version of the CWCBQ were developed following the same translation procedure as described in stage 3. A complete version of the English, German, and Italian CWCBQ can be found in the appendices. This current version of the questionnaire represents an attempt to further improve the psychometric properties of the CWCBQ. To the best of our knowledge, this questionnaire has not been tested towards construct validity so far.

Table 2. Standardized factor loadings and unstandardized item intercepts for each country (based on the partial scalar invariance model of Stage 3, $N = 3970$).

Subscales and Items	Standardized Factor Loadings			Unstandardized Item Intercepts		
I would …	CH	ITA	IRL	CH	ITA	IRL
Distal advice						
…go to the police *	0.615	0.504	0.692	2.085 *	2.794 *	1.724 *
…seek professional advice	0.778	0.705	0.755	2.184	2.184	2.184
…inform a teacher or the principal	0.741	0.708	0.691	2.695	2.695	2.695
Assertiveness						
…ask the bully why he/she is doing this	0.750	0.642	0.746	2.992	2.992	2.992
…tell the bully to stop it	0.800	0.754	0.847	3.292	3.292	3.292
Helplessness/self-blame						
…think that it is my fault	0.690	0.606	0.680	1.352	1.352	1.352
…not know what to do	0.646	0.464	0.677	1.766	1.766	1.766
…accept the situation as it is because there is nothing you can do to stop bullying *	0.558	0.484	0.621	1.502 *	1.342 *	1.221 *
Active ignoring						
…ignore all messages/pictures so that the bully would lose interest *	0.730	0.692	0.771	2.265 *	2.719 *	2.177 *
…pretend that it does not bother me at all	0.651	0.625	0.627	2.101	2.101	2.101
Retaliation						
…write mean and threatening things to the bully	0.711	0.689	0.775	2.055	2.055	2.055
…get back at him/her personally	0.895	0.827	0.924	2.423	2.423	2.423
Close support						
…go to someone who accepts me the way I am	0.764	0.610	0.757	2.887	2.887	2.887
…spend time with my friends to take my mind off it	0.714	0.625	0.747	3.048	3.048	3.048
…go to someone who listens to me and comforts me	0.769	0.651	0.741	2.796	2.796	2.796

Notes: * = Item intercept not invariant among the three countries; CH = Switzerland; ITA = Italy; IRL = Ireland.

Table 3. Descriptive statistics and reliabilities (Cronbach's alpha) of the subscales of the Coping with Cyberbullying Questionnaire (CWCBQ) at Stage 3 ($N = 3970$) and Stage 4 ($N = 358$).

Subscales	Switzerland (Stage 3)			Italy (Stage 3)			Ireland (Stage 3)			Italy (Stage 4)		
	M	SD	α	M	SD	α	M	SD	α	M	SD	α
Distal advice	1.86	0.70	0.75	2.79	0.65	0.69	1.48	0.44	0.73	2.96	0.68	0.77
Assertiveness	2.68	0.82	0.72	2.99	0.73	0.65	2.84	0.70	0.81	3.04	0.74	0.79
Helplessness/self-blame	1.59	0.62	0.62	1.34	0.32	0.52	1.78	0.63	0.72	2.53	0.79	0.66
Active ignoring	2.73	0.78	0.64	2.72	1.06	0.60	3.15	0.71	0.62	3.11	0.93	0.63
Retaliation	1.95	0.80	0.80	2.04	0.73	0.72	1.86	0.79	0.82	2.17	0.93	0.78
Close support	3.15	0.81	0.76	2.78	0.68	0.70	3.33	0.59	0.79	3.12	0.60	0.77
Technical coping [1]										3.46	0.53	0.68

Notes: [1] Included only at Stage 4; M = mean; SD = standard deviation; α = Cronbach's alpha.

Table 4. Correlations between the subscales of the CWCBQ at Stage 3 ($N = 3970$; below the diagonal) and Stage 4 ($N = 358$; above the diagonal).

Subscales	1	2	3	4	5	6	7
1 Distal advice	1	0.39 ***	0.60 ***	0.55 ***	−0.37 ***	0.67 ***	0.62 ***
2 Assertiveness	0.35 ***	1	0.21 *	0.12	0.17 *	0.54 ***	0.54 ***
3 Helplessness/self-blame	−0.01	−0.13 ***	1	0.61 ***	−0.36 ***	0.68 ***	0.60 ***
4 Active ignoring	−0.01	0.17 ***	0.34 ***	1	−0.52 ***	0.55 ***	0.53 ***
5 Retaliation	−0.17 ***	0.15 ***	−0.09 ***	−0.08 **	1	−0.33 ***	−0.26 ***
6 Close support	0.29 ***	0.42 ***	0.21 ***	0.58 ***	−0.17 ***	1	0.69 ***
7 Technical coping [1]							1

Notes: * $p < 0.05$; ** $p < 0.01$; *** $p < 0.001$; [1] included only at Stage 4.

Table 5. Standardized factor loadings and unstandardized item intercepts for the Italian sample (based on the data from Stage 4; $N = 358$).

I would ...	Loadings	Intercepts
Distal advice		
...go to the police	0.613	2.957
...inform a teacher or the principal	0.711	2.673
...seek professional advice	0.647	2.392
...call a helpline	0.630	2.197
Assertiveness		
...let the bully know that I do not find it funny at all	0.786	3.038
...let the bully know that his behaviour is not acceptable at all	0.687	3.215
...tell the bully to stop it	0.610	3.337
...ask the bully why he/she is doing this	0.732	2.933
Helplessness/self-blame		
...be completely desperate	0.705	2.528
...ask myself why this happened to me	0.709	2.948
...not know what to do	0.523	2.180
Active ignoring		
...get around that person	0.866	3.113
...avoid any further contact with the bully	0.805	2.874
Retaliation		
...get back at him in the real world	0.843	2.169
...get back at him in the virtual world (online, e.g., SMS/email)	0.586	1.727
...write mean and threatening things to the bully	0.639	1.978
...get back at him/her personally	0.897	2.215
Close support		
...talk to my friends because it's good for me	0.664	3.120
...go to someone who listens to me and comforts me	0.759	3.111
...spend time with my friends to take my mind off it	0.668	3.316
...go to someone who accepts me the way I am	0.604	3.142
Technical coping		
...pay more attention to who gets access to my data	0.650	3.457
...block that person so that s/he cannot contact me anymore	0.646	3.336
...put less information on the Internet	0.658	3.095

Note: These items were exclusively used in Italy. The translation into English was done for the purpose of this publication only.

3. Discussion

The aim of the present study was to describe the entire process of the development of the CWCBQ in a transparent way, including a qualitative pilot study and assessments of its validity and reliability using data that were collected in Switzerland, Italy and Ireland and during different progressive stages of questionnaire development. The CWCBQ went through a total of five stages of development. In the first stage, open-ended responses from a qualitative pilot study were used to develop a first version of the questionnaire with six subscales and 14 items. In Stage 2, this questionnaire was used in the second wave of data collection of the longitudinal netTEEN study and was revised and expanded to six subscales with 18 items. The revised version was used in the third wave of the netTEEN study and, after a translation into English and Italian, was also used in two studies carried out in Ireland and Italy. The data that were collected in the three countries were used to examine the construct validity of the questionnaire among the three countries. Configural, metric and partial scalar invariance were found after deleting three out of 18 items. However, some items were found to be problematic. In Stage 4, the questionnaire was revised and extended to seven subscales and a total of 34 items, and it was used in a follow-up assessment among the Italian sample. Herein, a large proportion of the items was found to have good psychometric properties, but others were not found to be satisfactory and were revised for the current version of the CWCBQ. The current version of the CWCBQ encompasses a total of seven subscales (*i.e.*, distal advice, assertiveness, helplessness/self-blame, active ignoring, retaliation, close support and technical coping) with a total of 36 items.

In sum, the development of the CWCBQ was initiated by taking a qualitative approach and an inductive strategy (*i.e.*, content analysis based on open-ended answers). The results were then complemented by deductive elements (*i.e.*, theoretical considerations) and led to the development of a quantitative questionnaire that was continuously revised using a combination of inductive and deductive methods for the development of new items and the revision of existing ones. As a result, the CWCBQ can be considered as a promising instrument for the assessment of coping strategies in the context of cyber victimization. However, it is important to note that the current version of the CWCBQ (see the Appendixes) has not yet been tested towards its validity and reliability. Thus, the current CWCBQ represents the result of an extensive process of questionnaire development in which items were partly revised from one version to the other. Nevertheless, the assessment of the construct validity of the CWCBQ among the three countries during Stage 3 represented a very strong and conservative test of the questionnaire's psychometric properties. Not only the configural structure of the questionnaire was tested towards invariance, but also the pattern of the loadings and of the item intercepts. These results show that the six constructs that were assessed with the version of the CWCBQ in Stage 3 were the same in the three countries. Therefore, it would be possible to carry out mean comparisons of these strategies, although this was beyond the scope of the present paper. Unfortunately, this test could not be replicated using the version from Stage 4, as no additional assessments were done among the Swiss and the Irish sample. Further, the results from the Italian sample in Stage 4 represented a strong improvement from Stage 3 to Stage 4, as 11 out of the 15 items that were kept in the analyses in Stage 3 were found to be satisfactory in Stage 4, as well. Moreover, the model fit obtained in Stage 4 was found to be much improved compared to Stage 3. In sum, although the items were slightly changed from one version to the other in order to obtain a more coherent questionnaire in terms of wording, there was evidence that a core of items exhibited good psychometric characteristics and that an overall improvement in validity and reliability was progressively achieved from one stage to the other.

The coping strategies that were assessed with the CWCBQ referred to a hypothetical cyber victimization scenario. This approach yielded an insight into what the adolescents would do/think if they experienced cyber victimization. Knowledge about coping strategies in hypothetical situations among individuals that never experienced cyber victimization is important, as individuals that do have a repertoire of coping strategies might be those who actually never experience cyber victimization. Considering that cyber victimization represents a very particular form of aggressive behaviour that encompasses power imbalance and repetition [1], it might be that those who know how to cope with situations that might end in cyber victimization might be able to prevent it in the first place. Thus, coping might be a competence that reduces the likelihood of experiencing cyber victimization and, therefore, does not just protect from negative outcomes when cyber victimization has already been experienced. Besides coping with hypothetical cyber victimization, another important insight would be what those adolescents that experienced cyber victimization actually did to cope with it. To this end, the current CWCBQ also includes a question that asks if the scenario that is described in the questionnaire (or a similar one) has ever been experienced. This would make it possible to examine if the CWCBQ is equally well suited to assess coping strategies of both adolescents who did and who did not experience cyber victimization scenarios similar to the one that was described in the questionnaire. Further, assuming that cyber victimization was also assessed in the same study, that there is detailed information on the kind of cyber victimization that was experienced and that the sample is large enough, one might explore what kinds of coping strategies were used in different kinds of cyber victimization. This knowledge would be of high value for prevention and intervention, as different forms of cyber victimization and victimization in general have different degrees of severity [21,48], and it can be assumed that different coping strategies are differentially adaptive depending on the exact circumstances and the available coping resources [23].

Knowledge on the effectiveness of different coping strategies is widely lacking to date, especially with respect to actual cyber victimization. Future research might use the CWCBQ to assess how different coping strategies moderate the impact of cyber victimization on well-being. This research aim can be addressed in different ways. One approach might be to conduct interviews with cyber victims and to focus on how they handled their experience and what they think about how effective their coping strategy was. Similarly, it might be interesting to work with experimental studies using different written scenarios, vignettes, videos or maybe games and accompanying them with questions about potential coping strategies and their expected effectiveness. Another approach might be to examine the longitudinal interplay between cyber victimization, an outcome of interest, and coping strategies, with a focus on the longitudinal moderating role of coping strategies. Finally, besides asking adolescents, it might be insightful to ask parents, teachers and practitioners about their perception of the effectiveness of different coping strategies that adolescents might use in the case of cyber victimization.

4. Conclusions

The current version of the CWCBQ results from an intensive development process and is currently being used in a follow-up study in Italy. Although, it has not been tested towards its psychometric characteristics so far, the results of the development of the CWCBQ described above suggest that the current version of the CWCBQ is a promising instrument that might be useful for future research and for prevention of and intervention in cybervictimization.

Acknowledgments: The netTEEN study (Switzerland) was supported by a grant from the Swiss National Science Foundation (SNF No. 100014_130193/1) to the fourth author (Sonja Perren). For the Italian data collection, we wish to thank the Province of Lucca for the financial support. The authors would like to acknowledge the collaboration of all students involved in data collection. Furthermore, we would like to thank all study participants and teachers for the participation over the whole duration of the study.

Author Contributions: Fabio Sticca helped with designing the study in which the CWCBQ was originally developed (netTEEN, Switzerland), organised and performed data assessments in Switzerland and helped develop the German, Italian and English version of the CWCBQ during all stages. He also performed the analyses for the present paper and wrote the main part of the paper. Katja Machmutow developed the original German version of the CWCBQ and was significantly involved in its further development (German and English version) at all stages. She also wrote a significant part of the present paper. Ariane Stauber wrote a significant part of the present paper and helped develop the German and English version of the CWCBQ during the final stages. Sonja Perren designed and supervised the study in which the CWCBQ was originally developed and supervised the work of Fabio Sticca and Katja Machmutow in all aspects. Benedetta E. Palladino organised and performed data assessments in Italy, helped develop the Italian version of the CWCBQ and with writing the present paper. Annalaura Nocentini and Ersilia Menesini designed and supervised the study in which the Italian version of the CWCBQ was used and supervised the work of Benedetta E. Palladino. Lucie Corcoran designed the study that was conducted in Ireland and organised and performed data assessments in Ireland, helped develop the English version of the CWCBQ and with writing the present paper. Conor Mc Guckin supervised the work of Lucie Corcoran in the study in which the English version of the CWCBQ was used.

Conflicts of Interest: The authors declare no conflict of interest.

Appendixes

Appendix A. Appendix 1: Current English Version of the CWCBQ

Sometimes, the Internet or mobiles are used to bully others.

Imagine that for a few weeks, you have been receiving nasty and threatening text messages. Aside from that, you found out that embarrassing pictures of you are being spread around.

Did you ever experience something like that? (Yes/No)

What would you do in this situation? "I would . . . "

Table A1. Current English version of the Coping with Cyberbullying Questionnaire (CWCBQ).

Item Name	Subscale	Item Label (Response Options: 1 Definitely Not, 2 Probably Not, 3 Probably, 4 Definitely Yes, 5 No Answer)
COCY00	TC	report the incident to the website owner or to the telephone company (e.g., YouTube)
COCY01	DA	go to the police
COCY02	TC	change my contact details (phone number, email address, chat name, profile on social networking sites)
COCY03	HS	be totally desperate
COCY04	RE	write mean and threatening things to the bully
COCY05	AI	avoid any further contact with the bully
COCY06	DA	seek advice on an online platform
COCY07	CS	go to someone who listens to me and comforts me
COCY08	AS	tell the bully to stop it
COCY09	AI	keep out of the bully's way
COCY10	CS	spend time with my friends to take my mind off it
COCY11	HS	think that it is my fault
COCY12	AI	pretend that it does not bother me at all
COCY13	CS	talk to my friends about it
COCY14	HS	accept the situation as it is because there is nothing you can do to stop bullying
COCY15	AS	tell the bully that this is not ok at all
COCY16	DA	inform a teacher or the principal
COCY17	RE	get back at the bully in the real world (offline, e.g., at school)

Item Name	Subscale	Item Label (Response Options: 1 Definitely Not, 2 Probably Not, 3 Probably, 4 Definitely Yes, 5 No Answer)
COCY18	AI	ignore all messages/pictures so that the bully would lose interest
COCY19	HS	ask myself why this is happening exactly to me
COCY20	HS	not know what to do
COCY21	AS	tell the bully that I don't think this is funny at all
COCY22	DA	seek professional advice
COCY23	TC	pay more attention to who has access to my data
COCY24	AS	tell the bully that his behaviour is hurting me
COCY25	RE	get back at the bully personally
COCY26	CS	go to someone who accepts me the way I am
COCY27	TC	block the bully to prevent him from contacting me again
COCY28	RE	get back at the bully together with my friends
COCY29	AI	try not to think about it
COCY30	TC	post less personal information on the Internet
COCY31	DA	call a helpline (e.g. Kids Helpline, CyberBullyHotline)
COCY32	RE	get back at the bully in cyber space (online, e.g., text message, email)
COCY33	AS	ask the bully why he/she is doing this
COCY34	CS	go to someone I can trust
COCY35	TC	save messages/pictures as evidence (e.g., copies or screenshots)

Notes: DA = distal advice; CS = close support; RE = retaliation; AS = assertiveness; AI = active ignoring; HS = helplessness/self-blame; TC = technical coping.

Appendix B. Appendix 2: Current German Version of the CWCBQ

Das Internet oder das Handy werden manchmal benutzt, um andere zu mobben.

Stell dir bitte vor, dass du seit einigen Wochen immer wieder gemeine und bedrohende Nachrichten erhältst. Außerdem hast du erfahren, dass peinliche Bilder über dich verbreitet wurden.

Hast du eine solche Situation schon mal erlebt? (Ja/Nein)

Was würdest du in dieser Situation tun? "Ich würde ... "

Table B1. Current German version of the Coping with Cyberbullying Questionnaire (CWCBQ).

Item Name	Subscale	Item Label (Response Options: 1 Sicher Nicht, 2 Eher Nicht, 3 Eher Schon, 4 Sicher, 5 Keine Antwort)
COCY00	TC	den Vorfall bei den Besitzern der Internetseite bzw. bei der Telefongesellschaft melden (z.B. YouTube, Swisscom)
COCY01	DA	zur Polizei gehen
COCY02	TC	meine Kontaktdaten ändern (Telefonnummer, E-Mail, Chatname, Profil bei sozialen Netzwerken)
COCY03	HS	total verzweifelt sein
COCY04	RE	dem Mobber ebenfalls gemeine oder bedrohende Dinge zurückschreiben
COCY05	AI	jeden weiteren Kontakt mit dem Mobber vermeiden
COCY06	DA	in einem Internetforum nach Rat suchen
COCY07	CS	zu jemandem gehen, der mir zuhört und mich tröstet
COCY08	AS	dem Mobber sagen, dass er damit aufhören soll
COCY09	AI	dem Mobber aus dem Weg gehen
COCY10	CS	Zeit mit Freunden verbringen
COCY11	HS	denken, dass ich selbst schuld bin
COCY12	AI	nach außen so tun, als ob mir die ganze Sache nichts ausmacht
COCY13	CS	mit meinen Freunden darüber reden
COCY14	HS	die Sache akzeptieren wie sie ist, denn man kann nichts gegen Mobbing tun
COCY15	AS	dem Mobber sagen, dass das überhaupt nicht ok ist
COCY16	DA	eine Lehrperson oder den Schulleiter informieren
COCY17	RE	mich in der realen Welt am Mobber rächen (offline, z.B. in der Schule)
COCY18	AI	alle Nachrichten/Bilder ignorieren
COCY19	HS	mich fragen, warum das genau mir passiert ist
COCY20	HS	nicht wissen, was ich tun soll
COCY21	AS	dem Mobber sagen, dass ich das gar nicht lustig finde
COCY22	DA	zu einer Beratungsstelle gehen, um mir Rat zu holen
COCY23	TC	besser darauf achten, wer Zugang zu meinen Daten hat
COCY24	AS	dem Mobber sagen, dass mich sein Verhalten verletzt
COCY25	RE	mich persönlich am Mobber rächen
COCY26	CS	zu jemandem gehen, der mich so akzeptiert wie ich bin
COCY27	TC	den Mobber blockieren, sodass er mich nicht mehr kontaktieren kann
COCY28	RE	mich zusammen mit meinen Freunden am Mobber rächen
COCY29	AI	versuchen nicht daran zu denken
COCY30	TC	weniger persönliche Infos ins Internet stellen
COCY31	DA	bei einer Hilfehotline anrufen (z.B. 147 Pro Juventute)
COCY32	RE	mich in der Cyberwelt am Mobber rächen (online, z.B. SMS/Email)
COCY33	AS	den Mobber fragen, warum er das macht
COCY34	CS	zu jemandem gehen dem ich vertrauen kann
COCY35	TC	Nachrichten/Bilder als Beweismittel speichern (z.B. Kopien, Screenshots)

Notes: DA = distal advice; CS = close support; RE = retaliation; AS = assertiveness; AI = active ignoring; HS = helplessness/self-blame; TC = technical coping.

Appendix C. Appendix 3: Current Italian Version of the CWCBQ

Ogni tanto internet e cellulari sono utilizzati per fare i bulli o i prepotenti.

Immagina che da alcune settimane ricevi continuamente dei messaggi cattivi e minacciosi. Hai anche scoperto che sono state diffuse alcune tue immagini imbarazzanti.

Ti sei già trovato/a in una situazione del genere? (Sì/No)

Cosa faresti in questa situazione? "Io . . . "

Table C1. Current Italian version of the Coping with Cyberbullying Questionnaire (CWCBQ).

Item Name	Subscale	Item Label (Response Options: 1 Certamente no, 2 Piuttosto no, 3 Piuttosto sì, 4 Certamente sì, 5 Nessuna risposta)
COCY00	TC	comunicherei l'accaduto ai proprietari del sito internet o alla compagnia telefonica (per esempio YouTube)
COCY01	DA	andrei dalla polizia
COCY02	TC	cambierei i miei dati personali (numero di telefono, indirizzo email, nickname in una chat, profilo in un social network)
COCY03	HS	sarei completamente disperato/a
COCY04	RE	manderei a mia volta dei messaggi cattivi e minacciosi al bullo
COCY05	AI	eviterei ogni contatto con il bullo
COCY06	DA	cercherei aiuto online
COCY07	CS	andrei da qualcuno che mi ascolta e mi consola
COCY08	AS	direi al bullo di smettere di farlo
COCY09	AI	starei alla larga dal bullo
COCY10	CS	passerei del tempo con i miei amici in modo da pensare ad altro
COCY11	HS	penserei che é colpa mia
COCY12	AI	farei finta che non mi importa nulla di tutto ciò
COCY13	CS	ne parlerei con gli amici
COCY14	HS	accetterei le cose come sono, perché contro il bullismo non si può fare nulla
COCY15	AS	farei capire al bullo che il suo comportamento non va per niente bene
COCY16	DA	informerei un docente o il preside
COCY17	RE	mi vendicherei nel mondo reale (offline, per esempio a scuola)
COCY18	AI	ignorerei tutti i messaggi e tutte le immagini in modo che il bullo perda interesse nel farlo
COCY19	HS	mi chiederei perché è successo proprio a me
COCY20	HS	non saprei cosa fare
COCY21	AS	direi al bullo che il suo comportamento non é per nulla divertente
COCY22	DA	cercherei consulenza professionale
COCY23	TC	starei più attento/a a chi ha accesso ai miei dati
COCY24	AS	direi al bullo che il suo comportamento mi ferisce
COCY25	RE	mi vendicherei personalmente
COCY26	CS	andrei da qualcuno che mi accetta così come sono
COCY27	TC	bloccherei il bullo in modo che non possa più contattarmi
COCY28	RE	mi vendicherei con l'aiuto dei miei amici

Item Name	Subscale	Item Label (Response Options: 1 Certamente no, 2 Piuttosto no, 3 Piuttosto sì, 4 Certamente sì, 5 Nessuna risposta)
COCY29	AI	cercherei di non pensarci
COCY30	TC	metterei meno informazioni personali su internet
COCY31	DA	chiamerei una linea telefonica d'aiuto (per esempio Telefono Azzurro)
COCY32	RE	mi vendicherei nel mondo virtuale (online, per esempio SMS, email)
COCY33	AS	chiederei al bullo perché lo fa
COCY34	CS	andrei da qualcuno di cui mi posso fidare
COCY35	TC	salverei i messaggi/le immagini come prove dell'accaduto (per esempio ne farei una copia o uno screenshot)

Notes: DA = distal advice; CS = close support; RE = retaliation; AS = assertiveness; AI = active ignoring; HS = helplessness/self-blame; TC = technical coping.

References

1. Smith, P.K.; Mahdavi, J.; Carvalho, M.; Fisher, S.; Russell, S.; Tippett, N. Cyberbullying: Its nature and impact in secondary school pupils. *J. Child Psychol. Psychiatry* **2008**, *49*, 376–385.

2. Modecki, K.L.; Minchin, J.; Harbaugh, A.G.; Guerra, N.G.; Runions, K.C. Bullying prevalence across contexts: A meta-analysis measuring cyber and traditional bullying. *J. Adolesc. Health* **2014**, *55*, 602–611.

3. Didden, R.; Scholte, R.H.J.; Korzilius, H.; de Moor, J.M.H.; Vermeulen, A.; O'Reilly, M.; Lang, R.; Lancioni, G.E. Cyberbullying among students with intellectual and developmental disability in special education settings. *Dev. Neurorehabilitation* **2009**, *12*, 146–151.

4. Sourander, A.; Brunstein Klomek, A.; Ikonen, M.; Lindroos, J.; Luntamo, T.; Koskelainen, M.; Ristkari, T.; Helenius, H. Psychosocial risk factors associated with cyberbullying among adolescents: A population-based study. *Arch. Gen. Psychiatry* **2010**, *67*, 720–728.

5. Ybarra, M.L.; Mitchell, K.J. Online aggressor/targets, aggressors, and targets: A comparison of associated youth characteristics. *J. Child Psychol. Psychiatry* **2004**, *45*, 1308–1316.

6. Juvonen, J.; Gross, E.F. Extending the school grounds? Bullying experiences in cyberspace. *J. Sch. Health* **2008**, *78*, 496–505.

7. Katzer, C.; Fetchenhauer, D.; Belschak, F. Cyberbullying: Who are the victims? A comparison of victimization in Internet chatrooms and victimization in school. *J. Media Psychol. Theor. Methods Appl.* **2009**, *21*, 25–36.

8. Yang, S.-J.; Stewart, R.; Kim, J.-M.; Kim, S.-W.; Shin, I.-S.; Dewey, M.E.; Maskey, S.; Yoon, J.-S. Differences in predictors of traditional and cyber-bullying: A 2-year longitudinal study in Korean school children. *Eur. Child Adolesc. Psychiatry* **2013**, *22*, 309–318.

9. Patchin, J.W.; Hinduja, S. Bullies move beyond the schoolyard: A preliminary look at cyberbullying. *Youth Violence Juv. Justice* **2006**, *4*, 148–169.

10. Topçu, C.; Erdur-Baker, O.; Capa-Aydin, Y. Examination of cyberbullying experiences among Turkish students from different school types. *Cyberpsychol. Behav. Impact Internet Multimed. Virtual Real. Behav. Soc.* **2008**, *11*, 643–648.

11. Tokunaga, R.S. Following you home from school: A critical review and synthesis of research on cyberbullying victimization. *Comput. Hum. Behav.* **2010**, *26*, 277–287.

12. Beran, T.; Li, Q. The relationship between cyberbullying and school bullying. *J. Stud. Wellbeing* **2008**, *1*, 16–33.

13. Ybarra, M.L.; Diener-West, M.; Leaf, P.J. Examining the overlap in Internet harassment and school bullying: Implications for school intervention. *J. Adolesc. Health Off. Publ. Soc. Adolesc. Med.* **2007**, *41*, S42–S50.

14. Pelfrey, W.V.; Weber, N.L. Keyboard gangsters: Analysis of incidence and correlates of cyberbullying in a large urban student population. *Deviant Behav.* **2013**, *34*, 68–84.

15. Brunstein Klomek, A.; Sourander, A.; Gould, M. The association of suicide and bullying in childhood to young adulthood: A review of cross-sectional and longitudinal research findings. *Can. J. Psychiatry Rev. Can. Psychiatr.* **2010**, *55*, 282–288.

16. Olweus, D. Cyberbullying: An overrated phenomenon? *Eur. J. Dev. Psychol.* **2012**, *9*, 520–538.

17. Hoover, J.H.; Oliver, R.; Hazler, R.J. Bullying: Perceptions of adolescent victims in the midwestern USA. *Sch. Psychol. Int.* **1992**, *13*, 5–16.

18. Machmutow, K.; Perren, S.; Sticca, F.; Alsaker, F.D. Peer victimisation and depressive symptoms: Can specific coping strategies buffer the negative impact of cybervictimisation? *Emot. Behav. Difficulties* **2012**, *17*, 403–420.

19. Singh, P.; Bussey, K. The development of a peer aggression coping self-efficacy scale for adolescents. *Br. J. Dev. Psychol.* **2009**, *27*, 971–992.

20. Gradinger, P.; Strohmeier, D.; Spiel, C. Traditional bullying and cyberbullying: Identification of risk groups for adjustment problems. *Z. Für Psychol. Psychol.* **2009**, *217*, 205–213.

21. Sticca, F.; Perren, S. Is cyberbullying worse than traditional bullying? Examining the differential roles of medium, publicity, and anonymity for the perceived severity of bullying. *J. Youth Adolesc.* **2013**, *42*, 739–750.

22. Sticca, F.; Ruggieri, S.; Alsaker, F.; Perren, S. Longitudinal risk factors for cyberbullying in adolescence. *J. Community Appl. Soc. Psychol.* **2013**, *23*, 52–67.

23. Lazarus, R.S. Emotions and interpersonal relationships: Toward a person-centered conceptualization of emotions and coping. *J. Pers.* **2006**, *74*, 9–46.

24. Lazarus, R.S.; Folkman, S. *Stress, Appraisal, and Coping*; Springer: New York, NY, USA, 1984.

25. Perren, S.; Corcoran, L.; Cowie, H.; Dehue, F.; Garcia, D.; Mc Guckin, C.; Sevcikova, A.; Tsatsou, P.; Völlink, T. Tackling cyberbullying: Review of empirical evidence regarding successful responses by students, parents, and schools. *Int. J. Confl. Violence* **2012**, *6*, 283–292.

26. Livingstone, S.; Haddon, L.; Görzig, A.; Olaffson, K. Risks and Safety on the Internet. The Perspective of European Children. Full Findings and Policy Implications from the EU Kids Online Survey of 9–16 Year Olds and Their Parents in 25 Countries. Available online: http://resourcecentre.savethechildren.se/library/risks-and-safety-internet-perspective-european-children-full-findings-and-policy (accessed on 13 February 2015).

27. Folkman, S.; Lazarus, R.S.; Gruen, R.J.; DeLongis, A. Appraisal, coping, health status, and psychological symptoms. *J. Pers. Soc. Psychol.* **1986**, *50*, 571–579.

28. Hampel, P.; Manhal, S.; Hayer, T. Direct and relational bullying among children and adolescents: Coping and psychological adjustment. *Sch. Psychol. Int.* **2009**, *30*, 474–490.

29. Yamasaki, K.; Uchida, K. Relation of positive affect with emotion-focused coping in Japanese undergraduates. *Psychol. Rep.* **2006**, *98*, 611–620.

30. Cassidy, T.; Taylor, L. Coping and psychological distress as a function of the bully victim dichotomy in older children. *Soc. Psychol. Educ.* **2005**, *8*, 249–262.

31. Völlink, T.; Bolman, C.A.W.; Dehue, F.; Jacobs, N.C.L. Coping with cyberbullying: Differences between victims, bully-victims and children not involved in bullying. *J. Community Appl. Soc. Psychol.* **2013**, *23*, 7–24.

32. Völlink, T.; Bolman, C.A.W.; Eppingbroek, A.; Dehue, F. Emotion-focused coping worsens depressive feelings and health complaints in cyberbullied children. *J. Criminol.* **2013**, *2013*, 1–10.

33. Ruggieri, S.; Friemel, T.; Sticca, F.; Perren, S.; Alsaker, F. Selection and influence effects in defending a victim of bullying: The moderating effects of school context. *Procedia Soc. Behav. Sci.* **2013**, *79*, 117–126.

34. Sticca, F.; Perren, S. The chicken and the egg: Longitudinal associations between moral deficits and bullying. A parallel process latent growth model. *Merril Palmer Q.* **2015**, *61*, 85–100.

35. Frydenberg, E.; Lewis, R. *The Adolescent Coping Scale: Practitioners Manual*; Australian Council for Educational Research: Victoria, Australian, 1993.

36. Tenenbaum, L.S.; Varjas, K.; Meyers, J.; Parris, L. Coping strategies and perceived effectiveness in fourth through eighth grade victims of bullying. *Sch. Psychol. Int.* **2011**, *32*, 263–287.

37. Kollbrunner, G. *Cyberbullying im Jugendalter: Erleben und Coping*; Zurich University of Applied Sciences: Zürich, Switzerland, 2010.

38. Camodeca, M.; Goossens, F.A. Aggression, social cognitions, anger and sadness in bullies and victims. *J. Child Psychol. Psychiatry* **2005**, *46*, 186–197.

39. Palladino, E.B.; Nocentini, A.; Menesini, E. Evidence-based intervention against bullying and cyberbullying: Evaluation of the Noncadiamointrappola! program through two independent trials. 2015; manuscript under review.

40. Corcoran, L.; Mc Guckin, C. Traditional bullying, cyberbullying, and cyber aggression: The experiences of Irish post-primary school students. In The Manuscript presented at the British Psychological Society Northern Ireland Branch 2014 Annual Conference, The La Mon Country Hotel, Castlereagh, Belfast, 3–5 April 2014.

41. Horn, J.L.; McArdle, J.J. A practical and theoretical guide to measurement invariance in aging research. *Exp. Aging Res.* **1992**, *18*, 117–144.

42. Jöreskog, K.G. Simultaneous factor analysis in several populations. *Psychometrika* **1971**, *36*, 409–426.

43. Steenkamp, J.-B.E.M.; Baumgartner, H. Assessing measurement invariance in cross-national consumer research. *J. Consum. Res.* **1998**, *25*, 78–90.

44. Cheung, G.W.; Rensvold, R.B. Evaluating goodness-of-fit indexes for testing measurement invariance. *Struct. Equ. Model. Multidiscip. J.* **2002**, *9*, 233–255.

45. Davidov, E.; Schmidt, P.; Schwartz, S.H. Bringing values back in the adequacy of the European Social Survey to measure values in 20 countries. *Public Opin. Q.* **2008**, *72*, 420–445.

46. Little, T.D.; Cunningham, W.A.; Shahar, G.; Widaman, K.F. To parcel or not to parcel: Exploring the question, weighing the merits. *Struct. Equ. Model. Multidiscip. J.* **2002**, *9*, 151–173.

47. Little, T.D. *Longitudinal Structural Equation Modeling*; Guilford Press: New York, NY, USA, 2009.

48. Slonje, R.; Smith, P.K. Cyberbullying: Another main type of bullying? *Scand. J. Psychol.* **2008**, *49*, 147–154.

MDPI AG
St. Alban-Anlage 66
4052 Basel, Switzerland
Tel. +41 61 683 77 34
Fax +41 61 302 89 18
http://www.mdpi.com

Societies Editorial Office
E-mail: societies@mdpi.com
http://www.mdpi.com/journal/societies

CPSIA information can be obtained
at www.ICGtesting.com
Printed in the USA
BVOW05*1937220317

479200BV00001B/1/P